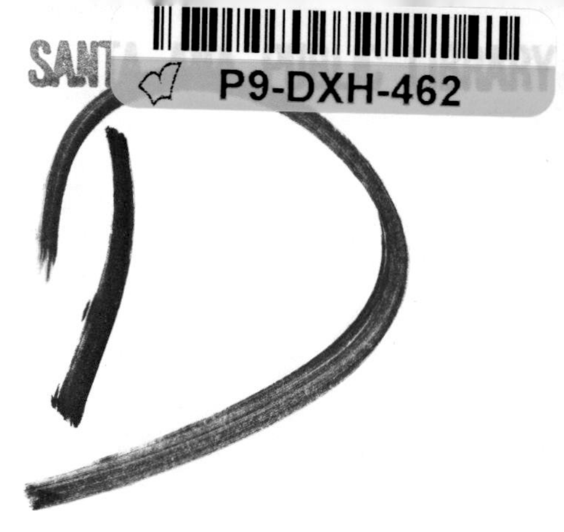
P9-DXH-462

ENDORSEMENTS

"*What Parents Must Know and Can Do About Teenage Alcohol & Drug Abuse* is an excellent no-nonsense guide for parents about drug problems. Hopefully, it will help wake people up to the problems involving substance abuse among both parents and adults. Thanks for your excellent work."

James R. Milliken, Juvenile Court Presiding Judge
Superior Court of California

"Parents love their children and want only the best for them. We tend to look for and see the positive and overlook and rationalize the negative. Unfortunately, that denial does not serve our children's best interests...I hope that parents will read and heed the valuable information, take action and get help sooner, rather than later. Perhaps if they do less damage will be done both to the child and to the family as a whole."

Charles M. Granger, Ph.D., Staff Psychiatrist
Naval Drug Rehabilitation Center San Diego, CA

"This is a reality check--A source of information and support for parents who care enough to accept their responsibility to help their child navigate beyond a major hazard to obtaining a happy and fulfilled life: Substance Abuse."

Dr. Jan Fawcett, Chairman & Professor
of Psychiatry
Rush Presbyterian St Luke's Medical Center--Chicago, Il

"I have been part of work with addiction for over twenty years now, and the most common questions that I am asked when I work with families with addiction are outlined in this book. Parents need to have hope that somewhere there is an answer. This book is written by the true professionals, the parents who have been there. Together, we help find answers. There is no other way today."

Dr. Marvin Prigmore, Program Director
Scripps Center For Quality Life and Work
San Diego, CA

"Don't go to pieces, go to PARTS These people know more about dealing with substance abuse than most professionals. Most of what I learned about substance abuse, I learned at PARTS"

Dr. Allan Rabin, Adolescent Psychiatrist
Mesa Vista Hospital
San Diego, CA

"In eleven years of working with chemically dependent patients PARTS has proved to be the most comprehensive effective support and education system I have found."

Dr. Steven Rudolph, Child Psychiatrist
UCSD Hospital
San Diego, CA

Parents Praise PARTS

"During this year PARTS has become my family. I no longer feel isolated, guilty, or scared of the future. I am sure of myself. Our family has become strong and we will make it. Now it's time for me to move on to the real world."

"Before PARTS we had retreated from all our hopes and dreams for our son. Our despair was exceeded only by our inability to make any positive differences in his life. We feel that, as it has been for us, PARTS can be a vital resource for other families."

"At PARTS I was able to see other people express their feelings which made mine more acceptable and understandable. We learned to discuss situations and feelings and to present a united front to our son."

"I value the simpler things in life more, and utilize information from the support group daily. I feel blessed that I am a part of such a valuable organization."

"PARTS has been a safe haven for us as parents to go and share our feelings with other parents going through similar experiences. It has been a lifesaver for my husband and myself, our relationship with each other and our son though it is an up and down battle.

We continue to go for support and to help others. Its comforting to know that we are not alone."

"We need to take care of ourselves and not put other people's needs above our own. While that may sound selfish, I now know it is the only way a person can have meaningful relationships with anyone, or be an effective parent"

"One of the most important aspects of my experiences is my involvement with PARTS...I have learned more from these people than from any other source about recovery and positive life styles. The parents who I have become close with are dear to me and will always hold a special place in my heart."

"The bottom line is that our son...is the one person who has to make the decision to save himself and realize that it has to come from within."

"I am so grateful for PARTS. Because of this program we came to believe that a power greater than ourselves could restore us to sanity. The tide one again flows between us and I can honestly look at my son today and say: I truly love you son."

"At PARTS I was able to see other people express their feelings the way my husband and I did, which made it more acceptable and understandable. We learned to discuss situations and feelings and to present a united front to our son."

Adolescents Praise PARTS

"The first thing you want to do when you get clean is ditch all your old friends and make new ones that are clean and sober. PARTS is excellent for that. PARTS has a lot of kids working on their sobriety. There are at least thirty or forty kids that I can hang out with."

"I have learned that I'm not the lowlife I thought I was. I am somebody. I am somebody that can make it, and that I am gonna make it!"

“They’ve helped me out a lot. Sometimes I come in with a problem and someone will call me on it. They say the answers are right in front of you and you just can’t see it.”

“PARTS is a place where you can open up in front of your peers, your parents and other parents and get feedback. Its nice to know there are other people like you and you’re not the only one.”

“When I think about “PARTS, I think about different parts of your sobriety, different parts of your addiction that come together as a whole with your family and you. Parts of the puzzle that match up.”

“I have a fresh start on life. Slowly you earn all your privileges back. I am doing well in school and I just started my senior year. For the first time I am actually taking my life seriously.”

“This is the best meeting I go to. It's here we all hang out. This is where I found my big sister and we help each other and our parents.”

“I finally realized that my addiction affected the whole family and that we needed to work on recovery.”

“I'm prepared. I have learned so much from this place that it's almost a guarantee. I'm gonna make it!”

“My one year token which glowed at night
To show that I worked for my life in recovery
My final word to the searchers of light
If you find your sobriety, then your life”

[What] Parents Must Know And Can Do About Teenage Alcohol And Drug Abuse

Parents Who Have Been There Offer Help and Hope To Parents Who Are There

Written by
PARTS–San Diego Board
of Directors

Edited
by
Alan Sorkin

BLACK FOREST PRESS
San Diego, California
(619) 656-8048
August, 1997
First Edition

PARTS Disclaimer

PARTS offers this information based on insights we have learned from our resources and from our parents over the past ten years. Answers to most of the questions in this book are highly subjective, and solutions vary from parent to parent and adolescent to adolescent. Our intent is to provide you with some additional choices for your own personal, unique circumstances. There are no easy answers to these questions, so consult a professional before making important decisions. Best of luck!

Publisher Disclaimer

This document is an original work of the author. It may include reference to information commonly known or freely available to the general public. Any resemblance to other published information is purely coincidental. The author has in no way attempted to use material not of his own origination. Black Forest Press disclaims any association with or responsibility for the ideas, opinions or facts as expressed by the author of this book.

Printed in the United States of America
Library of Congress
Cataloging-in-Publication

ISBN:1-881116-70-0

Chapter Two

WHAT SHOULD I DO ABOUT AN ALCOHOL OR DRUG ABUSE PROBLEM?

Chapter Three

WHAT MUST I DO FOR MY ADOLESCENT?

Chapter Four

WHAT MUST I DO FOR MYSELF?

Chapter Five

WHERE AND HOW DO I GET INFORMATION?

Chapter Six

WHERE DO I GO FOR LEGAL ADVICE?

About The Authors

Parents and Adolescents Recovering Together Successfully

PARTS, a non-profit organization dedicated to reducing adolescent alcohol and other drug abuse, believes that proactive prevention and intervention within the family is the best solution to fight the devastating, long-term effects of substance abuse. We have helped thousands of San Diego families recover and reunite since 1984.

This book contains our answers to all of the questions PARTS parents ask. Unfortunately, with substance abuse today, there are many more questions than answers. We hope you find our answers insightful, useful and thought-provoking. Hopefully, these will assist you in making some of your own difficult decisions.

We would like to hear from you. Please give us your feedback, with any suggestions and other questions you would like answered, on the feedback page of this book so we may improve future editions. Thank you.

Dedication And Acknowledgments

"Take a risk, change your life"

We dedicate this book to all "newcomers." Usually, adolescents with an alcohol and/or other drug (AOD) abuse problem and their parents are both in crisis. Sometimes they know it and sometimes they do not. PARTS offers both hope and the day–to–day tools you and your adolescent will need for coping with one of the most difficult situations your family will ever face.

We urge you to visit PARTS or similar organizations. Parents in crisis usually isolate themselves because they are angry and afraid, sense a loss of control, and feel guilty. Often they do not seek out resources and thus remain isolated, sometimes out of control and often unable to help their adolescent. If you have questions, get help today!

Open up your mind and use your network of friends, family and professionals. If you reach out, then you will find the resources to deal with your crisis. Find a support group such as Al–Anon, Nar–Anon or PARTS and begin to take control of your life. Adolescent users need parents who have their act together, so get the answers that are out there. You need better information than your adolescent has. There are three requirements for success: Awareness, Understanding and Action. The hardest part is getting started!

The authors would like to thank and dedicate this book to Dr. Allan Rabin, Art Aragon and Gene Battalia whose vision has inspired us. Through their tremendous support, tireless efforts and countless hours, they have helped PARTS become an organization that helps thousands of parents and adolescents yearly.

Thanks also to Jonathon Hulsh and Mark Watkins for their help with graphic design and illustrations.

We would also like to thank James Burke, CEO of the Partnership for Drug Free America, and John Schwarzlose, CEO of the Betty Ford Center, for their assistance in linking our Internet home page, and Alan Kidd, Neville Billimoria and Sean Dreilinger of Ark Enterprises for the creation of our Electronic Document and Internet Website, and Kris Land, CEO of LAND-5, for hosting and maintaning our Website.

The Board wishes to especially thank all the PARTS parents and adolescents past, present and future—those people who come back week after week to share their knowledge, insights and frustrations to help others navigate just a little better through troubled turbulent waters.

For the donation of services: Mike Martella, CEO of MARCOA Publishing for providing the graphics and printing of the book, and Black Forest Press for publishing the book. And lastly, to the Fieldstone Foundation for assisting us with the production and printing costs.

While some of this material is specific to California, many states have similar laws and organizations. For specific local information, consult your local White and Yellow Pages. If you wish to form a local PARTS organization, we can help. Our phone number is in the back of this publication.

PARTS—San Diego Board of Directors

Alan Sorkin, Editor

WHAT IS A SUCCESSFUL PARENT?

"A successful parent is one who has loved, one who has sacrificed, and one who has cared for, taught, and ministered to the needs of an adolescent. If you have done all of these and your adolescent is still wayward or troublesome or worldly, it could very well be that you are, nevertheless, a successful parent. Perhaps there are adolescents who have come into the world and who would challenge any set of parents under any circumstances."

Anonymous

Guilt holds you back from doing what is right. It's not fair to judge your worth on the basis of what your adolescent does. You are not accountable for other people's choices, and your children are not without choices.

Foreword By Art Linkletter

How I wish I had this book following the drug-related death of my 20-year-old daughter, Diane, in 1969. I was frozen by fear and anger and hurt. I was ignorant and appalled.

The shocking decade of the 1960s struck at many established customs by which we live and love and work. Emblematic was the "drug abuse problem." The national shock, frustration, search for quick solutions and scapegoats ensued as we found (to our horror) that no class, race, age, or person was safe from a damaging involvement with drugs.

The Linkletter family was no exception. Why had this awful, agonizing thing happened to us? My career and my home life were both full and rewarding. I had tried so hard to live life the right way, to be of service to my community, to be a good husband and father. Why had I been hurt so cruelly?

People in my profession are conditioned to conceal the unpleasant, to highlight the happy side of life. Show business personalities hire public relations people to gloss over the rough spots, to sweep the flaws and weaknesses and failures under the rug.

So, many of my "star" friends were surprised when I, the "old pro," decided to tell the truth and not hide behind a smoke screen by calling it an accident. We would let everyone know that the same kind of drug-related tragedy could catch up with them. My decision was to honor Diane by telling the facts as we knew them—and to memorialize her death by helping America's families to save their children from this new threat.

In the years that followed I studied the drug "epidemic," went into the pharmacological reasons and psychological urges for this insane desire to experiment with alcohol and other drug abuse. I became a member of President Nixon's Drug Abuse Commission, wrote books and articles, and lectured all over the U.S. in schools, churches, at conventions, and clubs.

It was a long and disturbing crusade. I did not have the knowledge and experience that this book contains. In fact, almost no one did: doctors, psychiatrists, preachers, and police were all fumbling in the dark.

Today we know so much more. But, tragically, a new generation is coming along, youngsters who are curious, experimental, and strangely ignorant.

Parents are still alarmed and confused about what to do. The new drugs, the stronger marijuana, and the liberal lifestyle invite our young people to follow Dr. Leary's old invitation to "turn on, drop out, etc."

In the past few years startling statistics suggest a new wave of young victims is rising again across America.

I hope and pray that this book will help at this critical moment. Only those of us who have lived through this unbearable experience can know the importance of the knowledge on these pages.

HOW DO I KNOW IF THERE IS AN ALCOHOL OR DRUG ABUSE PROBLEM?

"One day is worth one hundred tomorrows"

Abby's Story

Abby was 16 and living with her mother since her parents divorced. Abby was a good girl who had never been in serious trouble. In her sophomore year, she began to slide. She quit the basketball team because the kids were not cool. Her parents did not like her new friends, who looked terrible and had bad attitudes. She became sexually active, defiant, less responsible, more angry, more withdrawn and mean.

The doctor concluded she was depressed and probably had an Attention Deficit Disorder (ADD), but never mentioned the possibility of drug or alcohol use. Several months later, her mother found Abby's diary and confirmed that she was using drugs. Her mother called her father and said, "Our little girl has a horrible, uncontrollable addiction." Abby was out of control and her mother wanted her out of her house.

Her father knew that returning her to her former environment was not a good option. A psychologist recommended enrolling her in a thirty-month program at a therapeutic boarding school. The psychologist said, "If something is not done, Abby will never graduate from high school." Abby was sent away to school until her 18th birthday. At 18 she will decide whether she wants to complete the 30-month program.

In addition to schooling, the counselors began setting limits, confronting inappropriate behavior, and teaching her cause and effect. The school created many opportunities for Abby to improve her self–esteem, develop life skills, and meet and interact with positive role models.

Message: *Health care professionals without a background in alcohol and other drug abuse often overlook drug and alcohol problems.*

How Can I Tell If My Adolescent Is Using Alcohol Or Other Drugs?

"IT'S OKAY TO BE OCCASIONALLY DUMB, BUT NEVER BECOME NUMB"

It is very difficult to determine, even for professionals. Only .006% of the average physician's medical training is on alcohol and drug abuse. Parents are almost always shocked to find out that their adolescent is abusing alcohol or other drugs. Even parents with medical training often miss or DENY the signs.

Even if your adolescent exhibits several of the warning signs listed below, that does not necessarily mean there is an addiction problem. Substance abusing behavior is not significantly different from typical teenage behavior, so do not be too quick to blame what you think is "drug behavior" on alcohol and other drug abuse. All adolescents demonstrate many of the signs described below.

Much of your adolescent's behavior is age appropriate and normal (whether you approve or not). Jumping to the conclusion that your adolescent is an addict may not be helpful or proper, but please do not ignore the warning signs.

Because we usually wait too long to act on our own "gut instincts," there is a good chance that if you think your child is using, then the child probably is. Most parents of alcohol and other drug

(AOD) abusers display shock when they admit there is a problem, and cannot believe they did not add up the signs and recognize the problem sooner.

Many adolescents admit to using for years and are stunned that their parents never acknowledged the problem or did anything to check out their fears. Sometimes they attribute this to their parents' not caring. We believe it is due to naiveté. If this happens to you, you should not be too hard on yourself. Hindsight is always 20/20.

When you are fairly certain that there is a problem, don't over react or under react. The non–anxious presence of one parent (or a trusted family member) can offer some objectivity and sometimes present a rational perspective. Because this has probably been going on for a long time, there is no reason to overreact today.

What Are The Signs?

"BIG PROBLEMS BECOME SMALLER IF YOU PAY ATTENTION TO THEM"

Here is a list of symptoms, but please remember that the presence of many of these does not necessarily mean there is an addiction problem. We are often shocked to find out that our adolescent is using drugs.

Physical Signs

- Slurred speech, slow or unresponsive reactions, or very talkative
- Loss of motor skills
- Sudden weight loss or gain
- Change in appearance
- Pupil dilation or red eyes. Visine or eye

drops in the home
- Sweating, increased perspiration odor or bad acne
- Significant changes in sleeping and waking hours
- Insomnia or hyperactivity (may stay up or out all night)
- Isolation

Psychological Signs
- Noticeable personality changes such as unexplained mood swings, lying, arguing, withdrawing, inappropriate anger (such as punching holes in the wall), uncharacteristic irritability, giddi ness, depression, or hostility
- More complaints about medical or emotional problems, such as acute indiges tion, stomach disorders, paranoia, ulcers, or talk of suicide
- Difficulty in handling complex or multiple mental functions without becoming frustrated, violent or intimi dated by a task perceived to be insur mountable

Social And Behavioral Signs
- Lack of responsibility and lack of regard for house rules, parents, authority and curfew
- Dropping out of, or losing interest in, school or extra curricular activities, declining academics, or school behavior problems (truancy, respect)
- Withdrawn, sneaky phone calls, locking bedroom door
- Loss of old friends or new friends that you do not know

- Missing money or possessions that can be sold for illicit drugs or alcohol
- Hearing from friends, neighbors or relatives about drinking, "keg" parties where parents are not home
- Any other inappropriate behavior (being physically or verbally abusive)
- Trouble with the law (curfew, disorderly conduct, delinquency, drunk driving)
- Aggressive behavior or fighting with family members, peers or strangers (gives adolescent an excuse to leave home)
- Unexplained absences which provide opportunities to binge for a few days before returning home
- Defending the right to do as they please with "their body"
- Refusing to listen to you about alcohol and other addictions
- Reading drug-related books or magazines

What Should I Do If I Suspect My Adolescent Is Using?

"CHOICE NOT CHANCE DETERMINES DESTINY"

Addicts will do whatever is necessary to get their drugs or alcohol. *If you suspect a problem, it is appropriate to find out for sure by using whatever means it takes.* This includes searching your adolescent's room, night stand, closet or drawers. You may wish to contact school officials, teachers, and other students and their parents. This can be very risky, so be discreet and very careful so things are not blown out of proportion before you are ready to confront your adolescent.

Once you are certain, you may choose to contact the school and the parents of kids with whom your adolescent is associating. State your concerns in a non–judgmental way and let other parents draw their own conclusions. Do not let a personal fear of embarrassing your adolescent or yourself restrict your options. Remember, you are dealing with your child's life.

If enough signs are present, be prepared to believe them. Accepting does not mean approving. Accepting means acknowledging what you know. When we choose not to accept, we are living in the past rather than in the here and now. We all deny. Denial is lying to yourself about what you see. We deny because we are not ready to take action.

Because most of us have no experience with (AOD) abuse, we are afraid to deal with it. When we deny its existence, we do not have to act. Once we accept, we can begin to deal with the reality.

We see warning signs and we generally wait longer than we should before taking action. If you deal with your suspicions, you will often be right. You can pay now or pay later, but the price you pay increases as you wait. *Like the addict, you may choose the pain of discipline or the pain of regret.*

Beware of the "fair trap" that kids use—you're not fair, it's not fair, etc. Do not ignore your good judgment because of your adolescent's protestations. Try to stay out of "sparring contests," and do not let them draw you into a lose–lose match.
Here are a few suggestions you should implement immediately:

- Keep a diary. It will provide you one place to enter your thoughts and track your stress levels. It will be invaluable later on when you need to re-create information.

- Lock up your valuables, checkbook, car keys and credit cards. Your first reaction probably is: "Not my child," but it happens over and over again. It is okay to be suspcious. Be alert at all times.
- Make time for yourself because these problems can quickly become all–encompassing. You will have to make a concentrated effort to do what you used to enjoy (take a walk, exercise, meditate, listen to music, go to a movie, read a book, go out to dinner). Start with 15 minutes a day and try to maintain or increase that time.
- Learn as much about alcohol and other drug abuse and recovery as you can.
- Decide how and what you want to learn.
- Join a support group.
- Begin reading from the Recommended Reading List and use the Sources and Resources in the Appendix.

What Should I Do And Where Should I Go For Counseling And Advice?

*"KNOWLEDGE IS GETTING INFORMATION–
WISDOM IS USING IT"*

Take your adolescent for a physical examination and be sure to include a drug test.

We suggest that you have your pediatrician do a drug screen with every physical examination. Then you will know for sure and you do not have to get into the "You don't trust me" argument. Insist that someone observe your adolescent while they give a specimen. Ask your doctor to refer you to a specialist in chemical dependency (psychologist, psychiatrist or alcohol/drug counselor) if the test is positive.

Check into health coverage for restrictions from your insurance company or managed care provider.

If your adolescent is "using," you may be able to get the child admitted to a hospital. If the adolescent is out of control or a threat to himself or herself or to you, a doctor can admit him/her immediately.

Contact NA, AA, Al–Anon, Nar–Anon or PARTS.

NA is for narcotic addicts and AA is for alcoholic addicts. Al-Anon and Nar-Anon are for family members. PARTS works with the entire family. *Make your information as good as your adolescent's and find a support group.* Your adolescents have much more access to (AOD) information than you do (much is miss-information). You should make yourself more knowledgeable about (AOD) abuse than they are. Parents and adolescents who have been there can help you deal with every phase of the intervention and recovery process. Just ask...

Network with other parents.

You will find that these problems are much more widespread than you thought, so seek out others who have been there.

What Is Denial?

"KNOWLEDGE IS USELESS, UNLESS YOU ACT UPON IT"

Denial is not a river in Egypt. *Denial is the unwillingness to accept the reality of the situation.* Here is a graphic illustration of denial:

You walk into the living room of a house and see an elephant. You squeeze past it noticing that no one else comments on its presence. People are talking about everything but the elephant. We all know it's there, but no one talks about it. The elephant represents alcohol and other drug abuse.

How Does Denial Apply To Alcohol And Other Drug Abusers?

"SOMETIMES THE VERY THING WE'RE LOOKING FOR WE CANNOT SEE"

Denial about alcohol and other drug abuse may appear in different ways.

A parent:

- pretends that their adolescent's behavior is typical of all adolescents
- admits there may be a problem but it's not a very serious problem
- says all adolescents act like this or it's a phase they will outgrow
- will excuse, justify, rationalize or lie to himself or herself about their adolescent's inappropriate behavior

- becomes angry or changes the subject when someone points out their adolescent's inappropriate behavior
- sees a problem but blames the adolescent's friends for the problem

An adolescent says:

- I can handle it, it calms me down, I can concentrate better with marijuana
- everybody drinks or takes some type of drugs
- marijuana is proven to have medicinal effects, and it will be legal soon
- it's just pot, and I'll never try anything stronger
- it's my body, and I can do what I want
- I can quit anytime I want
- I am not any more irritable (rude, hostile, mean, etc.) than anyone else
- my old friends are nerds, my new friends are really cool

At What Level Does Alcohol And Other Drug Abuse Denial Occur?

"THE GREATEST FAULT IS TO BE CONSCIOUS OF NONE"

Denial about (AOD) abuse issues can occur at several levels:

- Individual denial of the user
- Denial by the abuser's family
- Society's denial as to the depth of the problem

These inappropriate responses all inhibit recovery, because until we all acknowledge that there is a problem we are unwilling to take action.

As kids start to use, they become great liars. Parents want to believe them because they are unable or unwilling to deal with the consequences of their child having an (AOD) abuse problem. The parents rationalize that they do not have enough facts until, sooner or later, they have more than enough facts and it's a huge problem.

Are They Just Experimenting Or Do They Have A Problem?

"THINGS ONLY HAPPEN IF YOU MAKE THEM HAPPEN"

Unfortunately, it is a fact of life today that almost all children will experiment with alcohol and other drugs. Professionals can conduct an assessment, but it is difficult to distinguish between experimentation and addiction. We believe that properly educated parents know their children better than anyone else, so they can identify the problem best.

You should decide whether there is a long history of using or they are just experimenting. Then you have to determine your own tolerance for their experimentation. Some parents are more tolerant of allowing their adolescents to experiment while others have no tolerance. Some families will allow some experimentation while others state that in this house there is a NO DRUG policy. *We believe that the prudent decision is for zero tolerance, but every family unit must draw their own line.* Experimenting is a problem and must be addressed because it leads to abuse and is evidence of a deeper problem. Remember that drawing a line with adolescents usually causes the adolescent to test your limits. Be real clear in your own mind as to what you are willing to do, or not do, if your child crosses that line. Remember, parents are most effective when they can agree on the rules and consequences beforehand. *It is best to talk to your adolescent so that everyone is clear on the rules and the consequences of experimentation and use.*

WHAT SHOULD I DO ABOUT AN ALCOHOL OR DRUG ABUSE PROBLEM?

"Addicts are not bad people trying to get good, but sick people trying to get well"

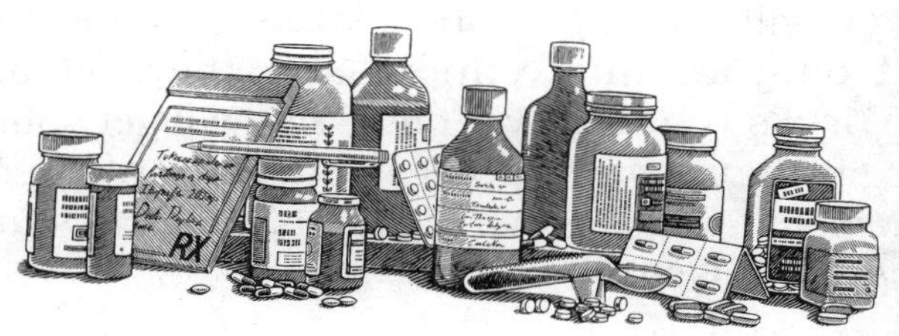

When Should I Drug Test My Adolescent?

"IT'S NOT A PERFECT WORLD, AND IT BECOMES LESS PERFECT AS WE GET OLDER"

Adolescents are masters of manipulation who learn to evade their parents. Some start using drugs today at the age of 9, 10 or 11, and by the time they are sophomores in high school they have been using a long time. Top athletes give up scholarships because they cannot give up (AOD), and they are unable to pass a drug screen.

Drug screens give parents in our communities a tool with which to identify adolescent drug use. The best advice is to bring your adolescent in for drug testing when YOU suspect there may be a problem. Because of the rampant use of drugs in high schools today, some drug counselors recommend random testing of every adolescent over 12. To avoid an argument with your adolescent, ask your pediatrician or family doctor to perform a urine test as standard procedure every time they conduct a physical examination. Kids often want to get sober, but they do not know how to ask for help.

A positive drug test often allows the adolescent to ask for help. If the child does not ask for help, the parent must intervene. If your adolescent asks why you do not trust him or her, your response can be: "If I'm wrong, I will apologize; but if I'm right, you will get help." Your adolescent's life may depend on your intervention, and they seldom give up drugs voluntarily. Some kids will get sober and begin the recovery process after an intervention. *Remember, this is not a trust issue, drugs are a life or death issue!*

In California, drug tests are confidential and results are released to parents only if the adolescent is under 18 years old. Federal law protects eighteen year olds and they receive their results directly. This information remains confidential unless:

- The patient consents in writing
- The disclosure is allowed by a court order, or
- The disclosure is made to medical personnel in a medical emergency, or to qualified personnel for research, audit, or program evaluation

What Type Of Drug Testing Is Available? Are Drug Tests Reliable?

The most common tests are for alcohol, marijuana, cocaine, opiates, barbiturates, amphetamines and benzodiazapines. The most commonly used specimen is urine. Some parents choose blood testing to decrease the likelihood of tampering. Blood levels and breath analyzers can also be effective for screening alcohol content. There are new procedures today based on hair analysis. Generally, there are qualitative and quantitative drug tests.

Qualitative

This is a general drug test and is the least expensive way to determine when your adolescent is using or has returned to drugs after being clean. It will not tell you how much is in the system and which substance is present.

Quantitative

This will show which drug is specifically in the system, and approximately how much of the substance is present. If an adolescent has been using over a long period of time, it takes longer to get the drugs out of the system. Each time you repeat the test the substance level should go down, and eventually the test should be negative. If it does not, you should assume your adolescent is probably still using.

Drug tests are only as reliable as the persons taking and giving the test. Sophisticated drug users may try using certain chemicals and procedures in an attempt to sabotage positive drug tests. You should be aware of the many tricks adolescents use to avoid a positive drug test, such as:

- substituting someone else's urine
- watering down their own urine
- dipping finger in bleach and touching urine
- using Golden Seal (purchased over the counter at any health store)
- drinking vinegar before the test
- drinking as much water as possible to flush out substances
- drinking herbal tea

If your adolescent has a copy of *High Times Magazine or Dazed and Confused,* he/she may be seeking new ways to beat a drug test. Because these techniques are continually changing in the drug culture, the most effective response is to have random tests.

If the drug screen is positive, contact a professional. Your personal doctor or a professional Chemical and Alcohol Counselor (CAC) or Chemical, Alcohol and Drug Counselor (CADC) can help. Go to a PARTS, Al–Anon, Nar–Anon or Tough Love meeting immediately for help.

How Long Do Drugs Remain In The System?

Different drugs remain in the body for different lengths of time. There is no hard and fast rule for this, as it depends on many factors:

- How recent the use,
- How much was used,
- How often the use, and
- The height, weight, metabolism and body fat of the user.

As a rule, marijuana stays in the system from 5 to 30 days (sometimes it is detectable for as long as 90 days). Crystal methamphetamines, cocaine, crack, LSD, PCP, heroin, amphetamines and barbiturates are generally detectable for about 2–4 days and alcohol lasts just a few hours. Since alcohol stays in the system for a short time, adolescents who do not wish to test positive often switch to avoid detection. The best advice is to test randomly and often.

How Should Drug Tests Be Administered?

"YOU ARE WHAT YOU PAY ATTENTION TO"

There are off–the–shelf drug tests, but we do not recommend them because they are not reliable, and false positives can occur. *Professionals who know all the tricks, and know what to look for, can best handle drug testing.* There is a high failure rate in a one-time test and a chance of a false positive reading even when the lab conducts a test. A false negative can give a false sense of security.

Parents may collect the specimen, but be sure that you control the entire test and never lose contact with the specimen. Be present while collecting the specimen and take it directly to a hospital or lab. *Be extremely careful of an adolescent using one of the above tricks. Addicts are very creative and resourceful.* In addition to determining whether your adolescent is using, random drug tests are a strong deterrent to his or her beginning to use again.

What If My Adolescent Refuses To Take A Drug Test?

"WE OWE IT TO OUR CHILDREN TO BE PARENTS IN CONTROL"

Drug testing takes away the: "You do not trust me argument." By testing, you no longer have to confront an adolescent who may be lying, and you no longer have to wonder whether they are using. You let the test speak for itself. Addicts will often refuse, but remind them their refusal is almost an admission of guilt. If the adolescent lives in your house, he/she must follow your rules. One of those rules should be NO DRUGS. You should have them take random drug tests or assume they are using and act accordingly. Please refer to Chapter 3, page 29, How Do We Go About Setting Limits?

Where Can I Get Inexpensive Drug Testing?

Chemical dependency units of many hospitals and Health Alliances offer drug testing. Simple qualitative tests are generally under $25, and specific quantitative tests start around $50. Immediate or emergency results are more costly. Some hospitals provide drug tests at no cost if your child is in treatment or is refereed by a staff doctor.

What Is An Intervention?

"IF YOU DON'T STAND FOR SOMETHING, YOU WON'T STAND FOR ANYTHING"

Contrary to popular opinion, you do not have to wait until an addict "hits bottom" before they acknowledge that they need help. The best interventions are done by a professional. They are well planned and highly structured. A poorly planned intervention can make things worse.

A family can offer help through an intervention. *An intervention provides a structured, organized message to the user that the family believes the individual needs help.* In this meeting the family clearly defines what they are going to do if the user refuses to change.

In an intervention most family members do not say anything that they have not said before, but they say things differently. People tend not to hear messages said in anger. We often give messages to users by yelling when we are angry and the user often responds in anger. Noise can distract the adolescent from hearing the messages. *When we deliver the message softly and lovingly, then the user can hear it differently.*

It is best to include several friends and family members who can demonstrate to the individual that they love him/her and they are doing this because they care about the adolescent's safety, happiness and welfare. A good intervention can often persuade an individual in denial to recognize that there is a problem, and how it has affected their life, family and friends.

An intervention is one of the most loving, powerful and successful methods that shows an adolescent they are loved. It is a group process that uses the power of the adolescent's closest friends and family group to put the user on formal notice that this family will no longer deny the existence of an alcohol and other drug abuse problem.

By intervening, the parents in crisis begin to move in the right direction by focusing on making the maximum impact on their adolescent. Because alcohol and other drug abusers almost always minimize their problem, you can sometimes reach them with a show of numbers at one focused meeting.

Dr. Allan Rabin, a well–respected San Diego child psychiatrist, suggests a variation: "You tell the adolescent that you are bringing four family members and friends to the intervention. If that isn't enough to convince the user, you will bring eight next time, and then, if necessary, sixteen the time after."

Both methods demonstrate to the user the depth of the problem and show the user that there are many people who truly care. It also provides clear boundaries as to what is or is not acceptable for this family. Honesty is the key, and concern is the vehicle.

Who Should Do The Intervention?

A family can conduct an intervention by themselves, but we do not recommend it. Find a professional.

It is better to use a professional intervention facilitator, or orchestrator, who sets up the process where each family member can share lovingly how they feel about what the user is doing. However, families can do them successfully.

Here is a classic story illustrating the power of an intervention. It occurred with a tough adolescent named Billy who was unmoved by every family member's presentation. Finally, his 8-year-old brother said, "Billy, I don't want you for a brother anymore. You stole money from my bank to buy drugs." Billy, after hearing this, decided he needed help.

The facilitator can also be helpful in suggesting a time and place where the user is most likely to hear the message. This maximizes your chance of success in trying to convince the individual "in crisis" that help is needed. *The intervention can also contain an element of coercion. The adolescent can be told that the next step is hospitalization, calling the police or going to court.*

When Should I Do An Intervention?

"CRISIS OFTEN PRESENTS AN OPPORTUNITY FOR CHANGE"

You may want to consider an intervention if your child:

- is experiencing falling grades, truancy or episodes with the law
- has broken off his relationship with you and/or other family members
- disappears for long periods of unexplained time

- exhibits enough of the signs above so that you reasonably decide there is a problem
- has little interest in school, work, outside activities, and family gatherings
- demonstrates inappropriate explosive or abusive behavior, fighting, or violence
- writes about drug activity in their diary or journal
- has drug paraphernalia in his/her room; or
- has publications like *Dazed and Confused or High Times*. This is clearly not proof of drug behavior, but it should wave a red flag.

If you discover or suspect any of the above or see any other abnormal behavior from your child, become a detective. Find out what is going on in their lives, including what is in their rooms. Snoop! You may be able to save your child's life.

You may conclude that some experimentation is permissible, but be careful you do not fall into the "Denial Trap." Often family and friends are in the same denial as the user. You must take action when the individual's life or health is at risk or they become a danger to others.

Once adolescents reach maturity (18 in most states) they can no longer be forced into treatment or a treatment facility unless they are a danger to themselves or others. Many states provide for a three-day psychiatric evaluation. With adolescents under 18 you can force the issue of treatment by doing an intervention or admitting them to a treatment facility. Many parents wish they had done something while they still had a chance. The earlier you intervene, the better chance you have of saving your child. *(AOD) abuse is a chronic progressive disease that seldom gets better and often ends in death.*

What Types Of Interventions Are There?

There are two types of interventions and they may precede hospitalization or occur once the adolescent is secure in the hospital.

Family Oriented Interventions

Family oriented interventions inform adolescents about current behavior or the addiction in the presence of families and friends. The family explains how the abuse is affecting the individual and their environment, families and friends. By having friends and families available, the adolescent is able to hear caring concerns that may possibly persuade them to take action about their problem.

Adolescent Interventions

This type of intervention is directed toward getting the adolescent to accept individual or hospital-based treatment. Parents often force their adolescents into treatment. While this may not always be fair or equitable from the adolescent's perspective, parents often initiate this action because they feel they must avoid a future crisis. Except in life-threatening situations, hospitalization requires a psychiatrist's (some states allow a doctor) consent. A doctor can sometimes convince an insurance company or HMO that hospitalization is prudent.

To start an intervention consult with doctors, friends, colleagues, Al–Anon or Nar–Anon, a local hospital or county mental health department. *There are no guarantees that an intervertion will work, but it's a good start.*

WHAT MUST I DO FOR MY ADOLESCENT?

"The only things we keep in life are the things we give away"

How Can I Keep My Adolescent Away From Drugs?

"EVERYONE HAS ONE LIFE TO LEAD, AND THEY SHOULD LEAD IT THEMSELVES"

We cannot keep kids away from drugs, but we can prepare a child to live in a drug-filled world drug free! The war on drugs cannot be won by the schools, churches or the judicial system because they do not have the vested interest that parents have. If the war is to be won, it will have to be won by the parents. Talk to your child about drugs. *If you do not know what to say, then find a book whose philosophy agrees with yours.* There are plenty of books on the market (consult our Recommended Reading List in the Appendix). Adolescents are going to experiment, but educated adolescents will recognize that the long-term risk far outweighs the short-term pleasure.

Adolescents who feel good about themselves are less likely to use drugs in the first place. *Let your adolescent know you love him/her unconditionally, but always give predictable, consistent boundaries and consequences.* You should expect your adolescent to follow appropriate expectations for living. Like it or not, the adolescent must realize that society has certain rules they must follow or they must accept the consequences. Set rules that allow your adolescent to be what he or she wants to be. Love them for who they are, not whom YOU want them to be. LEARN TO DEAL WITH THE ADOLESCENT YOU HAVE, NOT SOMEONE YOU WISH YOU HAD.

Some adolescents on drugs want to be sober. If you can recognize their cry for help or provide an environment that encourages communication, you can help them re–integrate back into society and your family. You must stick to your boundaries and let them know you mean business. *It's almost impossible to keep them totally away from drugs until they commit to doing it themselves. Expect the usual temptations, experimentations and probable relapse.* If you can open the lines of communication to discuss and educate them to the benefits of remaining sober, this is probably all you can do.

What Can I Do About My Adolescent's Friends?

This is difficult because you have no control once they leave the home. You cannot follow them to see whom they hang–out with at school, etc. You can only control who comes to your home. Talk to their friends' parents and make it difficult for them to get away with inappropriate behavior.

Sometimes, other adolescent parents may be in denial. It is best to converse with them saying your adolescent may be a potential bad influence on their child. Laying the blame on your child may not be fair or accurate but it may enable you and other parents to cooperate in keeping all users separate from each other. Parents should communicate with each other and make their information network better than their adolescent's network.

How Do We Go About Setting Limits?

"ACCEPT THE PERSON AND ACCEPT THEIR FAULTS"

There are different types of limits. You must distinguish between setting limits that will keep your child alive (i.e., drugs are not permitted in this house), as opposed to limits that will change behavior (i.e., you must treat me with courtesy and respect) and bring unity back to the family. You have to do whatever is necessary to keep your child alive. Often the (AOD) abuser is incapable of even making those choices.

Once you get to this stage, begin to *set the boundaries, but allow your adolescent to become what he or she wants to be.* Your expectations of what you want them to be are not always helpful. In fact, they may put too much pressure on your adolescent. You have a right to expect your adolescent to follow appropriate expectations for living. Adolescents need to live in a home where parents make the decisions. Do not be ambivalent. Do not let them decide for you.

You owe it to your adolescent to be a parent. Kids need boundaries and agreements to feel secure in the world. The orderly setting of limits allows the adolescent to experience life as they become ready for it. With abusers you must go back and re–set limits. Decide where you will draw your lines and then stick to them. *It is often better to confront the adolescent at lower levels of involvement in the hope that they will not get to a higher level.* If you give them too much freedom, it is almost impossible to clamp down.

Discuss what behaviors are acceptable in your home and agree on limits with your adolescent. Family meetings and written contracts are two devices that help you come to a mutually acceptable conclusion. Contracts can be as simple as one sentence. The most important agreement is staying clean and sober. There is a Sample Parent–Adolescent Agreement in the Appendix which covers many areas. Everyone should sign an agreement which is fair and workable. If you cannot get agreement, there is little chance of harmony.

Do not expect too much too soon. Adolescents who have been out of agreement for a long time take a long time to get into agreement again. *Get their input, agree on the rules and have a written agreement signed by everyone. This will avoid arguments. Think about setting reasonable limits that your adolescent can live with at that time.*

Lead by example. You need to be a role model with regard to agreements. Your adolescent will watch you closely and point out any inconsistencies between "your talk and your walk." Remember, *When The Student Is Ready, The Teacher Will Appear. The corollary is also true: When The Teacher Is Ready, The Student Will Appear.*

How Can My Adolescent Earn Back My Trust?

"THINGS BEGIN TO CHANGE WHEN YOU BEGIN TO CHANGE THE WAY YOU LOOK AT THEM"

Adolescents are more responsive to parents who are willing to give them some respect. Parents of substance abusing adolescents often feel they have no choice when it comes to trusting their child again. When you are ready, start by giving them some small opportunities and see how they handle those situations. We recommend written agreements to reduce areas left to interpretation. There are several areas that are negotiable, including chores and responsibilities, restrictions, personal belongings and their room, privacy, comfort, family activities, transportation and entertainment. Here are some examples of how your adolescent can begin earning back your trust:

- By being helpful, showing respect to you, the family and others (i.e., you may no longer raise your voice to me)
- By listening, following the rules and the routines of the house, and not arguing (i.e., no arguing about curfew or neatness)
- By acknowledging their addiction, committing to change, and changing their behavior
- By refusing to associate with user friends
- By voluntarily going to ninety NA, AA or PARTS meetings in ninety days
- By getting a sponsor, and working The 12 Step Program
- By consenting to random drug testing
- By being responsible, being at the appointed place at the appointed time and doing what they say they will do

How Can I Deal With My Adolescent's Anger?

"IF YOU DO NOT LIKE THE QUALITY OF YOUR RELATIONSHIP, THEN CHANGE IT"

A small change on your part will cause a "rippling effect" with your adolescent. One of your jobs as a parent is to teach your adolescent how to handle anger appropriately. Be the role model. The quality of your relationship depends on what you hear from them and what you say to them. A good guide book is: *How To Talk So Your Kids Listen and Listen So Kids Will Talk*, by Faber and Mazlish (See Recommended Reading List)

Listening vs. Hearing

> *Listening is a passive activity of allowing in words.* We spend most time listening while we are waiting to talk.

> *Hearing is active listening without an agenda.* You are reaching out for meaning. You do not have to understand or agree to hear, but you must actively reach out to your child. Hearing shows that you respect and value your adolescent as a person. You should hear the problem as your adolescent sees it. This is what they need from us.

Responding in anger is seldom productive and emotional outbursts can be extremely damaging to your relationship. You should always respond in a quiet and calm manner. Try talking quieter as they begin yelling louder. This can be difficult, but it is an important new way of communicating. Since anger is often about winning a point, it might be better to try and get what you want rather than to try to win an unimportant argument.

Take a "Time Out" if necessary before you respond. JUST BECAUSE SOMEONE ASKS YOU A QUESTION, YOU DO NOT HAVE TO ANSWER. When you are ready to respond, try to understand or have your adolescent restate the problem.

Hear the answer and offer choices for the solution. Addictive thinkers can usually think only of one choice. Try to give them several options. THERE ARE AT LEAST THREE BETTER SOLUTIONS TO MOST PROBLEMS. It is your job to indicate there are often several choices while your adolescent may only see one. After you hear their explanation of the problem, then choose your words very carefully. You do not have to agree that there is a problem. Try to remember that if your adolescent thinks it's a problem, it is a problem for them. Parents and children may see the same situation differently, and both be right.

WHAT MUST I DO FOR MYSELF?

"Knowing why changes nothing, acting differently is everything"

Martha's Story

Martha's 16-year-old daughter had been in treatment several times in the past. Numerous relatives were themselves alcoholic, using drugs and discouraging Martha from providing clear tough limits. Martha's daughter broke up with her boyfriend and began using marijuana regularly and stopped going to school entirely. She left home for several months and began living at a beach front home with several older drug abusing young women. Martha announced in a PARTS meeting that she would continue coming to meetings without her daughter.

Her daughter said she was ready to return home if her mother would let her continue using pot. Some parents suggested Martha let her daughter return home, even if it meant allowing her to smoke marijuana. Martha pointed out that several of her own relatives had continued to smoke marijuana throughout their young adulthood and they had never been able to support themselves. They continued to be dependent on other relatives. Martha insisted on breaking the long family tradition of dysfunctional drug use within several generations of her family.

Finally, her daughter returned home when she developed bronchitis. She needed a doctor and had no medical benefits. Martha's daughter was finally ready to accept the terms about sobriety. Martha's example of calm, focused, high–principled action made an impact on several of the parents who had been inconsistent and permissive with their own teenagers.

(Those parents who attend meetings regularly have an opportunity to think through their issues and to formulate successful plans.)

What Must I Do To Begin the Recovery Process?

"BELIEVE IN YOUR SELF, YOUR PLANS, YOUR GOALS AND YOUR ABILITY TO REACH THEM"

Parenting is one of the hardest jobs we have and is the one for which we receive the least amount of instruction or preparation. Help yourself by learning as much about (AOD) abuse and recovery as you can. Become an expert! Here are some suggestions.

◆ **Stop Denying And Begin Accepting**

"WE MOVE IN THE DIRECTION OF OUR CURRENTLY DOMINANT THOUGHTS"

The first step toward recovery is to stop denying, the second step is to accept, and the third step is to forgive. Denial always prevents the kind of action necessary to stop (AOD) abuse. (AOD) abuse is a chronic, progressive disease that does not go away. When you live in denial you have no choices, but through acceptance new choices appear.

Parents make the process so complicated. *Parents have to love their kids and give them rules and time and space to grow.* Recognize and accept your adolescent's behavior, but do not judge it. Direct the energy where it needs to be. We put too much energy into judging. Put your energy (and their energy) into the "here and now."

After the family accepts the fact that their adolescent has an (AOD) abuse problem, they can begin working toward recovery and forgiveness. *You must accept before you can forgive.*

"God, grant me the serenity to accept the things I cannot change, the courage to change the things I can and the wisdom to know the difference."

◆ Start Confronting

"DON'T DO TOO MUCH OR TOO LITTLE—BALANCE IS THE KEY"

First, and foremost, confront your adolescent about the problem. We recommend family counseling with either a doctor who understands (AOD) issues or a certified drug or alcohol counselor. As stated earlier, most Medical Doctors are under or misinformed about (AOD) addiction and recovery.

Recovery is a family issue, so the family should begin attending family meetings or multi–family group meetings like Al–Anon, Nar–Anon or PARTS. They offer great opportunities for families to begin communicating with other parents or adolescents who can offer excellent suggestions on how to handle most issues that typically occur with (AOD) abusers.

The adolescent should attend AA and/or NA and PARTS meetings on a regular basis. We suggest ninety meetings in ninety days. They must also find a sponsor.

◆ Rebuild Trust

"FIRST UNDERSTAND, THEN ATTEMPT TO BE UNDERSTOOD"

Trust almost always disappears when (AOD) abuse starts; however, it is critical to begin rebuilding trust on both sides. Trust is not given. *It must be earned, and you do not have to trust your child!* Kids feel that trust should be granted automatically as soon as they say, "I promise to be good." We believe an (AOD) abuser must earn trust back slowly. The trust issue is a big issue and it comes up often. We offer numerous suggestions in Chapter 3.

◆ Rebuild Communication

"RELATIONSHIPS DEPEND ON CONTACT. NO CONTACT=NO RELATIONSHIP"

Communication is a key to a family reuniting. If the adolescent stays clean, then communication is possible. As the adolescent works toward getting clean, communication opens up, and some adolescents choose to start spending more time with their family. You may encourage this but do not require it. Also, put fun things back into the family agenda. Set aside time for doing things together like going to movies, playing games, shopping, or whatever your family enjoys.

We suggest that you set aside a certain time each day for family time. You should meet in a quiet place in the home where the family can speak freely with one another. This time should have no interruptions from friends, phones, beepers, radio or TV.

◆ Stop Trying To Control What You Cannot Control

"TO THE DEGREE THAT YOU BRING VALUE, YOU CAN GIVE UP CONTROL"

As parents we are caretakers and caregivers. Except for life-threatening behavior, change your expectations and give up control (you never really have control of your adolescent anyway). Deal with the adolescent you have and not the one you would like to have. They are going to become who they choose anyway and giving up your expectations will make it easier on them and you.

Your expectations cause you to attempt to control your adolescent, and control naturally causes rebellion. When you let them become what they want to be you will gain influence with them. *Your goal is to bring power and empower your adolescent.*

◆ Give Approval

"BY SURRENDERING CONTROL YOU GAIN INFLUENCE"

We all need approval. *Many adolescents become addicted because they do not have enough self–approval.* They try to convince us they are individuals, and that they do not need or want our approval. They pretend to be "rebels" who want to stand alone (just like their 10,000 buddies). They will tell you they do not want or need approval, but in fact they do want approval from both you and from their friends.

Parents should give approval to their children, but only when they earn it. The most difficult people for adolescents to get approval from are their parents. If they do not receive approval from their parents, they seek it out from peers. It is easy to get approval from the losers. Kids convince themselves they do not need parents' approval, and they take the path of least resistance.

Kids take on images because they do not feel they will be accepted for who they are. They look for applause for that image and they get it, but it is applause for the image, not who they are. They still feel empty, so they will do anything for acceptance, including self–mutilation or self-destruction. They believe they deserve the pain because they hate themselves, so they take the pain in their gut (which is the worst pain) and move it to another body part. Suicide is second to accidents as a cause of teenage death. *Parents who begin paying attention to their children, often stop their child's pain.*

◆ Give Rules And Predictability, But Do Not Be Rigid

"LIFE HAS NON-NEGOTIABLE AGREEMENTS"

Have mutually agreed upon written agreements. *If you cut down their choices far enough, eventually they will make the right choice.* Kids need to make mistakes in a safe environment. When they make a mistake and do something to correct it, that is when they learn. This is when you need to ask them:

- How can I assist you?
- What do you need from me to support you?

◆ Become A Family

"DREAM, LIVE LIFE WITH A PURPOSE"

Family means hearing, boundaries, sharing, values, nurturing, loving, supporting and teaching by example.

- Be a positive role model for your adolescent
- Be real
- Do not just listen, HEAR
- Do not judge
- Do not have false expectations

◆ Do Not Expect Perfection

"IF YOU EXPECT PERFECTION, YOU ARE SETTING YOURSELF AND YOUR ADOLESCENT UP FOR FAILURE"

When you give up the need to control and bring value to your adolescents, then they will come back into your life.

- If you want respect, you must give respect
- If you want a friend, you must be a friend
- If you want love, you must give love

◆ Learn As Much As You Can About Recovery

"COMMIT YOURSELF TO LIFELONG LEARNING"

As your adolescent learns what recovery means, you must learn about recovery also. By understanding the process you can feel your adolescent's pain. *Recovery is a slow, frustrating process that requires all parties to be honest with and to care for each other.*

Remember that the hardest part for many of us is getting started!

What About All This Guilt?

"GUILT STOPS GROWTH"

Recovery is about choices, and you may choose to give up the guilt. Guilt holds you back from doing what is right. It's not fair to judge your worth on what your adolescent does. You are not accountable for other people's choices, and our children are not without choices. No one is a victim.

Things can happen that are beyond your control and theirs, but you still have choices. You can only choose your life, and the only real success is choosing your own life. You can choose to take charge of your own life, and they must choose to take charge of theirs. Once you recognize that there are choices, you will find three different scenarios:

- You may all choose to change
- You may change and your adolescent may not
- Your adolescent may change and you may not

If you choose to change, you will make things better. You have to change yourself. Most of us dislike change so much that we refuse to change until "not changing" hurts more than changing. By coming to PARTS, you are taking a first major step in beginning the change process and developing peace of mind.

Peace of mind does not mean happiness. If you have done the best you can do, that is all you can do, and that should give you peace of mind. Other people do not have to change for you to have peace of mind. *You have got to "own" your problems and let everyone else clean up their own mess.*

The attitudes you choose will determine where you and your adolescent will go. If you change your attitude, you change the way you view the world, and you will change your choices. THE ONLY ONE THING THAT CANNOT BE TAKEN FROM YOU IS YOUR CHOICE OF ATTITUDES IN ANY SITUATION.

We do not have the right, the need, or the ability to fix the world. We are just caretakers and facilitators for the early part of our children's journey. Our job is to give them roots and wings, but they have to make their own choices.

It might help to go back and reread What Is A Successful Parent? before Chapter 1.

What Happens To My Other Children While I Deal With My Addicted Adolescent?

You will probably neglect them to some extent, but do not forget them. It is very difficult to find time for anything else while you are in crisis, but try to make time for those children who are not causing problems. If you do not, siblings may choose to cause problems to get attention themselves.

You must explain to your other children that the "using adolescent" has an (AOD) problem. Let the younger children know that they can come to you with any questions. Answer them truthfully. Giving them this information is far better than trying to shield them from the truth or letting them draw their own conclusions. If you notice any behavioral changes, consult your doctor immediately. *The using adolescent may take a disproportionate amount of your time and energy, but try to make special time for your other children so they do not choose (AOD) to receive negative attention.*

Chapter Five

WHERE AND HOW DO I GET INFORMATION?

"All the information you need is out there, if you're willing to look for it"

Ben's Story

Ben, a 17-year-old boy, was verbally abusive to his parents. He would stay out all night long, miss school, and refused to change. He said his mother was incompetent as a parent and his father was physically abusive to him. His father had stopped disciplining him entirely after a therapist commented on the inappropriateness of corporal punishment.

Ben's father was reluctant to involve himself in any therapy or discipline after this. His mother, Beatrice, was overwhelmed by dealing with all the problems herself. Ben's younger brothers were also acting out and ignoring both parents. When Beatrice came to PARTS meetings she was overwhelmed and in great pain. Both parents stated they were being victimized by their son.

A friend of Beatrice allowed Ben to stay in her home which was much less chaotic than his own house. She established clear rules and limits that Ben agreed to follow. Ben did not follow the rules, and he was sent home. Shortly thereafter, Ben was taken to Juvenile Hall. The recommendation was for Ben to be placed in a long-term drug rehabilitation facility. His parents were afraid because Ben threatened to hurt them if he were sent there.

Beatrice attended parent meetings at PARTS regularly where she learned to voice her concerns. Other parents supported Beatrice, and she was finally able to send Ben to drug rehab. The parents coached her and made her ready to accept the recommendation to enroll her son in a program.

(Committed Al–Anon, Nar–Anon and PARTS parents and adolescents may serve as surrogates for families in crisis. A parent without the support of the other parent, or without support from other relatives or friends, has a difficult battle.)

Do All These AA, NA And PARTS Meetings Really Do Any Good?

Absolutely! They will support and educate you and help you through your adolescent's recovery. There are things you need to change also. AA, NA and PARTS helps teach you what has worked for other parents. They provide parents a place to share their feelings and frustrations in a safe, supportive environment, to vent feelings and to gain useful information. Some kids may be a little scary looking, but they are working on their recovery. At PARTS adolescents have an opportunity to replace their user friends with sober ones. They also have a new support group to call if they need help or feel like using. They can find positive role models, set structured goals and receive monthly recognition. *They can find safe, sober activities to replace just hanging around in unsupervised situations or with users.*

Should My Adolescent Have A Sponsor?

AA, NA and PARTS are based on a 12 Step Recovery Program that requires a sponsor. An adolescent who is serious about following the program must have a sponsor. *Abstinence from drugs or alcohol is not recovery.* Adolescents may be clean, but not necessarily in recovery.

Sponsors are not mandatory for recovery, but they certainly help. Parents cannot play this role. *It is far better for an addict to have someone to share their feelings with and to be accountable to.* By regularly attending meetings, it is much easier for them to stay focused on the recovery process. To recover, we suggest your adolescent work a 12 Step Program.

Should I Spend All My Time Taking My Adolescent To Meetings?

"RECOVERY IS A FAMILY ISSUE AND IT SHOULD BE DEALT WITH BY THE FAMILY"

Ninety meetings in ninety days is best, but that is very difficult. You are not responsible for getting them to meetings. The recovery belongs to your adolescent so he/she must take responsibility for getting there. However, meetings do help, and it's best if you can help your adolescent by driving when necessary and by arranging car pools, cabs, ride sharing, etc.

The more family members that attend meetings the better. Do not limit family members to mother and father. Families can be a single parent, foster parent, grandparent, aunt, uncle, or anyone with an interest in the child.

How Can Military Families Obtain Help For Their Adolescents?

"YOU CAN MAKE IT HAPPEN OR LET IT HAPPEN OR WONDER WHAT HAPPENED"

CHAMPUS provides excellent medical benefits to military families with an adolescent. However, getting these benefits may be difficult. Uncooperative clerks, poorly defined rules, arbitrary interpretations, bureaucratic red tape and unwilling insurance companies can often frustrate your efforts. *If you are willing to persist, and fight if necessary, you should prevail.*

The following suggestions come from PARTS military parents who were successful at championing their adolescents' causes and receiving the benefits they were originally denied. We hope this information is of assistance to you.

Begin collecting and sending a series of letters to CHAMPUS. These letters should be from teachers, counselors, advisors, doctors, psychiatrists and anyone else who will document the type of behavior your adolescent is demonstrating.

Life-Threatening Situations

In case of an emergency or life-threatening situation, proceed directly to the nearest hospital emergency room or call the police who can request an ambulance. A doctor can admit your adolescent immediately if he/she believes your adolescent is at risk.

Non–Life-Threatening Situations

If the situation is non-life threatening but you believe your adolescent needs psychological care:

- you may go to a Family Service Center and meet with a social worker who will recommend a therapist. Or,
- you may go to a Hospital Care Center (generally open 12 hours per day), who can recommend a therapist. Or,
- you may go to your family doctor who can recommend a therapist. Or,

- you may go to a military hospital and request treatment. If this facility does not have the necessary facilities, they will issue a "Non-Availability Letter" which will allow you to recieve benefits at a private hospital. The therapist should assign you an "Approval Number" which is necessary for you to receive medical benefits. Call within 24 hours later to verify that your number is in the computer.

If you still are not successful, go to your Commanding Officer.

REMEMBER: PERSISTENCE PAYS. CHAMPUS often denies and then pays the person who yells the loudest. Do not be timid. Do it for your adolescent! Good Luck!

How Can I Get My Insurance Or HMO To Provide Benefits For My Adolescent?

"WHATEVER HAPPENS, NEVER HAPPENS BY ITSELF"

You probably pay good money for your health insurance, but often the company is not there for you when you need it. Getting your entitlements is often tricky and may be extremely difficult. Uncooperative claims adjusters, poorly defined rules, arbitrary interpretations, bureaucratic red tape, and company policies often frustrate your efforts. *If you are willing to persist, and to fight if necessary, you can prevail.*

The following suggestions come from PARTS parents who were successful at championing their adolescents' causes and receiving benefits they were originally denied. We hope this information is of assistance to you.

Begin collecting and then start sending a series of letters to your insurance company or HMO. These letters should come from teachers, counselors, advisors, doctors, psychiatrists and anyone else who can document the type of behavior your adolescent is demonstrating.

Life-Threatening Situations

In case of an emergency or life-threatening situation, proceed directly to the nearest Emergency Room or call the police who can request an ambulance. A doctor can admit your adolescent immediately if he/she believes your adolescent is at risk.

Non–Life-Threatening Situations

If the situation is non-life-threatening but you think you need psychological care for your adolescent:

- you may go to your family doctor or find a licensed social worker who can recommend a therapist or Chemical & Alcohol Counselor. Or,
- you may go to an Urgent Care Center (they are generally open 12 hours per day and they can often recommend a therapist or Chemical and Alcohol Counselor). Or,
- you may go to AA, NA, Al-Anon, Nar-Anon or PARTS who can recommend a course of action.

If You Still Are Not Successful

Go to the next supervisor and keep going higher (do not stop until you speak to the Company President or CEO). REMEMBER: PERSISTENCE PAYS. *Insurance companies often deny and then pay the person who yells the loudest. Do not be timid, do it for your adolescent!*

If All Else Fails, Go To The Appropriate Governmental Agency

THE FOLLOWING MATERIAL IS COURTESY OF: *What To Do When You Can't Afford Health Care,* Matthew Lesko, Published By Information USA, 1993, P.O. Box E, Kensington, MD 20895

Under the Federal Hill–Burton law, hospitals and other health facilities that receive money for construction and modernization from the federal government must provide services for those who are unable to pay.

If you feel a hospital or other health facility is denying you coverage, you may seek relief. To register a complaint, you should contact:

U.S. Dept. of Health and Human Resources
Federal Office Building
50 United Nations Plaza
San Francisco, CA 94102
415/556–6746

If your HMO denies you coverage, contact:

The Office of Prepaid Health Care Operation and Oversight Office of Operation
Health Care Financing Administration
Cohen Building, Room 4406
330 Independence Ave., SW
Washington DC 20515
202/619–3555

For an Investigation, Mediation, Arbitration or Legal Advice in California, contact:

The Insurance Commissioner
100 Van Ness Ave.
San Francisco, CA 94102
800/233–9045

Or, **State Consumer Protection Office California**
Dept. of Consumer Affairs
1020 N, St, Sacramento, CA 95814
800/344–9940

Or, **Office Of The Attorney General Public Inquiry Unit**
1515 K St., Suite 511
Sacramento, CA 94244–2550
800/952–5225

(Non–California residents may find similar local agencies in their local White or Yellow Pages):

Or, **Your local Senator or Representative's Office**
Listed in the White Pages

Or, **U.S. Congress House Select Committee on Narcotics Abuse and Control**
H2–234 House Annex
2 Washington, DC 20515
202/226–3040

There are also groups of Physicians who volunteer medical services to the poor, contact:

California Medical Association
P.O. Box 7690
San Francisco, CA 94102
415/541–0900

(Non–California residents may find similar local agencies in their local White or Yellow Pages.)

WHERE DO I GO FOR LEGAL ADVICE?

"Seek good advice consistently, conscientiously, aggressively, and follow it"

NOTE: Start with your family attorney, or one recommended by someone who had a positive experience with an attorney. Your attorney may not know this area of the law, but can probably recommend someone who does. Additionally, County Bar Associations can provide you with a list of attorneys who practice that area of law. The best referral is from a satisfied client.

What Do I Do If My Adolescent Runs Away? Do I File A Report?

"HE WHO IS FLEXIBLE WILL NOT GET BENT OUT OF SHAPE"

Chronic runaways will return home to steal anything of value so they can run away again. To protect yourself and your family:

- change your door locks immediately
- do not leave cash, credit cards, jewelry or your car keys in the open
- do not give any keys to your adolescent
- warn younger children not to assist their siblings
- notify friends and parents of friends that your child is a runaway and that you will not tolerate them offering your adolescent a place to stay. Tell them that you intend to give the police their name as a possible haven, and
- notify the Department of Motor Vehicles. If your adolescent is under 18, most states issue a provisional license that may be revoked without parental consent. Furthermore, you may be held liable if your child is "driving under the influence."

Immediately call the police or sheriff, and file a report. Then, file a report each time. Do not let possible embarrassment limit your range of responses. Filing a report helps you document your adolescent's behavior, protects you legally, and sends a message to your adolescent that you are taking control. It also may keep your child off the streets for long periods of time. You must begin to create the necessary "paper trail" should you decide at a later date that your adolescent needs a treatment program, probation, or jail. It also tells your adolescent that you are not going to tolerate this type of behavior anymore.

Unless you report that your adolescent has committed a crime (for example, car theft), be aware that the police will probably not pursue your adolescent. If you file a report that your child has run away, the police will pick him/her up. Do not expect them to keep your child in jail because the police will not incarcerate a minor for any offense that they will not incarcerate an adult. The police will tell the parent their adolescent is in custody and that they must pick him/her up or they will sometimes bring them home.

Consult an attorney and learn about all the consequences of placing your adolescent into the Juvenile Justice System. *Do not make this decision when you are angry.* Forcing an adolescent to face the consequences of their own actions can be an effective 'wake-up call' that keeps them from escalating into the Adult Justice System. Sometimes a sympathetic judge will help by ordering drug tests or requiring your child to go to AA, NA or PARTS meetings.

DON'T EXPECT A LOT OF ASSISTANCE FROM THE SYSTEM. There is also great risk because the system can be a rigid, bureaucratic nightmare that may take control of your child, leaving you feeling frustrated and powerless. To a certain degree, you may lose control over what happens to your child. If you have already lost control, this may be your only alternative. Make sure you are ready to take this step.

What Is My Legal Liability For My Adolescent Under and Over 18?

Note that in California your duty to provide for your adolescent does not necessarily stop at the age of 18. Your duty to support your adolescent may continue until such time as the adolescent reaches the age of eighteen years or until the adolescent is emancipated. It may continue until the adolescent either ceases attending school full-time, or reaches the age of nineteen years, whichever shall first occur.

This is the rule, but you should contact an attorney before acting.

Duties To Your Adolescent Under 18

Parents are responsible for providing reasonable needs ("necessaries"), to wit: nutrition, clothing, shelter, health care, education, and attempt to keep them reasonably safe.

Over 18

If the adolescent is "incapacitated from earning a living and is without means," the parents have an equal duty to provide for the support of that adolescent. Otherwise, as a practical matter, the adolescent thereafter is on his or her own. (California Family Code, Section 3910)

However, the California Civil Code, Section 206, addresses the reciprocal duties of support between parent and adolescent. If either is unable to maintain himself or herself by working, it is based upon the ability of one to support the other.

Liability To Third Parties
Under 18

You have a duty to protect others from your adolescent, much like your liability for your dog. You can be held liable for damages incurred due to the actions of your adolescent.

Over 18

You have a duty to protect others from your adolescent, much like your liability to others (i.e., your brother, your friend, etc.).

What Is My Legal Liability When My Adolescent Drives My Car?

In California, assuming that the adolescent is a licensed driver, it is as if you loaned your car to your friend or neighbor whose car is in the shop. *If an accident occurs, your adolescent's liability as a permissive user (assuming he/she did not steal the car) is the same as yours.* Was your adolescent negligent? Just because the adolescent is in an accident does not mean the adolescent was the negligent party. *You, as the owner of the car, "allowed" the adolescent to use the car, so you can be liable along with the adolescent.* This is similar to your brother–in–law's use of your car with your permission.

You can be liable if you knowingly loan your car to someone who is incapacitated, drunk, medicated, blind, or a known careless or reckless driver. If you knowingly loan your car to someone whose license is revoked or who you knew was likely to engage in illegal behavior (racing on public streets) that is inherently dangerous, you may be liable.

Can I Throw My Adolescent Out Of The House Before He/She Is 18?

Probably not legally in California, but some parents do (if you have the mental and physical wherewithal to do so). Some states provide for emancipation. Be sure to contact an attorney before you do this so you know exactly what your legal liability is. *You may remain liable for their "necessaries" or perhaps for reimbursing a third party who provides the same. Additionally, there may be some criminal liability for not providing for the reasonable needs of the adolescent.*

When an adolescent decides to leave voluntarily, parents should let him/her know that you still love them and wish them the best. Give them a list of community support groups and sober living homes.

What Happens If My Adolescent Gets Into The Criminal Justice System?

"THEIR GOOD JUDGMENT MAY COME FROM THEIR BAD JUDGMENT"

Some parents choose to voluntarily place their adolescent in the California Criminal Justice System (other states have similar systems). Think carefully about this decision: never do it out of anger, and consult with an attorney before taking this step. Documenting your adolescent's refusal to behave is important, but placing your child within the criminal justice system can also create significant problems. Consider this option carefully.

If your child does enter the California system there are three levels:

> *Level 1: Your adolescent may receive informal probation with the local Probation Department sub–station.* There is an effort at educating abusers (discussions, essays done by the adolescent, films, etc.) and requiring them to do community service for a number of Saturdays.
>
> *Level 2: The adolescent receives informal probation with the Probation Department and he or she must satisfy additional demands of this department.* Usually this is less onerous and of shorter duration than Level 3.
>
> *Level 3: The adolescent is taken into custody. Within three business days there is a "readiness hearing" to see whether the court will look into the matter.* The adolescent has an attorney and the matter goes to trial. At the hearing, the court may be advised of an "agreed–upon plea–bargain." The judge may allow the plea–bargain or schedule a trial. *The court may order probation with certain terms and conditions of probation, education, or rehabilitation.* This may be either a day treatment program, a residential program or incarceration (either locally, or at California Youth Authority [CYA] juvenile prison).

As the levels increase, parental input and control decreases and your liability increases. Remember that you are liable for reimbursement to third parties for those necessaries. That third party is not just the little old lady in the next town who feeds and shelters your adolescent. It can also be the government.

What Happens At Juvenile Hall?

The adolescent receives a shower, clothing and a small room that he/she will share with several others. Usually the more senior roommates get the bed. There is regular visitation one evening a week and on Sunday morning. A few family members may visit and friends may not. There is an effort to provide some education.

WHAT SHOULD I DO WHEN THEY START ACTING RESPONSIBLY?

"Winners get up more often than they are knocked down"

What About Home Study Programs?

"IF YOU CAN'T GIVE UP THE PAST, THEN YOU HAVE TO GIVE UP THE PRESENT"

Parents must weigh the relative importance of getting education vs. keeping their adolescent alive. By removing your adolescent from public education you remove them from the main drug using venue. It is currently very difficult for a recovering adolescent to find a sober environment within the public educational system. Many parents choose home study to remove their child from "using" students. *However, it is important to remember that adolescents intending to use will find drugs anywhere.*

Home Study

Home study is available for adolescents from 6th grade through 18 years of age. It is for those who want to continue education but are unable or unwilling to do it through the regular educational system. Home study programs enable adolescents to receive school credit while they are working. The teacher gives assignments that are to be completed on a mutually acceptable date. Each completed packet of assignments earns credits toward a diploma. Students can also work on a GED if they desire. Teachers at home study sites work very closely with their students.

Some school districts have supervised home study programs. The student goes to a location where an instructor supervises the adolescent's individual study plan during the morning and then works during the afternoon in a job coordinated by the program. Parents can find information concerning education from the school counselor who has the information necessary for you to make a decision.

Positives

Students can work at their own pace. This is particularly helpful with adolescents diagnosed as having an Attention Deficit Disorder (ADD). Students can begin working while they are still in school and receive credits for working.

- It is more goal–oriented and less process–oriented
- It leaves less chance for interaction with others

Negatives

- The adolescent has a great deal of free, unstructured time. They only need to check in once a week with school, which leaves a lot of free time if they are not working at a job
- It is also very isolating and leaves little chance for interaction with others

How Can I Help My Adolescent's School Begin A Sobriety Program?

"THE CHOICE OF WHO ONE ASSOCIATES WITH IS ONE OF THE MOST IMPORTANT CHOICES ONE MAKES"

If you know of a drug problem in your adolescent's school, you need to take action, positive action. You can start by talking to other parents and then by making an appointment with the school principal. *State specifically what is happening and offer to help the principal, teachers and other staff. Be positive and not hostile or accusatory.* Make it easy for the school to be helpful and receptive.

- Many schools commit to a “zero tolerance drug policy,” but rarely is it enforced. See if there is a room available for a sobriety club.
- Approach the school about requiring a “mandatory intervention program” for first time offenders to possibly attend a drug program (like PARTS). This may allow first time offenders to remain in school.
- Try to establish an “(AOD) abuse Advisory Council” consisting of the principal, nurse, interested teachers, school officers, concerned parents, and community leaders.
- Stress that you know this is one of many schools with a problem, and you are here because your adolescent is here.

Where Can My Adolescent Find Part–Time Employment?

A successful job experience is one of the best ways to boost self–esteem. However, finding a job can be difficult and frustrating. The recovering adolescent is often lacking those skills necessary for finding and keeping a job. Parents and the adolescent should solve this problem jointly. Often adolescents want to work but do not make the effort because they do not know how and they are afraid of failing. Parents who assist greatly increase their adolescent’s chance for success. A successful job experience will aid the recovery process significantly. Help them to make this happen!

Don’t just tell your adolescent to get a job. Take the time to show them how. Show them how to read the want ads, how to ask for help, how to canvass the neighborhood commercial districts, and how to check local bulletin boards. It is very important that your adolescent have the skills necessary to present himself/herself best at the interview.

Often, adolescents who have used do not have good communication and presentation skills. Take time to help them select appropriate interview clothes. Advise them to bring a pen to the interview and practice completing an application. Show them how to answer an interviewer's questions. Remind them that many employers will require a drug test. Make sure they follow–up with prospective employers to let them know they really want this job.

Adolescent labor laws often limit options to adolescents. Sixteen-year-old adolescents will have their best opportunities with businesses like fast food restaurants, service stations, and grocery stores.

Where Can My Adolescent Find Summer Employment?

"EVERYONE WANTS MORE THAN THEY HAVE, AND YOU CAN HAVE MORE IF YOU WORK MORE"

Other options for 16-year-olds include movie theatres, local supermarkets, department stores, drug stores, mall stores, boys and girls clubs, and day camps. Encourage your adolescent to complete as many applications as possible. They should return them no later than April 15th or sooner if possible. Hire–a–Youth Programs, when they are funded, are a good resource also (consult your local White Pages).

Where Can My Adolescent Find Full–Time Employment?

"IT WILL WORK, IF THEY WILL WORK"

As adolescents turn 18, more jobs become available. They may try restaurants, movie theatres, super markets, and retail establishments. They will usually have more success than adolescents under 18.

Consider purchasing a copy of *Get Ready! Get Set! Get Hired!* by Drs. Jan and Dahk Knox, from Black Forest Press, 539 Telegraph Canyon Road, #521, Chula Vista, CA 91910, or call (619) 656-8048. Price is $24.95 plus $3.95 shipping/handling.

HELP AND HOPE FROM ADOLESCENTS BACK FROM HELL

We present the following real words and stories (with minor editing) of adolescents who deal with (AOD) problems daily.

Sixteen-Year-Old Adolescent Girl:

I remember being really happy in school and at home, but getting in a lot of trouble in the classroom. I always felt a little different than everyone else and felt bad because I thought I wasn't in the popular crowd. My mom and dad loved me. My mom took me to a lot of classes, but she didn't spend time with me playing games or things like that. My parents drank alcohol also, and I grew up thinking that it was okay to do that. I hardly knew my biological father, so my step-dad was my dad. He and I had fun when I was little. When I got older, he didn't talk to me much anymore.

When my sister was born, my mom spent a lot of time with her, and I just figured she was too busy to spend time with me. I felt alone so I hung out with my friend and drank alcohol sometimes. As time went on, I felt more and more like my mom and dad didn't care much about me, so I was mad at them for that.

We moved when I was in 7th grade, and I started going with kids who were drinking (even at school). I started drinking at school with them, and I started taking my mom's car to parties. I was only 12, but when we lived in the country my parents taught me how to drive a stick shift. One time I let another girl drive my mom's car, and when a signal changed, she froze and we didn't go. A cop pulled us over, and we were arrested. My mom had to come and get the car and pick me up. She told me I couldn't be with my friend anymore. I started feeling bad inside but didn't know why exactly. I was going to parties and drinking a lot, and sometimes I couldn't remember how I got to certain places.

One day I ditched school and got caught, and later that day my mom took me to a hospital. I hated her for making me go there and for not taking me out when I asked her. Now that I am older, I know that she was only trying to help me. I hated being in the hospital, and it was really hard to get along while I was there. I refused to listen to my doctor, and I kept losing privileges because I wouldn't do what I was supposed to.

I finally went home after two and a half weeks and started using again. I knew I couldn't drink alcohol so I smoked pot and eventually used crystal meth. My mom didn't know I was using because I learned how to hide it better. I became real depressed and tried to commit suicide. I hated the charcoal stuff they made me drink at the hospital, and I decided I wanted to be sober.

After that I asked my mom if I could meet my biological dad, so I went to Northern California to see him. He gave me pot while I was there, but after I came back I became sober. I've never understood why parents have to get divorced. This will be the second divorce, but it still hurts, and even though I've only seen my real dad once, I love him. He drinks too much, just like my step-dad. I feel that parents should set an example for their kids. My mom quit drinking for me.

I started going to a middle school after I came back from seeing my real dad. I worked very hard to stay clean, and I went to a lot of AA and PARTS meetings. I still kept taking dance and later started taking gymnastics, so I am very busy. My mother and I became closer, and we worked on the issues that had caused us problems. We still work on issues and probably always will.

I have been in a relationship for almost four years with the same person. We have broken it off twice but have gone back together. I met him at PARTS after my hospital stay, but almost drove him away when I continued using. I manage my own life now that I am almost 17, and I work a lot and go to school. I want to go to college.

Sixteen-Year-Old Adolescent Boy:

I'm an addict alcoholic, and I currently have 11 months, 14 days clean. I was living off the streets and was hospitalized when I was 15 years old. I found out I wasn't allowed to have any visitors other than my mother, and they were listening to my phone calls. I realized I must have a problem. I'm in the mental ward. I am trying to get through drugs or alcohol.

I started drinking at age five. My parents gave me alcohol in my milk to put me to sleep. I started stealing beers from my dad when I was five years old. I kept stealing until I was about ten. He would buy cases and never notice if one was missing. I would take a case and sneak it into my room and have one or two friends over for beers, and then drugs when I was about 11 or 12 years old.

My parents never knew, they had no clue. They thought I was a saint from heaven. They thought I had a learning disability and that's why I was having a hard time in school. It was really because I was bringing a water bottle full of vodka into class and drinking it. One of my teachers told me that she remembered me bringing water bottles, and she thought I was really thirsty. I'd be sitting there in the back of class drinking. She remembered my handwriting was pretty good at the start of the day and by the end it was so sloppy that she couldn't read it, so she would throw it away. One of the reasons I passed her class was because I did a lot of extra credit work. That's the way I passed most of my classes.

My mom found out I was drinking and doing drugs after I tried to kill myself. My mom and I got in this fight. I said, "@#* it" I'm just gonna leave this world." I grabbed the nearest pair of scissors and tried stabbing myself. My brother caught my wrist and sat on me until the ambulance and the police got there. I was carried off on a stretcher. No wounds or anything, but I came close. I was under a suicidal tendency watch. They gave me a drug test and found out that I had done a lot of crystal in the last few days. I neglected to tell them that the day I was put in the hospital I was to get four ounces of crystal to sell to people on the street. I had someone hold my money so my parents wouldn't get suspicious. I got my money from selling.

I thought, "I'm not an addict. I can quit whenever I want to. I quit pot six months ago." It's lucky they didn't test me a few months before because they would have found a lot of things in my system.

I was planning on bringing drugs in from Mexico and Germany, and bringing them over in cargo crates. I wanted a family and wanted to raise them with drugs and s—t like that. I thought I was gonna give them a better life than I ever had.

And now I see it different. I'm going to finish high school and then go to junior college. I'm going to San Francisco School of Arts to study architecture because I want to become an architect if I can. And then, from there, I'm hooked on getting married and having a family. I'm a family man.

I'm not going to raise my kids like my father raised me. He was drinking beers here left and right. I'm not gonna do that to my son, or my daughter. I'm a strong believer against child abuse. Children should not be beaten for any reason.

My family's very supportive. You know, the first person I met at PARTS was a good friend, and she's still is a good friend of mine. Yeah, they've helped me out a lot. Sometimes I'll come in here with a problem and someone will call me on my s—t. They tell me what's wrong with me. They say, "You know the answer's right in front of you, but you just can't see it. You're telling yourself the answer. Just get a hold of it." They have so many sayings, I swear, I've heard them all.

Sixteen-Year-Old Adolescent Girl:

I am 16 years old, and I go to an emotional growth boarding school. I guess you could say I messed up real bad to get here. I did drugs, lied and was not interested in school. My parents tried to threaten me with boarding school, random drug tests, and forcing me to stay at home. I refused to take my life seriously, and I was planning to smoke pot the rest of my life.

A typical weekend consisted of choosing what drugs to do on Friday night with my friends, scrambling to get to work on time Saturday morning, doing more drugs on Saturday night, and trying to recover on Sunday for school the next day. Compared to others, I did not call myself a heavily addicted teenager. However, I did my fair share. I smoked pot on a regular basis, and I drank alcohol whenever it was around. LSD was a drug I used on occasion, and I tried hash, mushrooms, crystal, and cocaine.

I liked experimenting and thought it was fairly normal. I had a boyfriend, for a little over a year, who I used drugs with. I was willing to stay clean if that's what it took to keep me at home. Unfortunately, I ended up in the hospital, on February 5,1995. After that I went to a 30 day treatment center.

When the time was up for my parents to make a decision of where I should go, they decided it would be best for me to finish school away from everyone and begin my recovery. Yesterday was my 7 month sober anniversary. I am very proud of myself for trying to turn my life around.

However, it isn't easy. I have had all my clothes, make-up, perfume, and cigarettes taken away. I can only have contact with my family. They do this so I can have a fresh start on life. Slowly you earn all your privileges back. I am doing well in school, and I just started my senior year. For the first time, I am actually taking my life seriously.

Sixteen-Year-Old Adolescent Boy:

I use to come to PARTS because there was a lot of good kids here. There were a lot of kids here because they wanted to be clean, and a lot of my friends were here. Most of those kids aren't here any more, and I'm still here. I started using drugs because I was the little kid who was hanging out with the big guys. I started hanging out with the wrong people and started doing drugs when I was 12, and I didn't quit till I was 15. All that peer pressure stuff is crap. I had the urge, and I had a desire.

My parents were clueless. Kids know every way in the world to hide drugs from their parents. That's just the way it is. I mean we have many tricks in the book. I didn't live at home from when I was 14. I had my own place, and I got my money for dope by stealing cars and other things. I don't miss the drugs and all the stuff.

I moved back home when I was 15 and got clean. My parents said, "Welcome back." After I started going to meetings for three days, I could tell my mom was still wondering. I sat her down, and I told her about my whole problem. I told her about my addictions, and then she started crying. I was really sad for her. The bottom for me was waking up one morning and realizing I was buying my drugs from 30-year-old white trash who had no life. All he cared about was buying and selling dope. I didn't want to be that 30-year-old man, so I stopped right then. For me it was, "I can't handle this any more. My life has turned into crap. It's turned to nothing, and I can't live like this."

I didn't have any plans. I just wanted to do dope and steal cars for the rest of my life. Then it just hit me when I was 15. It was February 3rd and I woke up. I had some friends and a girlfriend that were in the program so I knew where they were at. I went with her once, and I knew what was up. Another friend in the program said, "Try to be clean." I've been here for 445 days.

It was easy for me because I wanted to be clean. A lot of kids come here because they have to. Their parents lock them up in treatment centers, and they don't really want to get clean, but it kind of forces them to it. Eventually some decide, "Hey, maybe I should get clean."

You can't make a person go clean. All the drug tests in the world and all the yelling and screaming of the parents do not matter. If I saw some kids that were walking in my shoes, I'd tell them to shape up and take them to a meeting. PARTS can help you. Maybe that one percent who will actually stay around and say, "Hey, you know my life's messed up, and I'm gonna go clean."

I got my life back. I got my personality back. I'm still scrawny, but I've gotten a lot of my physical stuff back. I got trust back. I still mess up every now and then. I still have an awful lot of old behaviors, but nothing big. My mom and stepdad don't really get the whole idea of drug addiction. They felt that when I got around six months clean, I was cured. They said, "You know, you don't have that drug problem any more." They don't understand when you got a drug problem you're an addict and you're always an addict. I have to work my butt off to get out and go to a meeting, but they support me.

I love PARTS because when you're trying to get clean, lots of people there have more time than me. The first thing you want to do when you get clean is ditch all your old friends and make new ones that are clean and sober. PARTS is excellent for that. They have a lot of kids working on their sobriety. They are really good because they teach you how to go clean. You get a whole new life of sober friends.

Seventeen-Year-Old Adolescent Girl:

I'm 17 years old, and I started coming to PARTS with a friend of mine. I decided that since I was hanging around here a lot, it was time for me to get sober. I had been in treatment centers before, and it hadn't really helped. I was put in a hospital for recovery after I tried to commit suicide. I never dealt with my emotions. I used every kind of drug, except for PCP, and I lived on the streets for about a month. I felt my mom drove me out of the house when I was living with her.

I started drinking because my dad's hobby was wine tasting. I began sipping wine with another kid when I was seven. Then my cousin started smoking pot, so I began when I was eight years old. I went on to other drugs from there. I've been doing heavy drugs since I was about 15 years old, and I used to sell and steal a lot of drugs.

I never got caught, in fact, I used to walk up to a cop and say, "Hi, how are you doing?" It was really funny, living on the streets, because all the cops knew me and they never figured out that I was using.

Drugs really screwed up my family life. I don't have a relationship with my mom. My dad and I are just now getting back close. My parents are divorced. My mom's side of the family didn't know I was using, and it probably would kill my grandparents if they found out. My mom's side is not very supportive, so I've had more support from my dad, and he's more understanding now about my problems. He knew I was using, but he didn't know how bad it was.

Honestly, I'd rather have a relationship with my mom because she is my mom and I'd like to know her better. She will never support me at all. She says it's all in the mind, and you can just stop if you want to. She smoked pot with her friends in college, and she just doesn't understand.

Sometimes you can't stop. That's the definition of addiction. It wasn't easy to fit in for me. The only thing I knew was drugs. If I didn't have drugs on me, I would wait in a parking lot for five hours. I waited for the sale to go down, and it was really stressful. I started living on the streets, and one of my friends died of a heroin overdose. Another one of my friends shot himself in the head from crack. When I lost my friends, I hit bottom because I thought, "Oh, God, I don't want this to happen to me. I don't want to see anymore friends die, and I don't want to see myself die." I was in pretty bad shape, not in very good health at all. If I was still living on the streets, I wouldn't have a future, honestly, I would probably be dead. That's the bottom line. I wouldn't have survived more than three months if I was still living on the street, the way, the rate I was buying and using. It's pretty scary out there.

I'm working on my majors, psychology and music. My goal is to play each part of a symphony and be the principal base player in the Chicago Symphony Orchestra. I'm hoping to get to go to Australia this summer with the orchestra. I would never have never been able to do this when I was using.

PARTS has done so much for me. The support here is unbelievable. I didn't realize so many people out there had the same patterns I did. They've been there. I really like the support. They're there for me! When I need a kick start in the morning, they call me. If I have a problem, there is someone out there with an answer. And, I love to help people. People can call me whenever they want, and I'm there for them.

My dad was such a logical thinker. He could never understand what I was going through or know what my feelings were. He never showed emotion, and now he meets me at the airport and hugs and kisses me on the forehead. He would never do that before. The first time I did a double take and looked back at him and said, "What was that for?"

A couple of my friends said, "Yeah, he's changing a lot," which is good to see because he's showing more emotion toward me, and it makes me feel really good. Now I feel more love by him, and I can understand him more on his level.

PARTS is Parents and Adolescents Recovering Together Successfully and I'm a board member. I'm the only junior board member, and now I realize how much PARTS is involved with.

Sixteen-Year-Old Adolescent Boy:

It all started when I was 14. I started getting into smoking pot. I remember that I was never forced into smoking. I just had the urge to try it. I liked to smoke and got to the point where I was smoking everyday. At this point the questions started coming from my mom. She asked, "Are you using drugs?" My response was "No, Mom. What makes you think that?" She would respond, "Because your attitude has been changing a lot lately." I basically blew my mom off and just kept on smoking my life away. I was already to the point of caring about my dope more than family or anything else. Too bad it was just the beginning of my problem.

After the summer had passed, I was on my way into high school at age 15, just waiting to see how much fun I could have there. It took me not much longer than a week to find a new group of interesting friends that had done a lot of stuff I had never heard of. I was on my way to being introduced to a lot of stuff I probably did not want to see. I was already into dropping acid. I went through that experience before school had started. Little did I know I was going to be ditching five out of six periods of school almost every day so I could go drop acid and smoke more pot. It seems like every day I was doing more and more.

Things at home were not going so well. My mom knew I was using. She was very worried about me because she saw all of the changes I was going through. I pretty much did not care about anything but myself and my drugs.

About a month into school I guess I must have been really confused. I decided to run away from my house. I remember saying I would never go on my own. I went to my friends house because he was having a party. His mom was out of town for about a week, so he told me I could crash there until she got back. I was fine with that. Anyway, the first night I was away from home, I got into something I wish I would not have never heard about. I started doing crystal meth. Definitely the worst drug I had ever done. From that very first night of doing crystal, I became addicted to it. I was still doing a lot of acid and a lot of smoking pot. I was already so screwed up, I didn't even notice the changes in me. I ended up living at my friends house even after she got home. My friend's mom had no clue we were snorting lines of crystal every day. I ended up staying there for a little over two months. After that, things got even worse.

I ended up living in a hotel for about two weeks, living the life of a car thief, a drug user, and basically a bum. I wish I would have realized what was going on with me. I ended up in Arizona for a couple weeks because of all the stolen cars. We had to leave for a little while because our friend got caught, and we were traced to cars that were stolen. My finger prints were on some of the cars.

Arizona was terrible. The only thing I really remember about that place was me sleeping almost all day, everyday. I never thought I would be getting myself into this mess. I never believed I would become a drug user. I guess some things just happen.

Seventeen-Year-Old Adolescent Boy:

I can see the sun shining through the curtains, another day is coming, I guess. Eight hours ago I was happy, ready to take on the world, even though I'm still in this @#* apartment. I felt like I accomplished something. I guess I did, I drew the blood and kept myself going for eight more hours. I tried to talk to God again, but I guess the son of a bitch wasn't taking my calls. Obviously, since I'm still here, the devil wasn't either. Sometimes I wish he was on my shoulder so he could take me away from here, from the god awful pain I feel when my loads run dry and my sack is empty.

A long time ago when my mind was young and didn't understand death, I used to wonder what happened to the souls of the dying. I wish I could be so young again. Today death is nothing more than a companion who stands in the distance waiting for moments of weakness. He is everywhere, he carries no sickle and wears no robe. He's unseen and surrounds me every hour of every day, just waiting. I wish he would come for me now because I have nothing left to fight with. My veins are empty. I feel so alone, so sad and lost. Whatever happened to the promise of love, the future. Death is not to be feared—it is to be invited. My only thought is to leave this place, this world forever.

Seventeen-Year-Old Adolescent Girl:

The first time I drank alcohol was in fourth grade. By tenth grade, I found crystal, which was a new kind of a wonder drug that could get me through school and made everything okay. I was doing crystal for about six months. And it pretty much kicked my behind. My parents really didn't know. I kind of had a nervous breakdown and ran away from home. I hated my parents, and I hated my life. I moved in with a friend and tried to get clean. I kind of upset the whole family structure.

I wasn't a party girl, and I didn't stay out late. I just did my drugs at home. The crystal was a little upper for school. It was my homework helper. I could stay up all night, doing my homework, and it helped me get done really fast. It was fine and everything was taken care of. The alcohol was an escape. I didn't have to deal with anything when I was drinking.

My family attributed a lot of it to normal, teenage behavior. They didn't like the loud music, and locking yourself off from your family was pretty much what parents expect kids to do. I had a nervous breakdown because I emotionally couldn't handle it. I weighed 93 pounds and was an emotional wreck. I didn't know what was going on in my life. I was very scared, and I really wanted to get clean. When I ran away from home, my parents decided to go to PARTS. One of the requirements at the group was to go to one outside meeting a week. From the first moment we got here, things started to change. Within, about two months, I was back home.

I wasn't an inpatient anywhere. When I ran away from home, I made a phone call to my mom that went, "Hi, I'm trying to get clean, bye." They decided that meetings at Kaiser would be a good idea. Kaiser recommended PARTS, and we came here. Ever since the orientation meeting, things have gotten a lot better. The first few weeks we were here we yelled at each other all the time. At every multi-family meeting we looked at each other and yelled. Other parents explained to my parents what was going on and how they dealt with it. Other kids explained to me what was going on and how they dealt with it. It allowed the communication to get better.

And now, 18 months later, I've been clean for a year and a half. My parents come every week, and they come to help. My mom does the phone lists and the attendance sheets, and writes the letters to the Court for people who have to be here. It's important to me, it helps them, too. The thing about PARTS is that it helps everybody in the family. It's so important to come here with your parents. Addicts have other places to go, but addicts' parents don't have many place to go. They don't have a places where they can get the support they need. PARTS helps heal the family instead of just taking an individual outside the family and dealing with them. Parents are just as frightened and confused as anyone else would be.

I've learned that you can deal with life on modest terms and you don't need to escape, and you don't need something to get you through the day. You can deal with life. And it's okay. It's not happy all the time, but life happens and things are gonna happen that aren't what you want them to be. That's the way life is. I've grown really attached to PARTS. It's the place where I can get and give support, and it feels good to help other people. I'm going to be in college in the fall.

Seventeen-Year-Old Adolescent Boy:

It all started when I was 15 and things were okay. I felt like something was missing though, and after awhile I found out that it was drugs. I had been active in sports just about all my life: soccer, baseball, and football, but they were beginning to get real boring. The first time I was introduced to drugs I was not very interested in the idea of getting "high." My so-called "friends" insisted that I try it and I would not be sorry for doing it. I am ashamed to say this but they were right. Things got bad. All I could think about was when I was gonna get my next high. In time that came to be true, and I was barely getting by in school, church and my life.

I couldn't stay in school long. I felt like I had to get out of there. I was getting high every day. Sometimes not even eating lunch for a week straight just to get high. It got real bad at church. I was supposed to be a role model for the younger kids. Eventually, they figured out what I was. I had a bad "trip" at a church function one night, and I flipped out. I felt like I was homeless lying under the tables trying to get these orange bugs out of the carpet. That was when everybody started to laugh, and I felt like the biggest outcast in the world. I don't keep in touch with them anymore for a reason.

Life at home got really bad, I thought. My parents are very giving and loving, but everything they wanted me to do I was completely against, and I made them hate taking me along. I made it a point for them to hate me. I was very selfish, very selfish. It got to the point where I had to lie more frequently than most kids would. I couldn't get through the day by telling the truth. In fact, I didn't even know what telling the truth was. I have only been caught four times high and drunk combined. I had them pretty much fooled, but I couldn't fool myself. My mom had begun to have some real problems with me. I was "couch surfing" as a way of life. My thick head still could not get a clue that I had a problem.

I ran everywhere telling everybody what awful things she was doing to me to make the odds against her. As you can probably tell, that didn't matter at the time. I never left home until I went into treatment, but that came in later. I hurt my mom emotionally real bad. She went through her phase of being a bad mother. She thought she was. I tried to tell her that she didn't have to give a damn about me, which hurt her even more. I had no concept of what my actions were doing to her, but I didn't care either. I left on bad terms, which is the way I wanted it.

I was one of the best when it came to parties. My friends loved me when it was party time because I didn't care about anything except getting as drunk or high as I could possibly go. There were even times when I would even go past that point. When I got high, I got high, and I did crazy and stupid things. My friends wanted to do them also, but they cared about what others thought of them. I didn't.

I can remember one night when my best friend tried to help me, but he turned his back and I ended up in a blackout for I don't know how long. I don't even know how I got home that night. I woke up from my blackout at the front door of my house puking. I remember asking my mom for help with my drinking problem. I had a good thing coming, but I got blasted the next day at school.

That was the way everything went when it came to parties. I would wake up in the morning. Sometimes not even home wondering where I was. I remember another night when my uncle, aunt and cousins, who look up to me, were in town. I was out with my best friend getting high, and we came home. My parents were leaving to put my dog to sleep, and I felt like death. That's when I think I realized that I had a problem with drugs.

My plans were to be the biggest clown of all times! I did everything in my power to be the biggest goof-off. I eventually reached that point, and I thought I was, but I wasn't. Throughout the whole school just about everybody knew who I was. I had finally gotten my reputation as clown. I didn't get much out of school, except how to survive among the wild. I even got a rep at school as the "party king". Now I am only two tests away from getting my GED in Omaha, Nebraska.

I guess that in my own little sick way, I was trying to tell my parents that I needed help. The night that I used for the last time was March 27, 1995. My parents were sitting on the couch and I played the song "Liar" from the Rollins Band. The ending is what summed it up for me: "If you give me one more chance, I swear I'll never lie again. Now I see the destructive power of lies. They are stronger than truth, I'm sorry I can't believe I ever hurt you. I will never lie again, I promise." The next day I sobered up and have been since March 28, 1995.

The dream that I had was very disturbing, maybe even a nightmare. It was about killing a certain someone, slowly and very painfully. That happened for two weeks straight one week while using.

That's when I thought something was wrong, and I went into inpatient treatment.

I was 18 years old, and I didn't catch on too quickly, but eventually I did. Things were real hard at first, everybody was free except me. I would stare out to the freeway, thinking, "Look at all those innocent people going home." The day when I was moving downstairs to outpatient, I woke up with a little bit of reality. I did really well. I did my homework and everything else expected for the most part. It wasn't too much time until I found out that I would soon be leaving there.

This is the best meeting that I've been to in a long time. It's where we all hung out. The best part about the meeting was before and after. I am real happy to hear that my old gang is still sober!

Moving was real tough on everyone. I set my mind on not thinking about leaving all my friends behind. It was something that I had to do, good or bad. My family and everybody behind was too hard to look at, but the day came. It was time to leave. I said "goodbye" to everyone. I didn't want to leave because it hurt. I felt alone, real alone. When I was on the plane, I cried just about the whole way there, and I haven't cried much since that day.

Seventeen-Year-Old Adolescent Girl:

I started smoking pot when I was 15 years old, and I continued to use more and more every day, until my life was unmanageable. I was almost 17. I did it because of peer pressure, to be cool in school, to be popular, and to have fun. I thought that drinking and smoking pot was the only way to have fun. It was the only way to make friends easily. I didn't have much of a relationship with my family until I become clean, so it affected my family tremendously.

I would come home drunk or stoned, and I would lie about it. I moved out of the house for seven months because I was right and they were wrong. I ditched school, and I didn't have any trust. I did numerous, deliberate evil things. I hit bottom when I realized that every dime in my paycheck was going for drugs and alcohol. I didn't save any money, and I wrote bad checks. I was only 16 years old, and I already had bad credit. I was writing checks so I could get cash to buy beer. I didn't take school seriously, and I didn't care about anything. I isolated myself from my family, and I kept to myself. My friends were always pressuring me to use drugs, and they were always coming to my rescue.

If I needed drugs they would help me, and they would give me a place to stay. They were my scapegoats. It was easy to use drugs because I would say, "Oh, I'm going over to my friend's house." So I could say I was there, and do something else. We would have contests, and we would play games. We wouldn't just sit and use, we would play Quarters, or other social using games.

My parents and I made deals like if you have two months sober you will get rewarded. If you have three months, you will get rewarded more. They did this as opposed to grounding me for negative things. I was rewarded for doing things that were right. That was a big change because it's a lot easier to do the right thing than getting in trouble. I have a lot of trust in my family now, and my family has a lot of trust in me. I feel like I can tell my parents a lot of things that I could never tell them before. I've developed good relationships with my parents, not negative relationships.

I don't have many friends anymore, and I used to have a lot of friends. It's a slap in the face when you become sober and find out who your real friends are. It comes down to a handful, or not even that. My friends now are strictly from PARTS and different support groups. I don't really have a best friend or anything like that. I don't trust that easy. The best friends I have right now are my family.

PARTS makes me a person, it gives me wholeness, and it fills up the despair I had. I'm more content. I trust myself, and I trust my own intuition. This program and other programs have taught me a lot about my disease. I know that we're not responsible for our disease, but we are responsible for recovering. PARTS is a foundation where you can open up in front of other peers, your parents, and your parents' peers. You can ask how people relate to different situations with different families and get feedback. You learn there's other people in the world that have the same problems you do. It's nice knowing that even their parents know about it, and everybody knows so it's not a secret. And it's nice to know there are other people like you, and you're not the only one. And, neither are your parents. I know it helps the parents to know they can go in their own room and talk, and we go in our room and talk and swap stories.

Be cool. It's cool not to do drugs. Don't forget to go to school. I have knowledge now about alcoholism and addiction, and I advise other young people. Drugs are for people who can't handle reality, and reality is for people who can't handle drugs.

PARTS stands for Parents and Adolescents Recovering Together Successfully. When I think about PARTS. I think about different PARTS of your sobriety, different PARTS of your addiction that come together as a whole with your family and you. PARTS of the puzzle that match up.

Eighteen-Year-Old Adolescent Boy:

The weather report called for rain. A storm was approaching steadily and should arrive by nightfall, they said. It was already bitterly cold, and I could not help but shiver. The streets were lonely that night and I the same. A fiery hatred filled my eyes that gazed at the people who had somewhere to go. My heart was as empty as my stomach, but I had no food, I had nothing, almost nothing.

I knew of a park near me, there was a restroom there. I needed to escape the winds, the now falling rain. But most of all I needed to escape from my reality. Somewhere shots rang out, somewhere else I heard sirens. I was almost there. I turned the corner that led to the park. Poor lighting caused me to stumble across the floor to the first stall. Between flickers of lights I could only make out the well-vandalized walls of the restroom. If you knew me then you knew I kept my money in my sock. I struggled to find a vein that hadn't been beaten and bloodied. The needle was so dull and fired and caused so much pain I had to wince. After this time I'm throwing it away, I told myself, but so many times I did not.

As a child the sight of my own blood being drawn in a syringe frightened me. Sometimes I wish it still did.

The flickering light in that bathroom now showed the blood that ran down my arm dripping on my tattered clothes. With my head against the wall, I thought I'd entered paradise (for the time I had). I spoke to God, and all of heaven overwhelmed my spirit. For the first and only time since my last load did I smile, did I feel alive.

This incident is only one of many; I can tell you that this was one of my best nights on the street. So many people who knew me said that I had the look of a dead man, the icy stare of a corpse. Some said my destiny was to die from the one thing I had grown to love, some said nothing, perhaps that scared me the most. Death was an invited friend most of the time. An escape to a better world for me.

Me, the liar, the thief, the violent criminal at times. I was the inmate, always in the close-watch cell, I was the inpatient strapped to the white bed in that damn white room. I was the one who would kill you for ten dollars and a pack of cigarettes. I was the one without remorse, I was the one in the shadows, on the news. I was barely seventeen years old. I was rapidly moving toward becoming another statistic, another lost youth. The boy next door who no one talked about.

When all the meth and heroin ran out, when all my bridges were burned and old friends grew to hate the sight of me, when no more color could leave my face and eyes and I could lose no more weight, can you guess what I did?

No, I got high. But this time was different. This time I had to watch my friend die before me. His lifeless body laid there, his eyes still open, his arm still holding the very thing that killed him. His needle was mine five minutes earlier. I shed no tears, I just left.

This was going on two years ago now. Shortly after, I returned home and entered rehab again. Now after eighteen months of sobriety, I am here to pass on my experiences. I won't say that it was easy or that life is great now because it wasn't and life is a roller coaster. Sometimes I still dream about it, sometimes nothing else is on my mind. I can never forget those feelings, I can only deal with them. Because forgetting may mean starting over, and starting over will mean death.

Chapter Nine

HELP AND HOPE FROM PARENTS BACK FROM HELL

We present the following real words and stories (with minor editing) of parents who deal with (AOD) problems daily.

Mother Of A Fifteen-Year-Old Son:

I have a son, 15, and he has eight months clean. We've been going to PARTS for about a year and a half. He was having lots of problems in school, and we were having a lot of problems with his whole change in behavior. Things were real different as far as the change of friends, the change of attitude, the change of his perspective on life, and his values. Maybe if I had known more I would have had him drug tested earlier, but I just thought these were normal teenage problems. I wasn't really looking for drugs entering our family life.

It was about two years ago. He probably first tried marijuana a couple of times when he was 12 in the sixth grade. In seventh grade it became more regular, and in eighth grade it was like milk and cereal to some of us. A daily habit. I have to be very thankful for the school counselor because we were talking about his lack of motivation, ADD, and being a teenager. Then he asked my son, "Have you tried any drugs?" He said, "Oh, yeah, a couple of different times." The counselor took me aside and said, "Any time they say a couple of different times you can probably multiply or cube that number."

That's when we started taking a different look at him and realized that with addiction, they're going to lie to you. One time, within a week or so, he must have taken something that was a whole lot stronger than marijuana, probably crystal, or whatever, and he was very, very nervous. He talked very fast, and he could hardly contain himself. He seemed like he was so excited, and that was such an antithesis of his lack of motivation. I point blank said, "I'm gonna take you to be tested." And he said, "You don't have to. I'm higher than a kite." We sat down and talked about it and it hit us between the eyes that he didn't think anything was wrong with this kind of life. He said, "Hey, it's just Marijuana. I'm not gonna do anything heavy," and "marijuana is not any different than people having a glass of wine." We realized that there was a real difference between his values and those of our family.

We really felt like we needed to do something, and very quickly. He was just 14 years old. So we got him right into a program at Kaiser. Kaiser told us about PARTS, and it opened up our eyes as parents. At PARTS I was able to see what other parents had gone through with kids that were 12 or 13 and what happened to them at 16 and 17. It gave my husband and I the strength to say, "We need to do something right now, not go ahead and decide whether he's got a problem, or how much he's doing it, or find out more information. Let's not accept any part of his lifestyle and do everything possible to let him know that it's unacceptable. And tell him there is help here and go from there."

It was almost as if I was going through something terminal. I mean it was very traumatic. We weren't looking for drugs to be part of my 13 year old's life. I have known people, but it was always somebody else. Now it was me, and I had to face that. I was devastated, but only for awhile. When I came to PARTS, I was able to see that there were parents from every economic strata and every ethnicity. We were all devastated. No matter who you are, this tears the family apart. You have something hanging over you that is unacceptable. I had a whole new problem to deal with and it wasn't teenage behavior, it was drug addiction. Whatever your son or daughter is going through, you're all going through it at the same time. I didn't want to accept it, and yet here we were going to meetings and going to counseling. We also found out that we were working a whole lot harder than my son. We wanted him to recover, and he didn't. There was a period of time that was pretty difficult because with something like cancer you want to get well. You don't know whether you're going to or not. We didn't know whether our son was deciding to stay clean. He proved us wrong for a long time.

He's not into recovery. There are a lot of changes in attitudes and he's working through the steps, but he's abstaining. He does some of the things toward recovery. He was out of the home for six months at a Christian boarding school. We decided to get him away from all of his friends and out of the environment. He was not making an effort to stay clean, and we said over and over, "In order to stay in our home you have to be clean." We realized we had to do something that would prove our point. We said, "As long as you're not going to make the effort to stay clean, you can't stay home. We'll make sure that you are in an environment where we can guarantee that you're gonna be clean, and that's not in our home. It will provide you with your food, structure, housing, and it will provide with some values. You won't have a whole lot of choices, but you'll be clean."

There's been a big improvement because he wants to be home. Previously he thought it was a right that he had, and now he knows that he doesn't have that right. He thought just because he's our son, and we love him, we're gonna turn over and say, "Oh, gee, this is fine. You can live with us and stay dirty." He knows now that we're serious about when we say, "No drugs!" And that's the only reason he's doing this. He isn't saying, "I know that recovery is for me, and that I'm gonna be clean." He knows that as a 15 year old he would like to be able to drive. He knows that he would like to be free. He likes having free time with his friends, and he doesn't have any of those privileges unless he can be home. He knows that the only way he can stay home is if he's clean. So it's a matter of consequences and rewards. I wouldn't ever say that his light bulb is turned on or that he says, "I think marijuana isn't good for you, and it ruins your life, and I'm not gonna have any future." He lives day to day, and it's amazing that he's got eight months clean right now. But day to day, he has decided that, "Wow! This is a whole lot better than being in boarding school."

PARTS helps families to identify with people who've gone through the same pain and teaches things that are not in textbooks or that counselors offer. There are people who say, "This is a painful experience, and I'm able to get through it and survive, and actually even have a life of my own." And you can, too. That's the real strength parents need. They need to know that they're going through this as well, and they've had certain expectations about what they want for their family and for their life and those have all been blown apart. They need to rethink about how they're parenting, and about how they're living their life.

In order to rethink you have to be able to talk to people and listen to what others have gone through and pick up some of their ideas. Try them out. Parents have to have a place to cry and a place where somebody else can say, "I understand why you're crying. I know what it feels like."

A Parent's Story Of Their Adolescent Son:

My wife and I kicked our son out of our home on his eighteenth birthday. The kid who walked away that day, and who shivered, and sometimes slept, on the beach for two December weeks, came home a young man focusing on the life ahead of him instead of on the next high he could achieve. His remarkable turnaround is his achievement, but I believe its genesis was only made possible by the decisions and actions his mother and I took in the several months leading up to his birthday. At the suggestion of our school's counselor, I would like to share with you some information about PARTS, the program our son became involved in that gave us the determination to take the steps we did.

PARTS is an acronym for Parents and Adolescents Recovering Together Successfully. It is run by families for families, and offers support and information to parents trying to deal with their children's (AOD) abuse. It offers support to adolescents with professional and peer support for those striving for sobriety. Weekly programs vary in format, including separate meetings for adults and kids, multi-generational meetings, and issue-specific meetings covering such topics as stop-smoking, job search and ADHD therapies. We learn from and support each other. We gain perspective and knowledge about alcohol and other drug abuse, creativity in our problem solving, and growing up in the '90s.

Before we found PARTS, my wife and I had retreated from all our hopes and dreams for our son. Our despair was exceeded only by our inability to make any positive difference in his life. We feel that as it has been for us, PARTS can be a vital resource for other families.

A Parent's Story Of Their Adolescent Son:

When I was twenty-five years old, my wife gave birth to a baby boy. He was born two months premature, weighing just over two pounds. For thirteen days he struggled to survive, but it was not to be. When we buried him, we thought that nothing could ever again hurt our family like that. How wrong we were. We had another son two and a half years later. There was never a child who was more wanted and loved. He was raised with sound morals and values. We were pleased with the kind of person he was becoming. After all, he was achieving most of our expectations.

If we try to trace when our painful experience began, we would have to guess it started when our son was fourteen. The warmth that was once part of our relationship was gone. The changes were gradual. Or, were they there, and we just didn't see them? They were unexplained, but we suspected. Was it just a phase that he would outgrow? We knew that entering adolescence meant separation. However, we were unprepared for the person he had became. The smiles were replaced by cold stares; the hugs by hitting, and "I love you" by filthy, belligerent language. When the behavior escalated to physical abuse and rage, we could no longer look the other way. He was admitted to a hospital for youths and adolescents who are chemically dependent or self-destructive. He was sixteen years old.

There are days in your life that you always remember. Usually, they are marked by an event that changes your life dramatically. The day that we were informed by his doctor as to the extent of his drug use is one that we will never forget. Our son was an ADDICT! He was using crystal methamphetamine. He was a male bulimic, and he didn't like purging. As a result he used crystal to suppress his appetite. He was also "huffing" gasoline four times a week. That explained all the headaches he was having. The week that he spent in the lockdown unit in the hospital, and the weeks that followed, were ones filled with desperation and despair. We had no idea why he was so depressed. Why was he abusing his body and mind with drugs?

The vision of our life as a family was shattered. Our son didn't feel loved or valued. He truly felt that he did not belong. We often question if we were strangers for more years than we can remember. Grief was constant, and we were all suffering in our own private ways. Some of the questions were hard to ask. Some of the answers painful to hear. How do you live with your child in the same house for all those years and look into the face of a stranger? We already knew that losing a child was one of the cruelest heartbreaks that could happen to a family. We were not going to let it happen again. We were determined to do everything within our power as parents to save our son.

Then, miraculously, our search for knowledge and answers brought us to PARTS, (Parents And Adolescent Recovering Together Successfully). We as a family, started our journey to recovery; we, were all looking for answers. However, we needed support for what was to come. No one who has not gone through this could really understand what was happening. How desperate this time was. The members of this support group, PARTS, took us under their wing; they provided us with understanding. There was warmth and compassion. We could express our fears, cry our tears, and come away with self-respect. No one judged us as parents or as people. We borrowed their strength and it became ours.

As communications opened, we dared to hope that our family could be reunited. At this time we took the very best of ourselves and gave it to our son. There were times when we were saddened to think that our family was cheated out of life's expectations. Those occurrences that most of us take for granted. That pain stays sedated because we have gained so much since that association started.

We are grateful that our son has made positive life choices. He has been clean and sober for over two and a half years. After getting D's and F's in school while under the influence of drugs, he just recently graduated from high school with a solid B average. He is working; he plans to continue his education. We know that we are extremely fortunate that he chose sobriety. We are the lucky ones. We thank God every day for our son's health. And we thank PARTS for helping us to become a family again.

PARTS continues to grow. That's because of the increased use of drugs and alcohol by adolescents. Hospitals, doctors, judges and law enforcement agencies continue to refer families to PARTS. Its unwavering mission is to assist, educate and empower parents and adolescents during their crisis and ongoing recovery. PARTS also conducts drug awareness seminars within the community to make parents understand that addiction is a disease.

This happens many times in many other families. It could be your son or your daughter. It's a scenario that we wish all other families never have to experience. However, it's a reality that is constantly lurking at your door, or in your neighborhood. And it is a family issue.

Mother Of A Sixteen-Year-Old Daughter:

At 21, I had experimented with marijuana, LSD, cocaine and alcohol. By the time my daughter was born, I knew I was an alcoholic. Because I promised myself to raise my children differently, I knew I had to leave their father because of his alcoholism and marijuana use. I also knew I wanted to quit drinking, so I began trying to limit my intake of alcohol. During my pregnancy I cut down substantially, but I now believe that using any alcohol or other drugs during pregnancy may increase chances of addiction for the unborn child. This conclusion is based on many stories I have heard from other parents.

When my daughter was ten I finally quit drinking, but the years of alcoholism had taken its toll. When my second child was born, my daughter felt as though I didn't love her anymore. She began experimenting with alcohol. I didn't know this at the time, but I did notice that she was drifting away from me. I felt we had been extremely close. In her earlier years, I provided as many activities as we could afford, including four to six dance classes a week, acting, voice, and piano lessons. I participated with her in Campfire Girls and as many other activities as I could. I tried to protect her self-esteem as completely as I could, as I remember the misery I felt from low self-esteem when I was young.

When my daughter entered middle school, I became aware of her extremely belligerent attitude and her hostility toward her sister and stepfather, and myself. I attributed this to normal adolescent behavior, but now I know that it was inappropriate and that she was acting out for help. I discovered she was taking my car out at the age of 12, and I began feeling very powerless, depressed and sad. I knew our family was out of control but was at a loss about what to do.

One day I received a call from a counselor at her middle school. The counselor called to tell me that my daughter had ditched school and had been picked up by a deputy sheriff. The counselor called me and told me my daughter was in a serious mental state and that I should not bring her home, but take her to a hospital. I didn't know it at the time, but my life was about to dramatically change forever.

When I picked my daughter up from her school, I took her directly to the hospital. She was still behaving in a belligerent and obnoxious way, so she didn't notice the locked elevator and other security devices. She was clueless about where she was. She didn't have any clothes, so I went home, picked up clothes, and returned to the hospital. By this time she realized that she was somewhere where her freedom was completely restricted, and she pleaded with me to take her home. She said she was sorry and promised she would behave better from now on. These were the most difficult moments of my life. I was torn between my desire to protect and nurture her myself, and the realization that she was in serious trouble and needed to stay. When I told her she would have to stay and be evaluated, she became hostile again, and I knew I was doing the right thing.

She stayed in the hospital for two and a half weeks, which was probably the most painful time of my life. She celebrated her 13th birthday in the hospital by calling me every name she could think of and telling me she never wanted to see me again. She said she hated me for leaving her there, and I decided that I was not going to take this behavior anymore. During hospitalization, parents were invited to meetings and I learned the most important concept. That concept was that we need to take care of ourselves and not put other people's needs above our own. While that may sound selfish, I now know it is the only way a person can have meaningful relationships with anyone, or be an effective parent.

After my daughter came home from the hospital, her behavior was wonderful, and I mistakenly thought we were past the nightmare. We began attending a weekly meeting called PARTS (Parents and Adolescents Recovering Together Successfully). After a few months home, however, my daughter started staying up late and her grades started slipping again. She ditched school again and almost was expelled from a new school I had moved her to. She then tried to commit suicide by swallowing a bottle of Tylenol. Fortunately her friend made her call 911. At the hospital my daughter told me she had been using since she was released from the hospital, but now she was using crystal meth. She had to swallow charcoal to offset the Tylenol, and from that day on she began working an intense program. She attended PARTS faithfully and attended AA or NA meetings at least twice a week. She began a relationship with a young man with three years of sobriety.

My daughter is sixteen and just became a senior in high school. She is working an independent study program rather than attending a conventional high school due to the pressures that exist in the public schools for using (AOD). She also has nothing in common with these high school students. She also works 30 hours a week and pays for most everything in her life. She is looking forward to college, and this motivates her to push to finish high school as soon as possible. While it saddens me somewhat that she will miss traditional high school experiences, I am thrilled that she has been able to continue her education. Many recovering young people lose this experience entirely. Her relationship with her boyfriend has endured almost four years. I hope she can find true happiness in her life.

Of all the things I have been blessed with throughout this experience, the most important aspect is my involvement with PARTS. I have developed relationships with many parents and adolescents from PARTS. I have learned more about recovery, relationships and positive lifestyles from these people than from any other source. The parents who I have become close with are dear to me and will always hold a special place in my heart.

I also have learned that most children completely imitate their parents and take to heart all of their behaviors, bad or good. We need to pay attention to each detail of child rearing. If we get lax about setting good examples and spending enough time with our children, our children and society pay the price. I have also learned that we must not let our children manipulate us into submission for things we know are not in the child's best interest (easier said than done).

All of the parents I have met through PARTS tried to be good parents and did their best to protect and teach their children. Through PARTS we have learned to be even better parents and, hopefully, we have taught our children how to be better parents.

Mother Of An Adolescent Son:

You never dream that when your baby boy is born, and you go to check him to make sure he is still breathing, that seventeen years later you will be looking at him on the floor. He was unconscious, surrounded by paramedics, and it was due to alcohol poisoning. This is not when our story begins. It started many months before this. First we noticed the personality changes. He didn't let us know when he was coming in late or when he was not coming home at all. We began calling the police and got to know them on a first name basis.

We then went through psychiatric visits where we were told that our son fell through the cracks. There were many very serious trips to the emergency room. There was the unrelenting stress that he put on the whole family, including his younger brother.

Our son was admitted to rehab, and then we made the difficult decision to put him in an out of state program. He was in three out of state programs. Each time we were hoping and praying this was the one that would finally help save our son.

After our son returned home we, reluctantly, wanted to give him the chance to move ahead with his life. It didn't work, and we ended up asking him to leave our home. This was the worst thing I've ever had to do. My heart felt like it was being ripped out of my body. The bottom line is that our son is the one person who has to make the decision to save himself and who has to realize that it has to come from within.

We believe that all the programs that he went through were a learning process for him. As parents it's impossible to describe, in words, the feelings that consume your body when you see your child taken over by drugs. PARTS has been a safe haven for us as parents to go and share our feelings with other parents going through similar experiences. It has been a life saver for my husband, myself, and our relationship with each other. Even though it is an up and down battle, we continue to go for support and to help others. It's comforting to know that we are not alone.

My husband, myself, and his brother have a great amount of faith that our son will continue to fight this wicked disease of addiction, that he will beat it, and he will discover the wonderful, talented person he is. We love him very much and will continue to support him in his sobriety and recovery for as long as it takes, but he has to want it.

Mother Of An Adolescent Son:

In the book *The Prophet* there's a beautiful passage which reads, "Love is the tide that flows between two souls." Four months ago the only thing flowing between my son and I was raw sewage. His drug addiction was tearing us apart. We couldn't stand each other. There was so much insanity in our home that one day, out of desperation, I told my son to take his drugs and his booze, his bong, and his "dead head" friends and get out of my house! When it's that crazy, the abnormal becomes normal.

After about a week he came to the door with his hat in hand asking to come home. He was scared, and so was I. We didn't know what to do. We finally decided drug rehabilitation was the way to go. Little did we know that rehab would become recovery and a whole new life for both of us. I am so grateful for PARTS, Narcotics Anonymous, and Nar-Anon. Because of these programs we came to believe that a power greater than ourselves could restore us to sanity. The tide once again flows between us, and I can honestly look at my son today and say, "I truly love you."

Father Of Twenty-Year-Old Son:

I have a son, 20, who is an addict in recovery. His primary drugs of choice were crystal and pot.

Three years ago he was admitted to the hospital where they have a program where parents and adolescents come together. It's called PARTS.

He was caught at school with a small amount of pot. We had suspected that he was using, but we couldn't find any evidence. He had changed his friends, and the new friends did not come to our house. His grades started dropping, but we blamed that on his learning disability. He had been in special education since first grade. The pot affected his memory and learning process.

When he was caught with the pot, he was smoking it on a daily basis and using crystal. He was caught with pot at school, but there was not enough for the police to arrest him. There was a school board hearing. We signed a contract where he agreed to go to meetings and agreed to do community service. Things got worse and two weeks after that incident, he was in the hospital. He flipped out at home. He became very angry, shouting obscenities, slamming doors, throwing things, running out of the house and violating curfew. He was totally out of control.

We were angry, scared, frustrated, and we knew nothing about drug addiction, NA, or PARTS. It was a nightmare come true. We felt we had provided him a safe home with good standards and morals and had given him love and support. He went to Little League, Boy Scouts, church and Sunday school. We thought we had done all the "right" things, but it doesn't matter what you do or what kind of family you're from. Other factors often determine whether your adolescent becomes an addict.

He was frustrated in school because of his learning disability, and after years of struggling in school he had a poor self-image. When someone offered him drugs, they took away his pain, helped him to escape and feel good. To this day he's only shared a little bit about what was going on. I don't want to know everything, but he needs to explore his feelings and find out that he is a good person who can contribute to society.

He's had many relapses. Most of them have been minor, but several major relapses put him in emergency rooms.

We kicked him out of our house last July when he was 18. He was treating us like servants and using our house as a hotel. After coming home from an out-of-state recovery program, he figured that he was cured, but he wasn't ready to come home. We had a contract with him, but everything just went to hell. A lot of his old friends were using, and he could not handle it, so we said, "You have to be out!" He left on July 4th. Asking our son to leave our house was the hardest thing that we've ever done in our lives.

I know that PARTS has helped my wife, me and our son. We see him once a week at PARTS. Even though we're not living together, we come together in a group setting. Our relationship has gotten better since he is out of the house. He has been gone now for almost a year. There was a period of time when he was homeless, sleeping on the beach or on the sidewalk with no place to go. He has friends that he's made at PARTS who have provided him with a place to stay. Now he lives with other people in recovery looking for a job. He has a hard time because he has trouble following up. This is particularly true for young adults in recovery who focus more on clean time than getting on with their lives.

We believe in giving back to other families. We came to PARTS every week while he was out of state for nine months. We have a much better understanding of addiction, recovery programs and what adolescents go through when they use. We were more comfortable and confident in what we were doing, even though he wasn't at home. My wife and I are committed and dedicated, and we want to help by sharing our experiences with other parents. We came on the verge of hysteria or a break down, and we were at our wit's end. Other parents brought us out of absolute despair. We have gone public in our community and other people contact us. We bring them to PARTS.

Mother Of An Adolescent Son:

My son is 17 and has been coming to PARTS for five months. PARTS has done wonderful things for him and it's changed him a lot. He's not in recovery, but he's abstaining from drugs. It's helped us as a family to communicate better.

We were court ordered to come here as a family, and I'm really glad. It opened up a lot for us so were able to talk, and we've learned to communicate with our son instead of fighting with him. Because he's getting clean, he can talk and now things are a lot better, and I recommend it to everybody (everybody who will listen).

I've gotten a lot out of listening to other parents and realizing that I'm not alone, and that I didn't cause his problems. It's gotten me into other groups like Al-Anon. As a result, my son is no longer drinking. He realized that he was an alcoholic. He was using crystal, but he also smoked pot, and drank, and used anything he could get his hands on. Crystal was the main drug. He got arrested for being drunk in public. And that was the beginning. It was a blessing in disguise because he was doing a lot of other stuff that we weren't aware of until that happened.

As our son approached the ninth grade his behavior became belligerent and secretive. His attitude worsened over the year, even though we went to family counseling through our health plan, as well as privately. We didn't suspect drugs to be the root of the problem, and no one else mentioned it. Sometime in our son's sophomore year we realized drugs were involved, and so we went through a multi-family program provided by our HMO. At that time it was almost a relief to know it was drugs, we thought it might be a mental problem because of the wild rages. Our HMO said they still couldn't rule out mental problems. We had a lot of ups and downs, mostly downs! He became abusive and scary, and we were afraid of him and what he might do.

We wanted our insurance company to put him in a drug treatment program but they said he had to want to go. We heard about a long-term live-in program, but he refused to be interviewed. He was impossible to carry on a conversation with, and he blamed everything on us. He was jumping out a window at night to go who knows where. We had totally lost control. We searched for help and isolated ourselves from friends. We didn't want to talk about what we were going through. I hid from my co-workers, except my immediate boss.

Our son threatened to kill my husband during one of his wild rages. We tried to have the police intervene on several occasions, but the timing was never right. We were desperately trying to get him in the system to get him some help. Our insurance company told us he had to be "off the wall" to get into a locked program against his will. He was off the wall but never before the proper witnesses.

Somehow he managed to continue with school. By now he was in classes with all the other "goof-offs," and he never did homework. I was constantly getting calls at work from his teachers and it was difficult to talk to them, especially at work. Many times on the verge of tears, I would go into the restroom to regain my composure. Our son was suspended for a year from high school in the middle of the eleventh grade. The vice principal told me that he had the worst behavior that she had ever seen. Our sons used to play together in grammar school.

We were told to report to continuation school in a week. At orientation my son refused go to this continuation school and insisted on entering the Career Development Center (CDC), an option through the school district we hadn't been told about. This program offered a supervised two-hour home study program in the mornings and a job in their warehouse in the afternoon. I can't say enough about this program. Everyone there treated my son with respect and a caring attitude. He did well there and became very close to some of the instructors.

But he still continued to use. After several months he stopped going to CDC to be with his using friends. This, of course, increased the tension at home, and finally just before his seventeenth birthday we gave him these ultimatums: "Go to school or work. Show respect for us and abide by our curfew, or go out on your own." He left for parts unknown. We found out that he was in Alpine, California, but didn't know where. After four months he and his newfound family ran into an acquaintance of ours at the Colorado River. Finally he came home.

Our son wasn't home too long before he overdosed on LSD. According to the police report, it took five grown men to hold him down and hog-tie him. He was berserk, ranting and raving. When we went to pick him up at juvenile hall, my once-handsome son looked like the wild-eyed Charlie Manson. He said he wanted help. Thankfully the health evaluator said he would be allowed to enter an in–patient program. They paid for one week and by the end of that week he was a willing participant in a month-long day treatment program.

During this period we found PARTS. After years of floundering, we found the support and the education we needed. This program enabled my husband and I to see how others were handling the same problems we were having and to have friends to talk honestly to. Seeing other kids achieve sobriety gave us encouragement that recovery was possible.

I had always felt deep sadness over our son's behavior, while my husband expressed what seemed to me as hate. We separated for a short time over differences in dealing with our son. At PARTS, I was able to see other people express their feelings the way my husband did, which made it more acceptable and understandable. We learned to discuss situations and feelings and to present a united front to our son.

After leaving the treatment program our son seemed to know he had to give up the hard drugs, but he thought pot was okay for him. He re-entered the CDC program and gained more credits toward his high school diploma. He went to NA meetings and PARTS meetings but drifted back to his old friends. It didn't take long for him to revert to his abusive ways, but we were stronger this time.

One day I was driving him to take a test and he went into a rage and beat on the dashboard of my car so hard it cracked. This was the wake-up call for me. That night he was told he would have to find his own transportation and that we expected him to move out the following week. His departure was calm. We told him how much we loved him, how much we wanted him to get help, and when he was ready we would be there for him. He said he knew that we loved him. So at 18 he was out again. This time he was armed with $500 for the first month's rent. He moved into an apartment with friends.

We soon heard chilling stories, including encounters with guns during drug deals. We were terrified. We tried intervention with family members, but he refused to participate. Every time we talked to him we told him we loved him and would help him when he was ready to give up the drugs. He and his friends were evicted within three months. He was never able to get a job, so he survived by selling drugs. Months went by with stories of more criminal behavior and of living at different motels. Several of his friends were in jail. We saw him occasionally, and we we're further saddened by his sunken-eyed, gaunt look.

One day my husband came home and saw a body laying on our front lawn and it was our son—alive—wanting help. He said he would go wherever it was necessary. He de-toxed for five days and went to a private live-in facility where he received treatment for two months. After that he transitioned to a sober living home where he lives today. It is quite structured. He has a full-time job, a driver's license, and he is making his truck and insurance payments. He is supporting himself.

Now at 19, our son has nine months of sobriety. He has a lot of strength and determination. I never thought he would have such a wonderful recovery. We are honest with each other, and our lives are slowly mending. He said he always wondered why his dad and I kept going to PARTS, until he finally realized that his addiction affected the whole family and that we needed to work on recovery, too.

Father Of A Seventeen-Year-Old Daughter:

My daughter started using drugs between junior high school and high school. My wife and I had never been around that type of situation at all and so when it came up, we were just totally lost. We didn't know what to do, what the behaviors were like, and what was going on. We went to a counselor who suggested PARTS. It seemed like a wonderful format because it gave us the opportunity to talk and to learn, and to find out what things were about. At the same time, we could bring our daughter to a meeting and we knew where she was.

She was truant all the time ditching school. She was running around and leaving the house at night doing who knows what. She was violent and angry if we confronted her or forbid her to leave the house. All we knew was that she was angry about something, she was paranoid, and there was strange behavior. We weren't really sure that she was using drugs. She masked it and would use at times when we wouldn't be around. Coming to PARTS was really an eye-opener. Once we started talking to other people and hearing what was going on in their households, we could see, "That's going on in our house, too." PARTS gave us insight, and that's when things really started changing.

She was using marijuana, methamphetamines, and possibly LSD. She's never admitted to that in our presence, but she was. She's a runaway. At first she started working a program, and she had eight and a half months sober before she had a relapse. Since then her behavior has gone downhill, and she ran away. So, we're currently waiting for her to hit bottom. The good part for us is we're no longer going out of our minds trying to deal with the fact that she has run away. We're saying, "Okay, she's run away. She's almost 18 now, so our stress level's pretty low. We're gonna let her go, and we're not gonna chase her down. We tried that once and brought her back when she ran away about a year and a half ago. She said she was gonna stay. She lied and lied and then left. So we're not chasing her anymore."

Now, I'm letting go. I know she's out there. We've had people talk about her coming by their house. They've seen her, and she's not in any great physical harm, but she's not living a fun life. A year ago I would have been stressing out over this, but now I'm saying she's out there doing her thing.

PARTS is sharing. You learn that people have similar problems. By talking with others you find out that you're not the only one out there. You're not the only one having these problems. You know somebody else is dealing with it, and you learn some of the strategies they're using. Their strategies don't always work, but you don't go down blind alleys, and sometimes the strategies do work. That's what PARTS is about. It's given us the insight to know what to do when situations arise.

Never assume you're the only one, because you're not. Never assume it's not gonna happen to you. Don't stick your head in the sand and say, "It isn't happening." Open your eyes and take a clear look at what's going on around you, realizing that you may not be seeing everything. If you see the tip of the iceberg, don't be afraid to dig in a little bit deeper to find out what's really going on. Then, act on it. Not acting is the worst thing.

My daughter suffers from depression, and she used drugs to medicate herself. We didn't notice the depression early enough. If we had had our eyes open a little bit more, we might have dealt with this before she even started using instead of after the fact. Keep your eyes open, and assume it can happen to you.

CONCLUSION

"In the absence of certainty, there is nothing wrong with hope"

As we said in the beginning, there are many more questions about (AOD) abuse today than there are answers. (AOD) abuse is usually a symptom of something else going on in an adolescent's life. *Addiction is a family affair, so it is best to have the family find ways to deal with the problem, as well as the symptoms.*

Two major prerequisites to reunification are acceptance and communication. Acceptance does not mean agreement, it means acknowledgment. Communication is a lost art in many families today. Parents who learn to communicate with their children have a better chance of avoiding or repeating drug issues. Talk to your children about (AOD) abuse. Do not wait to talk until there is a problem. If you begin the process, you may prevent the problems from developing. Do not be afraid to admit that you do not have all the answers, because no one does.

We trust this book has given you some new ideas, some answers and hope. You are not alone. Many thousands of parents are fighting the war on drugs at this very moment, and there are many who have fought this battle and won. They will tell you not to give up on your adolescent.

Two important ingredients are persistence and hope. If you persist, hope, and search for solutions, you will find most of your answers. You may not be able to help your child as much as you would like, but you will increase the level of your own emotional maturity and develop better coping skills.

Hopefully, your adolescent will also mature and become a contributing member of society. Best of luck!!

"It works if you work it. It doesn't work itself."

FEEDBACK

Please Help Us To Help Other Parents By Giving Us Your Opinion

Constructive Criticism

1. Was this material useful and helpful for you?

10 9 8 7 6 5 4 3 2 1
Very Useful Good Ok Fair Not Helpful

2. What did you like least?

3. What did you like the best?

4. What questions should be added or expanded upon in future editions?

5. May we use your comments? ☐ Yes ☐ No

Optional

Name: ____________________
Telephone: ____________________
Facsimile: ____________________
Postal Address: ____________________
Email address: ____________________

Please fax your response to:

(619) 259–2862

Or mail to:

PARTS, 12815 Stebick Court
San Diego, Ca 92130

Or Call:
(619) 793-4673

Additional copies of this book may be ordered from the above address for $14.95

Please include $3.95 for shipping and handling and California residents include 7.25%

Visa and Mastercard Accepted

RECOMMENDED READING LIST

How To Raise Drug Free Kids And Growing Up Drug Free: A Parent's Guide To Prevention. Washington, DC :U.S. Dept. of Education,[1992]. http://www.health.org/pubs/parguide/Call (800)/624–0100 for a free copy.

Budd, Linda S. *Living With The Active Alert Child: Groundbreaking Strategies For Parents.* Prentice-Hall, Inc; New York, New York, US, 1990.

De Sisto, Michael. *Decoding Your Teenager,* William Morrow and Co., 1991.

Faber, Adele. *Liberated Parents/Liberated Children.* New York, Grosset and Dunlap, 1974.

Faber, Adele [et al]. *How To Talk So Kids Can Learn— At Home And In School.* New York: Rawson Associates, 1995.

Faber and Mazlish. *How To Talk So Your Kids Listen and Listen So Your Kids Will Talk.* New York: Rawson Associates, 1994.

Goleman, Daniel. *Emotional Intelligence.* New York: Bantam Books, 1995.

Glenn, H. Stephen and Jane Nelsen Ed.D. *Raising Self–Reliant Children in A Self–Indulgent World.* Prima Publishing, 1987.

Ginott, Haim G. *Between Parent and Child.* Avon Book, 1969.

Ginott, Haim G. *Between Parent And Teenager.* New York: Macmillan, 1969.

Lesko, Matthew Research Director; and Sharon Zarozny. Rev. ed. *What To Do When You Can't Afford Health Care.* Information U.S.A New York: Viking Penguin, 1986.

Knox, Jan Ph.D. and Dahk Ph.D. Ed.D.. *Get Ready! Get Set! Get Hired!*. 4th ed. California, Black Forest Press, 1994.

Kushner, Harold S. *When Bad Things Happen To Good People.* 2nd ed. New York: Schocken Books, 1989.

Yoder, Barbara. *The Recovery Resource Book.* New York: Simon and Schuster, 1990.

Hazeldon Pamphlets—Call 800/328–0098 for Hazelden Catalogue http://www.hazelden.com/

- *Setting Limits—Parents, Kids and Drugs*
- *Let's Talk—Communicating With Your Teen in Recovery*
- *When Your Teen Is in Treatment*
- *Enabling Change—When Your Child Returns Home From Treatment*

SOURCES AND RESOURCES

Al–Anon Group Headquarters, 800/356–9996

Alcoholics Anonymous—Worldwide, Consult your White Pages

Child Protective Services 800/344–6000,

Cocaine Helpline, 800/COCAINE

Crisis Team–24 Hour Intervention,

800/479–3339, 619/557–0500

"Just Say No" Clubs, 800/258–2766

National Council on Alcoholism Info Line,

800/NCA–CALL

National PTA Drug and Alcohol Abuse Prevention, 312/577–4500

Narcotics Anonymous, 800/479–0062,

619/584–1007

Nar–Anon Family Group, 213/547–5800

National Runaway Hotline, 800/231–6946

PARTS, 619/793-4673

Tough Love, 800/333–1069

Youth Crisis Hotline, 1–800/HIT–HOME

YMCA Childcare Resource Services

800/481–2151

These numbers were current at the time of publication, but may change, so please verify.

The following sample agreement offers some issues to be dealt with. You may ignore certain areas or add additional ones.

SAMPLE PARENT-ADOLESCENT AGREEMENT

This agreement is intended to improve communication, reduce family conflict and to begin rebuilding trust. It is agreed upon by
______________________________________ referred to as (PARENT or PARENTS) and _________________________ referred to as (ADOLESCENT).

Parent or parents agree:

- Be open and honest in their communications.
- Attempt to put aside past behavior and deal in the present.
- Not be punitive or angry.
- Treat their adolescent with courtesy and respect as an individual just as they expect to be treated.

Tone of Voice & Arguments

All parties will speak in conversational tones at all times. There is to be absolutely no *YELLING, SWEARING, VERBAL OR PHYSICAL ABUSE* by either side during any argument or difference of opinion. During an INTENSE discussion that becomes TOO HEATED, either side can call a "TIME-OUT. " This will be an automatic cooling off period for________ (15 minutes, 24 hours, etc.) before discussion continues. Discussions may continue sooner only if:

- Both parties agree that everyone has cooled off sufficiently to continue discussions, or
- Both parties have stated their respective positions in writing.

Bedtime, Curfew, Sleeping Out or Others Sleeping Over

Adolescent is fully responsible for punctuality. To begin establishing trust again, when going out adolescent will state: where, with whom (phone #'s as necessary) and when planning to be home.

Conditions of curfew shall be determined by local ordinance. Adolescent is allowed to stay out until______ p.m. on school nights (after homework completed) and_________p.m. on weekends.
Punctuality shall serve as a guide to adolescent's showing good faith in keeping agreements.

Suggestion: Five (5) successful returns in a row adds 15 minutes to future curfew time, but two (2) unsuccessful (late) returns results in loss of 15 minutes to curfew. Special Occasions—Late Curfew: Adolescent must let parent know at least one week in advance of any special events that would keep him/her out beyond normal curfew, and an extended curfew may be negotiated.

Job, Support Groups, Meetings and Extra-Activities

If adolescent is working, he/she should be given ________ hour or hours for relaxation. Parents and adolescent agree to attend the following support groups or meetings on a regular basis:

____

____

____

Mealtime

During dinner, there will be no arguments and no radio or TV. Adolescent will assist as much as possible in dinner preparation and share responsibilities for cleaning up.

Room Condition

Adolescent's room is part of our home, so he/she will maintain his/her room in a neat and orderly fashion.

Phone Calls

Using the phone is a privilege that may be revoked at any time. However, adolescent may use the phone for __________ hours/minutes per day, however, calls may be limited to ______ minutes each.

Chores & Responsibilities

As parent is providing room and board, the parent and adolescent will mutually agree upon any chores and responsibilities for adolescent. Adolescent shall be responsible for the following (circle as appropriate):

- Keep his/her room and bathroom clean and neat
- Perform kitchen duties (i.e., cooking, clean-up, table setting, general kitchen cleanliness, etc.)
- Work together on keeping house clean and doing the wash
- Bring in mail daily and dispose of garbage daily, if necessary
- OTHER:

____

____

____

Privacy

Each party will do their best to respect the privacy of the other.

Marijuana & Drug Paraphernalia

Adolescent will remove any marijuana or other drug-related paraphernalia, inappropriate posters, pictures, magazines, etc., and not have such items in our home. We will renegotiate items, such as pictures, after 6 months.

Restriction Conditions

Restriction is confinement to the house except to (a) attend school, (b) go to work, (c) attend daily exercise, (d) perform chores requiring leaving the house. Restrictions also may mean limited phone use.

For exercise, adolescent is permitted to ______________ (run, skate, walk, etc.) for an hour within ______________ (one block, 1/2 mile, etc. of the house).

Restriction period will be determined by the severity of the misconduct and will be levied in the form of the number of days of the week of restrictions (i.e., a minus five (-5) restriction means restrictions for 5 days of the week).

Reduction of restrictions will occur weekly if everything is OK (Begin reducing by -5 to -4 to -3, etc., until 0, which is no restrictions. If a week does not go okay, the minus level can remain or increase. If adolescent performs in an extraordinary manner, the minus can be reduced accordingly.

Family Activities

Adolescent agrees to participate in the following family activities:

____

____

Other Issues:

____

____

____

We promise to abide by the above conditions and do our utmost to promote faith, harmony and trust in our family. This agreement is agreed upon ____________________ (Date)

______________________________ ______________________________

Parent Adolescent

____

Parent

P9-DXM-041

CASEY FLANAGAN comes to spend the summer in the small southern town where her grandparents live, not knowing a soul her age, shy about making new friends, wishing she could just turn around and go home.

Then she meets Dwayne Pickens. From the very first day, Casey and Dwayne form a special friendship. But Dwayne is a man thirty-three whose mind has never grown beyond that of a boy twelve. He loves baseball, hates girls, and simply assumes Casey—with her short hair and jeans—is the new boy in town. In time, Casey comes to protect Dwayne as she enjoys his easy ways and shares his one big fear of being sent away again to the "home," a place he dreads.

It is a summer of surprises for Casey whose life weaves in and out of the lives of many other people who love her: Jane and Ben Flanagan whose home is a solid comfortable place; the wreckless Taylor Flanagan, her stock-car racer uncle, who draws Casey into the center of things; Hazard Whitaker, the middle-aged loveable loser his name typifies; Pansy, the prim but warm-hearted spinster whose courtship with Hazard is awkward, loving and irresistible to Casey and all those who watch it unfold.

Casey affects these people indelibly, and cannot help being affected in turn, especially by Dwayne who is unforgettable to her. Dwayne's happiness is infectious, but his vulnerability leads to a disaster that pulls Casey, her family, and the community together in an unselfish act to save him.

In a remarkable way, Sue Ellen Bridgers' new novel is a sensitive portrayal of a girl approaching adolescence, as well as a heartfelt story of a community. Her ability to show simple, innocent people doing what they have to do with courage and foolishness and love and pain is unparalleled. By defying categorization, *All Together Now* is a hopeful story for everyone, a book to be long remembered.

Also by Sue Ellen Bridgers

➽ *HOME BEFORE DARK*

All Together Now

A NOVEL

Sue Ellen Bridgers

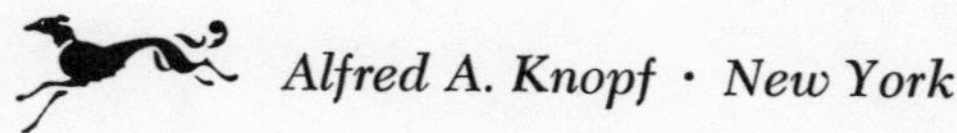

Alfred A. Knopf · New York

Grateful acknowledgment is made to the following for permission to reprint previously copyrighted material:
Copyright Service Bureau, Ltd.: An excerpt from "You Made Me Love You" by James McCarthy and James Monaco: © MCMXII Broadway Music Corp. ® MCMXL Broadway Music Corp. © 1973 Broadway Music Corp. International copyright secured. All rights reserved. Used by permission.
Jefferson Music Co., Inc.: An excerpt from "Too Young" by Sylvia Dee and Sidney Lippman. © 1950 Jefferson Music Co., Inc. Copyright renewed. All Rights Reserved. Used by permission.
Warner Bros. Music: An excerpt from "It Had To Be You" by Gus Kahn and Isham Jones. Copyright 1924 Warner Bros. Inc. Copyright Renewed. All Rights Reserved. Used by Permission.

THIS IS A BORZOI BOOK PUBLISHED BY ALFRED A. KNOPF, INC.

Published in the United States by Alfred A. Knopf, Inc., New York, and simultaneously in Canada by Random House of Canada Limited, Toronto. Distributed by Random House, Inc., New York.
Manufactured in the United States of America 10 9 8 7 6 5 4 3 2 1
Library of Congress Cataloging in Publication Data. Bridgers, Sue Ellen. All together now. Summary: Casey spends her twelfth summer visiting her grandparents in their small town while her father serves in the Korean War and her mother works two jobs. [1. Grandparents—Fiction] I. Title.
PZ7.B7615Al 1979 [Fic] 78–12244 ISBN 0–394–84098–4
ISBN 0–394–94098–9 lib. bdg.

For
Elizabeth
Jane
Sean
in exchange for smiles

All Together Now

1

*Casey came unwill-*ingly. So, when the bus pulled into the station after six hours of farmland, sky, and trees seen through the gray tinted glass that made everything look artificial, she sat still while the people around her got up, stretching, sighing, lifting down packages from above their heads. She sat there, hands folded in her lap, unable to look out the window, unable to reconcile herself to a summer away from home even though she knew that when she did look, a familiar face would be there to greet her.

Perhaps her grandfather with his summer hat pushed back on his balding head, rimless glasses slipped beneath the hump of his thin nose. Maybe her grandmother in her black lace-up Sunday shoes, her pocketbook like a weapon at her side, her hand raised against the sun in her eyes. Or Taylor, off the job for a few minutes to deliver his niece home, in shirt sleeves and with pants bagging at the knees, grinning at her, his hand out to pull her off the roaring bus like a knight rescuing a lady from a belching dragon.

It was her grandmother. Jane Flanagan stood there with her hand shading her eyes, the solitary welcomer in the empty bus station, waiting for a granddaughter who would be her child for the summer because her real child, Casey's father, was off in Korea fighting his second war.

Jane waited for a child's face, a girl's face, to appear at the window and look down at her as the bus spewed exhaust on the splotched concrete. But there was no face. The bus shuddered, growled, died. The door opened, and passengers started out. Moses from down the street, back from visiting his sister; the Farmer girls, home from a shopping trip; two strangers.

Her heart rose just like it had when she'd heard her mother was dead twenty-two years ago, just like it had when the lumberyard burned in 1938 and she hadn't known for hours if her husband and son were safe. Like it did when she knew David would be flying in yet another war. Her heart rose, pushing in her chest, cutting off her breath. And then a head appeared, tiny it seemed to her, like an infant's head, smooth with short shiny brown hair. A cheek, a profile that made her heart stop, then two eyes turning toward her hesitantly. David's eyes. Deep set, wrapped in shadows of their own making. Her husband's eyes, her son's.

My goodness, she's shy, Jane thought, opening her arms. That's the difference between eleven and twelve, between Christmas and summertime. Long legs and arms, gangliness, a face turned away from kisses.

She was wearing pants, too. Long pants to hide in, as if dresses exposed too much. A boy's shirt opened at the neck. And saddle oxfords that looked the size of Taylor's.

It was a mistake to call her Casey, Jane thought as she held the thin body close to her. She knew that only she held on; Casey merely stood in her embrace resolutely, doing her duty. It's too much a boy's name, Jane said to herself.

"Sweetheart, I'm so glad you're here at last! I almost had a fright when you weren't the first one off the bus!" She turned the girl away from her but kept her arm about her.

"I have to get my suitcase," Casey said uneasily.

"Of course you do," her grandmother said. "What am I thinking? The truth is, Casey, I'm not at all accustomed to meeting buses. Usually I send your grandpa or Taylor on errands like this. But then there's never anyone quite so important to meet as a granddaughter coming by herself all the way from South Carolina." Jane hugged Casey again while the driver unloaded the baggage. "Which one is yours, honey? Can you carry that big old thing all the way home? Why, goodness gracious, it weighs a ton! I should have brought the car, but it's such a nice day and I thought you'd like to stretch your legs a little." Jane pretended to tug at the suitcase.

"I can carry it," Casey said.

And with the suitcase banging against her leg, they went down the walk toward the edge of town and the tree-shaded street where the Flanagans had always lived. Her grandmother talked on and on about how glad they were she had come and how her grandfather and Taylor would be home at suppertime.

Casey watched the street silently, looking for familiar signs, a tree she remembered, a house she'd once visited in, some obvious signal that she should be here at all. The houses were large and looming and very quiet at mid-afternoon. She wished she hadn't come.

The wish almost brought tears to her eyes when she remembered how, at home, she'd be in the club pool right now or riding her bike to her best friend's house, where they'd eat ice cream off sticks and catch bees in pint jars or make clover chains.

She could see the edge of the Flanagans' yard and then the walk curving up to the porch, familiar but not dear to her. It wasn't her house.

"Well, we're almost home," Jane said as if she knew what Casey's silence meant.

Just then Casey heard a noise, a metallic ring, the thump of something hard and solid striking metal, the pounding of dirt, and then the voice, an announcer's voice, singsonging a mental picture she could not yet visualize.

"What's that?" She stopped to peer through the trees on the other side of the street, searching out the source of the chatter. The metallic clatter echoed again. A long swish—somebody sliding—a dusty voice sputtering.

"That's Dwayne Pickens, playing ball," Jane said, walking on.

"Who's he playing with? Is he new? I don't know Dwayne Pickens, do I?" Casey asked, heartened by the prospect of another kid in this neighborhood of ancient houses and, it seemed to her, even older occupants.

"Of course you don't. He just moved here. Dora Pickens and her family lived for years and years over on Plum. Dr. Pickens was a fine man, a good dentist, too, but he died a few years ago, not long after their other children were married. One of them lives in the big house on Plum now. Dora didn't see much point in keeping such a big place for her and Dwayne, so she bought that little house across the street from us a year ago. It's small, but there's an empty lot with it and a garage for Dwayne." Jane sighed.

"As for Dwayne," she continued, "he's in his thirties, your daddy's age, but he's got the mind of a twelve-year-old. Retarded but harmless. He likes baseball and toys just like a boy would. He goes all over town on his own. Everybody knows him so he never gets into any real trouble. Once, though, a while back, they sent him off to a home, an institution I reckon it was, but Dora got him back as soon as she could. She's a saint, but he's a burden on her any way you look at it. Makes me thank God every day my two boys were born healthy and right in the head." Jane turned up her walk, leaving Casey on the sidewalk.

Through the thin line of trees she could see a figure on the dusty vacant lot. He stood in the middle of the field, slightly elevated on what must be the pitcher's mound. He was adjusting his black cap over his eyes.

"Reese steps into the box, ready to see what Dickson will give him this time. Pee Wee's oh-for-three so far today. He's flied to left, walked, and grounded to third," he yelled to his invisible audience.

Casey could see the yellow baseball in his hand as he flipped it with short snaps of his wrist. He looked hard toward the plate, set the arch of his right foot firmly across the rubber, and swung both hands behind himself while sliding his left leg back and dropping his head down. Then he swung both hands high over his head, where they met and were hidden somewhere behind his black cap. He pushed off with his left foot onto his right, swung his left leg into the air in front of him, dropped his right arm behind his back while balancing his left hand high in the air, swung his glove down, and followed it in a windmill motion with the right hand.

"Here's the windup and the pitch!"

The ball flew high toward the plate, then darted to the left and dropped suddenly across the outside edge of the plate. It whammed into the bottom half of the empty oil drum behind the plate and bounced back sharply between first and second base.

"It's a curve! Pee Wee swings and hits a hard ground ball toward second!"

Balanced on his toes like a diver, his right arm still across his chest in the follow-through, the man sprang to the left after the bouncing ball, then threw himself headlong at it.

"And Basgall can't get it! Pee Wee rounds first and holds up there for a single!" he shouted from the ground.

"What's he doing?" Casey asked her grandmother, who was waiting for her halfway up the walk.

"I told you, honey, he's playing baseball."

"By himself?"

"Does it look like he needs anybody else? He's got the Dodgers and the Pirates already." Jane came back to where Casey was standing. Together they watched as Dwayne picked himself up off the ground and trotted out into right field after the ball. Reaching down, he flipped the ball up into the webbing of his glove, tossed it into the air, and caught it in his bare hand. He was grinning when he walked back to the pitcher's mound.

"Hey boy, atta way to go, boy!" he called.

Jane stood watching him through the trees as if he

were something from another time, something dear and familiar and yet lost to her. "Do you ever go out by yourself, Casey, maybe to sit in a tree or on the porch swing or just to wander around, and out there, all by yourself, things happen to you? You imagine wonderful, exciting times. You dream in your head with your eyes wide open till you forget it isn't real. Well, Dwayne's like that, except he doesn't know enough to keep his dreaming quiet. He doesn't see people laughing at him. Or maybe he doesn't care. He's gullible, you see, and more honest than most of us."

"Maybe he'll let me play with him," Casey said almost to herself. "I could run the bases."

"I doubt it," Jane said, hoping to squelch any such notions before they had time to settle. "He's like a twelve-year-old boy, you remember. He won't have anything to do with girls. Besides, there're plenty of young people around for you. Not that I object to Dwayne. He's respectful and good-natured. But still . . ." Her voice trailed off, not knowing what else to say.

Run the bases, she was thinking. No matter how she tried, there seemed little hope of having a girl in her house. Two sons and now a granddaughter in pants and saddle oxfords who wanted to play baseball with Dwayne Pickens.

"Let's get you settled," she said to Casey, who was finally following her around the house to the kitchen door. "I thought you'd like to have your daddy's room. Oh, Casey, we had the nicest letter from him yesterday. I'll let you read it. Of course, he doesn't know you've come for the summer yet. We'll have to write him all about it. I know it'll make him feel better. You know, he seems so close when a letter comes, like he's right down there in South Carolina and not all the way in Korea. Who'd have thought there'd be another war, Casey?" They pushed through the screen door and stood in the middle of the kitchen. "Who'd have thought there wasn't enough learning done the last time?" She sighed, conjuring up memories of sad times, of Dwayne Pickens and her David growing up together and then leaving each other—at twelve, one mind slipped past the other—and now her David at war while Dwayne pitched baseballs at an oil drum.

"Well, let's get cheerful," she said suddenly. "A merry heart, you know. A happy house." She stopped short and let out a soft, round chuckle. "And just look who's coming!"

2

Looks like we're going to have a full house. A hat on every hook," she said, surmising her situation with a smile, "because here comes Hazard!"

They were standing in the kitchen, the woman in her straw summer hat and the girl with her hand still on her suitcase, as if she were trying to decide whether to go or to stay. They froze there like a painted audience before a make-believe show, the screen door making a gray haze between them and the awaited attraction.

Having reached the porch, the man called Hazard leaned forward on his toes, ready to knock.

"Sh-h-h-h," Grandmother whispered, and Casey released her fingers slowly from the handle of her bag.

"*Rap-p-p-p!*" One solid blow crashed against the door jamb and then they watched through the screen as the man sprinted off the steps and bent down to scoop up a handful of dry dirt from the flower bed below. Back on the porch, he shook the dirt onto the glossy painted floor to make it crunch under his feet, and took off his hat, which he held to his chest as if acknowledging the flag.

Casey looked from the apparition on the porch to her grandmother, who showed no sign of surprise. She was smiling like someone who knew the punch line but wanted to hear the joke anyway.

"What you doing out there, Hazard?" she called as if she were a great distance from him.

"You come on out here, Jane!" the man shouted back. "You come on, now!"

Grandmother put her black patent pocketbook on the kitchen table and began slapping her thighs in response to some music in her head. Her bosom heaved happily to the alternating rhythm of her hands and the foot she had begun to pat on the hardwood floor.

"Hazard, Hazard, where you been?" she called out.

"Down the track and I'm going again!" the man sang back.

"What you gonna do when you get back?"

"Come in your house and hit the sack!"

Rhythm established and attention drawn, the man began to dance. The dirt crunched under his cheap wing-tips as he shuffled across the porch, hat flailing in his swinging hand. His torso, straining at shoulder and elbow against his ill-fitting blue plaid jacket, seemed confined, almost motionless, while his long thin arms balanced his agile legs between the screen door and the pots of geraniums that lined the porch railing. He seemed lighter than Casey could imagine a man being. And yet there was a kind of desperation in his movements, as if he felt he had put himself against impossible odds and must prove himself again. He whirled on his feet, slapped his hat against his thigh, and shook the other hand in the air as he did a kick step across the porch.

"Hazard, watch out!" Jane called.

But it was too late. The man's long white fingers,

spread wide and shaking, had collided with the first of the geranium pots, which in turn toppled onto the next one. Both pots leaned askew for a second and then fell over the railing into the dirt.

"G-D, I broke my hand!" he yelled, holding the injury to his chest and massaging it frantically with the other hand. "Get some soaking water! Get a splint! Get a doctor!"

Jane was smiling. "That's Hazard," she said to Casey. "His hand's not broken, but he knows my clay pots are."

"Just offering a little entertainment," Hazard was muttering, having noted that aid was not forthcoming. "Just getting off on the right foot." He cackled suddenly, his face mobile and bright. "You hear that, Jane?" he yelled through the screen. "Off on the right foot! Hah, hah, hah!"

Grandmother went to the door and swung it open, as if the man were just arriving and her geraniums were where they were supposed to be.

"Hazard, welcome home," she said and let out a gigantic happy sigh. She was smiling with unabashed pleasure.

"That's right kind of you, Miss Jane," the man said. He dropped his injured hand to his side as though he had no further need of it and bent himself through the door jamb although he was less than six feet tall. He seemed to stoop unconsciously, as if he'd spent many years getting into places that proved uncomfortable to him.

"Why, you've already got company," he complained, seeing Casey, who still stood beside her suitcase. He paused to look her up and down. "Great God, it's David's little girl, ain't it?" He was glad to see she was somebody he knew. He could feel like one of the family as long as there weren't other outsiders around to remind him that he, like they, wasn't blood kin to the Flanagans.

"Of course it's Casey, but I'm surprised you recognized her," Jane Flanagan said, putting her arm around her granddaughter. "She's twelve years old this past spring. All grown up."

"Don't believe it," Hazard boomed. "I don't believe it! Twelve, you say! Great God, and I'm just thirty-five myself. Just hitting my prime!"

"He can't even remember when he last saw thirty-five," Jane said to Casey. "Why, when your Uncle Taylor turns thirty-five, Hazard won't even recognize it on him, it's been so long since he's seen thirty-five."

"Listen to her! What did I come here for? To get talked about?" Hazard slouched into a kitchen chair trying to look dejected. "Here I am with this injured hand paining me something terrible, and this woman goes on, poking fun, taking advantage of my mistaking my age. Never was good at numbers. That's why I never made any money, girl. The only reason. I knew I wouldn't appreciate it like other folks. Didn't want to figure on it. Didn't want to count it. Five dollars. Now there's a good amount. Simple to figure on. Don't bulge in your wallet. You can set down on it easy. Nobody's gonna rob you for it, but it'll get you a place to sleep and some rat cheese to nibble on any day you're needing it."

"I reckon that means you're hungry," Jane said. "Everybody in this house eats at twelve sharp, in case you don't remember. But"—she smiled at him—"considering that Casey here just got off the bus from Fort

Jackson, South Carolina, and it's three good hours till suppertime, I suppose I could get you both something. Something cold, mind you, Hazard. Something cold and left over."

"Her leftovers are perfection," Hazard said to Casey, pulling out a chair for her with his injured hand. "Her leftovers are fit for kings. Her—"

"Her leftovers are just that." Jane put plates in front of them. "Casey, don't you mind him. He's always thought he had to flatter me. Goes on and on with this foolishness like I was paying attention to him. I don't pay you any mind, Hazard." She put a plate of sliced ham on the table, followed by potato salad and sliced cucumbers soaking in vinegar.

Hazard attacked the food like it was a foe to be reckoned with. Casey cut and chewed carefully, watching her manners and the man at the same time. She'd heard about Hazard all her life, so his performance on the porch didn't surprise her much. She was grateful he'd come, though. Here was somebody who would eagerly draw attention to himself, filling her grandmother's time with his antics so that Casey could slip away unnoticed and be by herself. Not that she wanted to be alone all the time, but she didn't want her grandmother hovering over her, either, like she was an orphan or a charity case. What she wanted was to be doing something, not talking about it.

After lunch she slipped out the back door, passed the broken geraniums, and went around the house toward the vacant lot where she'd seen Dwayne Pickens. Crossing the street toward the trees in the Pickenses' yard, she wondered vaguely if she should have asked her grandmother's permission, or at least told her where she was going. She wasn't used to telling anyone where she was going at home. With both parents working, she had learned early what would do and what wouldn't, and she enjoyed both her independence and her parents' confidence in her. Besides, being around so many people in uniform had given her a special, if misplaced, sense of safety. It was like meeting a policeman on every corner. You never expected to be hit on the head midway the block.

She heard the ball hit the metal drum.

"And here's the pitch. Robinson *bunts!* Holy cow!"

Dwayne dashed to the plate, picked up the ball with his bare hand, turned and made a throwing motion toward first base, although he still held the ball in his hand. He raced off toward first himself.

"Garagiola's off with the mask! He grabs the ball and fires it to first! Is it in time?"

At first base, Dwayne toed the bag and then snared the ball from its invisible flight with a flick of his gloved wrist.

"They've got him. Garagiola throws out Robinson on a beau-ti-ful play! And that's all for the Dodgers! In the top of the ninth, it's three up and three down!"

Casey was at the fence now. She wrapped her fingers around the wire and leaned into it for a better look. The man was on his way back to the mound. He was wearing khaki work pants and a T-shirt to which dirt clung in sweaty patches. He was short, although still a head taller than Casey, and his body was hard and muscular. Casey tried to make out his face from under the bill of his cap, but she could see only his chin and cheeks, a rugged jaw without a hint of the weakness she'd expected him to expose.

Chapter Two

It must be in his eyes, she thought. That's where his stupid look must be.

But just then he took off his cap to wipe his forehead with the back of his head. She saw a full head of thick dark hair, a wide clear forehead, and then the eyes. She couldn't see their color, but even from that distance she knew they weren't wild.

He knocked his cleats on the mound and moved a wad of tobacco to his cheek, then sent a squirt of brown juice straight in front of him, right toward her.

"Hey boy," he called in a voice more gruff than his announcer's tone, but just as loud. "Whatcha doin' here, boy?"

Casey felt her stomach lurch. She loosened her fingers from the wire and moved back a step.

"Hey boy! Hey you! Whatcha doin'?" Dwayne was coming toward her, trotting like players do when they're heading for the dugout.

"Just looking," Casey said, still backing away. The gate to the fence was farther down, but she knew he could jump the chicken wire to get to her if he wanted to.

He stopped, leaned into the same spot where she'd stood, and looked out from beneath his cap at her.

"I've come to stay with my grandparents," she said, desperate not to show fear in her voice. It's like talking to an animal, she thought. I can't let him know I'm scared. "You know the Flanagans across the street, don't you?" Surely he knew and liked them. He'd been her father's friend years ago. Or could he remember after all these years of being twelve?

"Miss Jane?" He began to grin. "I like that lady. One time a boy, he come by here and pitched to me. I hit one clean across the street right up on Miss Jane's porch. Boy, I can tell you I was scared! How about if I broke something? What would Mama say? And Alva? You know my brother Alva? He gets so mad at me! Really *mad!* Anyhow, 'nothing broken.' That's what your grandma says to me. She says, 'It's all right, Dwayne Pickens. And you come see me sometime.' " He was beaming at her, having remembered the conversation so vividly that it gave him pleasure again. "I like that woman."

Now she looked right into his eyes. They were gray eyes, and although he squinted against the sunlight at her, Casey could see that they were clear, unshadowed by his slow-moving brain. He didn't look retarded at all. Only his speech betrayed his childishness, for he slurred over words, bobbing his head as if to help himself think.

"What's your name?" he was saying. "Hey boy, what's your name?"

Casey moved a step closer to him and took a deep breath. She had never done what she was now thinking to do. She had never lied, at least not a big lie, a gigantic lie, one that could change her summer. Yet the proportions of her dishonesty didn't scare her, for it seemed right, both for her and for Dwayne Pickens, that she should say the words that could give them both so much pleasure.

"K.C. Flanagan," she said slowly, testing the sound she made. "K.C.—I'm David Flanagan's kid. I'm spending the summer right across the street."

"Hot dog!" Dwayne was shaking the fence in his excitement. "You like baseball?"

"Yeah," Casey said, remembering girls' softball games. She knew baseball wasn't all that different.

"What position?" Dwayne wanted to know.

"Most anywhere. Not much of a hitter, though."

"Don't need a hitter," Dwayne said. He moved his tobacco against his cheek and spit on the ground at his feet. "Need a outfielder. Run myself ragged out there. You don't want to pitch, do you? 'Cause I'm the pitcher."

"Never been much on the mound," Casey said, gaining confidence. If she had already convinced Dwayne Pickens that she was a boy, surely she could convince him she knew baseball.

"Casey!" It was her grandmother. "Casey, where are you?"

"That's Miss Jane right there," Dwayne said. "She's a-callin' you for something."

"I got to go," Casey said. "Maybe I'll see you tomorrow."

"Yeah." Dwayne looked a little disappointed that she was leaving so soon. Then he brightened and slapped his cap on his thigh. "Tomorrow we'll go downtown. I can show you everything." His face seemed to expand as he envisioned the sights in store for them. "Maybe we'll go to the show."

"Well, 'bye, Dwayne," Casey said.

" 'Bye."

Casey started across the street to her grandmother.

"Hey boy!" She could hear Dwayne calling. "See you tomorrow, boy!"

"So you met him already," Jane said when Casey reached her.

"Yes," Casey panted, out of breath from excitement as much as from running. "Grandma, he thinks I'm a boy," she said softly.

"Now just how did that happen?" Jane wanted to know. She started down the sidewalk with Casey trotting after her.

"I just didn't say I was a girl," Casey said breathlessly. "Casey could be a boy's name, too, you know. He just never thought any different."

"Not telling him is the same as lying, Casey," Jane said slowly.

"I know, Grandma, but it won't hurt anything. How can it? When school starts I'll be gone. Besides, I don't intend to spend my whole summer with Dwayne Pickens."

"I should hope not." Jane walked on ahead, trying to decide what she should say. If Casey were one of her own boys, she knew what she'd do—send him packing across the street to tell the truth—but this was her grandchild, a little girl with a father fighting a war and her mother at work—an abandoned child was one way of looking at it—who'd come here to have a family. How many more summers would there be for her to enjoy herself? And if she wanted a retarded person for a friend, why should his poor stumbling mind and opinions stop her? "I won't tell Dwayne," Jane said finally.

"Thanks, Grandma," Casey said, and Jane saw her smile for the first time.

3

Hazard Whitaker lay on the bed in the Flanagans' guest room, his stomach resting easy with Jane's leftovers but his head troubling over the problem he always had when he came for a visit.

Arriving at this house always reminded Hazard of where he'd come from. Which was nowhere. At fifty-two, he was without almost anything that gave a man reason to look back on his life with pride—no wife or children, no home except two rooms above a restaurant, no career, no savings account, no automobile. Lately he'd even been feeling a little embarrassed about his occupation, a fate he'd never expected to come to because he'd always admired entertainers, people who could make others forget their troubles for a while and pat their feet a little. Now he wasn't so proud of being a dancing man.

Of course, he hadn't always been a dancing man. No, years ago when he first met Ben Flanagan in the railroad station, he'd been a salesman. Selling shoes back then. After that, a fine line of kitchenware. Then what? Borrowed money from Ben to take a three-months' photography course over in Charlotte and came out of there taking group pictures right in your family setting.

He tinted the pictures for two-fifty extra, and most people ordered themselves in color. Vanity took over when people got their pictures made.

But then everybody got a camera. Hazard considered going into the photography equipment business, selling tripods, fancy lenses, and light meters door to door, but he didn't really have his heart in it. People didn't care about taking fine pictures, just quick ones.

So he'd gone looking for his first love, his childhood fantasy—dancing—and had come as close to it as he thought he ever would. He got a job waiting tables. Never one to settle for a single gesture when he could envision two, Hazard spun between the tables at Papa Tutoni's Spaghetti House, twirling dishes and balancing trays with an acrobatic skill that came to him magically when he had an appreciative audience. Almost every Saturday night, Tutoni's cousin would come in to play the piano for tips. Then Hazard could really dance. The old piano would surge with a rumpled, thumping bass as the girl rippled through "Side by Side" and "Carolina in the Morning," and Hazard would start the slow, rocking steps that made heads turn and forks slip onto plates of pasta.

He knew he could dance. Great God, his head went light with the thought of faces turning to him above the blinking candles stuck in bottles. Then he would lose sight of the audience and just be out there alone, free of every worry known to man, while orders backed up in the kitchen and Papa Tutoni slapped his doughy fingers on his apron and lifted his eyes to the dingy ceiling. Who was to know how much business this crazy man brought in? Sure he was good, but so was the lasagne and the ravioli, not to mention the pizza. And who ever heard of a dancing Italian waiter? Not that Hazard could pass for an Italian even in the dark. If he were just an accordion player or a violinist. A singer even, Papa Tutoni would lament. Anything but a dancing man.

Still, Hazard could make the customers happy. They ordered more wine, a little dessert, another coffee. Hazard could stop arguments with his toes, mend romances with a little shuffle to the left. He could lift his head, eyes all dreamy, and make a roomful of eyes lift with him, going outside themselves just like Hazard was doing, with smiles they'd never recognized on their own faces.

Now he was in the Flanagans' house, in the room that had long ago come to be known as his, and he was staring at the ceiling with his mind on Pansy.

Over the twenty-five years since he'd first brightened Jane Flanagan's door on the heels of Ben—who'd found him asleep beside his shoe samples on a train station bench—he'd spent considerable time wondering what to do about Jane's best friend, Pansy, for she'd consistently poached on his feelings from the first moment he'd laid eyes on her.

He could remember to this day how she'd looked, her napkin in her lap, her wrists resting lightly on the table edge, her voice whispering amidst the clicking of fork and china plate. She came to supper every Thursday night. That Hazard learned when the two women had the dishes done and were finding their jackets to go to choir practice. It was a ritual of theirs nurtured through a teen-age friendship, on into the first years of their adult lives when Ben Flanagan was wooing Jane, through the newly married years when Jane, seeing no reason to give up a good and true friend, arranged her young mother's life to include another woman whom folks were still expecting to marry off just any day.

When Hazard saw Pansy coming in from the kitchen that autumn evening, his first thought was of her husband and where he might be. Maybe a traveling man like himself, or a doctor making rounds, or a fireman on duty. Or could it be that he was sick and she, just having touched his forehead with a damp cloth and cool hand, had left him sleeping to come down the street for a decent meal urged on her by a good friend. All this he imagined in an instant, never once thinking that she was as free as he, as able to love as he, as ready.

Oh, he would have married her by Christmas. Asked her, at least. But something held him back, pulled against his touching her, made his shoulders tense and his eyes refuse hers. Through all those years of sitting on her front porch, of picture shows and window shopping, of fountain lemonades and winter walks, he could have asked her—and yet he didn't, until he found himself a dancing man, a waiter, and no fit husband. Now at fifty-two he was unemployed altogether, jobless on account of Papa Tutoni's heart attack.

Business Closed through the Summer, the sign on the front door read.

"Collect unemployment," Papa's son, the sauce cook, had said. "We all need a rest," he'd said. He'd had tears in his eyes and his hands were white and smooth beneath the cuffs of his good suit. He was on his way to the hospital to see his father and didn't want to argue with a dancing waiter.

"I'll call you when Papa gets well," he said without much enthusiasm.

So Hazard left the Flanagans' telephone number in the kitchen and packed his bag. He didn't want to stay above the vacant restaurant all summer. He needed people around him. He needed family.

That's what he was thinking as he stared at the ceiling of his room. How he needed someone and how more than likely at six o'clock he would hear Pansy's voice below in the kitchen, pick her soft laughter out of Jane's rollicking loud humor, and know that she, pretending no surprise at finding him there, would offer him only a fleeting smile across the supper table. She wouldn't expect or demand anything.

There was a humming in the wall. Hazard raised up on the bed, cocked his head as if one ear heard better than the other, and stared out into space as though he expected to eventually see the sound. The humming stopped, paused it seemed for a shallow tremulous breath, and then started up again.

It was the girl Casey in her daddy's old room. Hazard had forgotten all about her. What was she doing here, anyway? He couldn't remember having seen her since she was a tiny thing and her mother, looking so young and bright-eyed, had brought her to spend an earlier summer while David was in the Pacific.

Surely they came more often than he knew, probably at Christmas, for Hazard made a point of avoiding the Flanagans' at Christmas. He always told them he couldn't get off from work, but the truth was that he felt uncomfortable with them on holidays. He didn't want to be included in the Flanagans' holiday because they felt sorry for him, so he always arrived after the first of the year, bringing gifts bought at the pre-inventory sales, to put under the tree Jane left up through Epiphany.

So their pasts had never touched, and he didn't know this Casey who'd sat next to him in the kitchen nibbling at her lunch while he and Jane had bantered, saying nothing but providing comfort to him in that moment of transition he always felt between standing on the back porch and being in his room upstairs.

Now it seemed to him the humming was somehow tearful, pushed out by sighs.

"Who's there?" he called, rapping lightly on the wall above his head.

The humming stopped.

"I say, who's there?"

Silence. He rapped again, determined to make contact with the voice that seemed so melancholy to him.

"It's me—Casey," a voice said finally. "I didn't mean to bother you." Her voice seemed close, as if she had pressed her lean cool cheek against the wall by his head.

Hazard lifted his hand to the wall again, a long bony hand with even, clean nails and a sprinkling of fine gray hairs. His hand surprised him, for it suddenly looked old, an undeniable evidence that he was truly fifty-two. What have I done? he thought suddenly. What can I account for since I was her age?

Instead of knocking again, he slipped off the bed and went down the hall to the door of David's room. The girl was standing at the head of the bed close to the wall as if she were still listening for him. Her suitcase was open on the narrow bed, and some of her clothes had been unpacked and were separated into piles on the spread. He knocked once gently and pushed it open.

"Oh," Casey said, turning her attention from the wall. "I'm sorry. I just start singing sometimes." She looked down at the underclothes on the bed, then lifted them quickly back into the suitcase and closed the lid. She wanted to be alone. Couldn't he see that?

"I don't want to bother you," Hazard said, easing in. The room looked like it always had. The rug on which David had long ago spilled chemicals from his laboratory set was still there, blotches of faded color around his desk. It looked vaguely like a boy's room, and yet more bland then he'd remembered, as if it were ageless, sexless, void of any personality. Casey looked ageless and sexless, too.

"Your daddy's room," Hazard said, nodding at the plaid curtains as if they especially reminded him of David. Actually he was remembering his first glimpse of the boy when he must have been eight years old, dark David of the shadowy eyes, the veiled face, the silent kitchen helper, solitary roamer. He had been at the table next to Pansy that first night. David was as much a part of Hazard's life as anyone. Now it looked like Casey would be, too. "Yeah, David's room," he said again.

"Uh-huh." Casey looked at the room, too. She seemed to be searching for proof that it really was her father's room. She sighed with defeat.

"I used to come in here sometimes when your daddy was a boy. We'd talk sometimes. He was quiet, though.

Always busy doing something and looked like he didn't want to be interrupted. You favor him, you know. Got those eyes and that mouth. Gimme a smile. Yeah, there it is. Just like David."

Casey sat down on the edge of the bed, and Hazard took it as an invitation to himself to settle in the only chair in the room. He turned the desk chair around so he faced the girl. "What were you humming?" he asked.

Casey looked down at her suitcase and then at her hands, which she rubbed together as if to warm them. "It Had to Be You," she whispered.

"That's it! That's right!" Hazard grinned and slapped his knees. "I knew I knew it, but I just couldn't bring it to mind. *It had to be you,*" he sang, slightly off key. "*It had to be you . . . I wandered around and fin-al-ly found . . . Some-body who . . . Could make me feel true . . . Could make me feel blue—*" He hesitated, running his tongue against his upper lip while he thought.

"*And even be glad, just to be sad—*" Casey sang softly, the beginning of a smile on her lips.

"*—Thinking of you.*" Hazard joined in with a snap of his fingers to show he'd remembered. He was on his feet, poised for action.

"Sing, sing," he urged. "You know it. Sing!"

"*Some others I've seen—*" Casey began louder than before. She was watching him move. The old rug was like glass under him as he spun and the afternoon light from the window spotted him gently. A hand here. A shoulder. Full light in his face. "*Might never be mean . . . Might never be cross or try to be boss . . . But they wouldn't do—*" Her voice rose to a torchy pitch while Hazard twirled. "*For no-bo-dy else gave me a thrill . . .*

With all your faults I love you still . . . It had to be you, won-der-ful you, had to be you—"

"Hot damn, you're good," Hazard said, collapsing in his chair. "Why, you got the voice of an angel. You gonna be a singer, I know it! I'm in show business myself, and talent don't have to knock me in the head before I see it!"

"That's what Mama's doing," Casey said. She had looked back to her hands; the spell they had created between themselves was broken.

"What's that?" Hazard leaned forward to hear her.

"Singing. She's singing in a club in Columbia. She works in the bank like she always did, but she's singing at night. This man heard her singing at a party she went to with some of Daddy's friends and he told her she could sing at his restaurant if she wanted to. She went down there the next day. It was a nightclub and that scared her a little, but the man was real nice and she says it's a nice place."

Casey paused to get her breath. Hazard thought it might be the most she'd ever uttered at one time.

"Daddy's in Korea," she went on. "That makes Mama nervous and she didn't like being home every night thinking about how Daddy might get hurt. She said she needed to keep busy. So she took this singing job and I came here to spend the summer so I wouldn't be by myself all the time. I didn't mind being by myself a bit, but Mama said she didn't want to have me to worry about too, so she wrote to Grandma about it and Grandma called up long-distance on the telephone and said I should come." She looked up, straight into Hazard's eyes. "Mama bought some dresses to wear when she sings. A red one and a black one and one with blue sparkles on it because it would look pretty under the lights. I don't like dresses. I wear pants, even to school. When the teacher complained, Mama went after class and showed her where there's nothing in the dress code except about being neat and clean and wearing shoes." She smiled, believing that if any need had arisen to do so, she had successfully redeemed her mother.

"Sounds real fine," Hazard agreed. "All summer here, huh?" He slapped his knees. "Me, too, I reckon. Haven't told Jane yet, so don't go blabbing to her. I work in a restaurant, too, you see, and the owner got sick and closed up until he's better. I didn't see much point in hanging around there, so here I am, ready to pickle, shuck corn, string beans. Whatever comes along."

Casey just looked at him.

"Well, I'm thinking how Miss Pansy just might be coming for supper tonight," he continued. He was feeling better. Having explained himself aloud, his situation didn't sound so bad. "You're acquainted with Miss Pansy, I reckon."

"I reckon I am." Casey couldn't help smiling at him.

"What you grinning about?" He looked pained and then turned on his grin. "You've heard about me! I know it! I can tell!"

"Just from Grandma and Pansy. Sometimes, like at Christmas, Pansy will get a worried look and say to Grandma, 'Wonder where that man is this cold winter evening?' and Grandma will say right back, 'Off somewhere, causing a hazard.' Then they laugh until Mama comes to see what's the matter and then they get quiet, like you're a secret between them. Grandma and Pansy get right silly together sometimes."

"There you go!" Hazard laughed. "Two little bantam hens!"

"That's not all," Casey said, beginning to enjoy herself. "Pansy said you were a millstone around her neck."

"Said what?" Hazard had the feeling he was hearing more than he wanted to.

"She said Hades could freeze over before she married you. She said she doesn't want to get married to anybody, but she's tired of waiting to turn you down."

"When'd she say that?"

"Just this afternoon. After you came upstairs, Grandma and I walked down to her house. Grandma said we were going because Pansy was so anxious to see me, but all the talk was about you."

"It was, huh?" Hazard rubbed his chin as if he were seriously contemplating this information.

"You and Uncle Taylor," Casey added. "And Taylor's new girl friend." Casey got up and went to the window. She ran her fingers along the edge of the plaid curtain while she looked out. "Grandma doesn't know what to do with Taylor, you know. Pansy says he's twenty-eight years old and what can anybody do with him? But Grandma says Pansy doesn't know what it's like having a grown son showing no more sense than Taylor does. He's always off racing that car of his, you know. Grandma says if Taylor would just settle down with some nice girl, she and Grandma would let him run the lumberyard all by himself. They'd turn these three rooms up here into a little apartment for them and not charge a bit of rent. They'd take a trip to Florida."

"My room!" Hazard said before he could stop himself.

"A sitting room, a bedroom, and I think a nursery," Casey said, "because Grandpa says that's the only circumstance that will get Taylor married. Grandma says 'God forbid' to that."

"My room!" Hazard boomed.

"Grandma says Taylor brings girls through her house like it was an inspection post, because he knows these racetrack girls aren't going to get any encouragement from her. Well, I'm supposed to be setting the table. You coming?"

"I've got to wash up," Hazard said.

He sat in the room after Casey had gone and watched dust mots stirred by her movement in the stream of light across the desk. All this talk about marriage worried him. It was like they had all latched on to the subject of his personal affections like fruit-flies on a spoiling peach. Even Casey seemed to be in on it. Well, he'd wanted to be prodded a little—he could admit that, at least to himself. But he didn't want to be peeled, pitted, and preserved. Not yet, anyway.

"Oh well," he sighed like a man who had already given up. He leaned back in the chair, his hands supporting his thin neck, and stared up at the ceiling. He was still sitting there when Jane called him to supper.

4

Jane Flanagan turned the turnip salad out of its steaming pot liquor and into a colander in the sink.

"Good Lord, it's hot in here," she said over her shoulder to Pansy, who had just come in the back door and was arranging curls around her face with a deft finger. "You'll just melt if you linger a minute. Go on in the parlor. Taylor's in there. Ben, too, I think. And Casey's around here somewhere."

They looked at each other, silently acknowledging the presence of Hazard in the house.

"I'll stay in here and help you," Pansy said, although she made no move toward the bubbling stove.

"Well, you can touch up the flowers on the table if you want to do something," Jane said. "It's been so dry lately, I don't have anything but some azalea sprigs."

Pansy stepped into the dining room. The air was close, faintly tinged with kitchen heat and smells from the stove. The shades were pulled, but a light evening breeze edged around them and sucked at their centers.

She went to the window and raised the shades. Light broke in soft patterns on the rosy wallpaper and the faded green rug. Jane's dining room was Pansy's favorite part of the house. She loved the heavy dark mahogany sideboard and breakfront that gleamed with old silver and delicately flowered crackled china. The table had been set and the chairs pushed into place.

Six places. Jane and Ben at the ends. Casey next to Ben. Taylor next to her. On the other side of the table, her own place at Ben's left. Hazard beside her, but with a space between. An empty space. She felt a sudden urge to fill that void and so she stepped into it, one hand on her own chair, one on Hazard's. The wood was warm, the fabric slick and worn with pulled damask threads from years of being sat upon. The cloth was warm, too, as if a body had just been there. Hazard, who slouched in his seat. Who always looked careless at the table, as if he wanted to prepare them for any mishap that might occur. Of course, his attitude was conducive to accidents—his was the water goblet that tumbled, his roll crumbled around his plate. His coffee cup sloshed onto the table cloth. And so he was apologetic and contrite and aggravating.

"Oh," she moaned, imagining him there, and pressed her palms to her face, fingertips against her eyebrows. Her forehead felt hot, flushed with thinking about Hazard, and with knowing he was somewhere in the house, maybe in the room above her.

She knew what that room looked like, for she'd passed it many times on her way to inspect new curtains, help fit a dress, visit a sick child. She knew how the washstand tilted a little on the uneven floor and how a block of wood was slipped under the back leg to steady it. She knew what the bed looked like, a double bed with a blue chenille spread washed to hard flat knots of cotton. She even knew the view from the window, how the Baptist Church spire showed above the trees to the left and how if one stood in just the proper spot, the beginning of her own walk was visible, a glimmer of a white post, a marigold or two.

She knew the room but she couldn't imagine Hazard in it, didn't want to think about his shabby clothes in the open wardrobe or his shaving kit on the washstand or the bed stripped of its chenille and laid white and crisp with sheets as slick as the tablecloth she was now touching. She dropped her hands to her sides. Oh, Hazard, she thought. What will become of us?

There was laughter from the parlor. It was Hazard. He was greeting Taylor and Ben with hugs. Slapping his thighs. Making a joke for Casey. All this while he waited for her.

As surely as she knew he was there, Pansy knew he stood expectantly, his feet shifting, his legs as weak as hers. And now his stomach curled, his hands sweated slightly, his grinning face contorted with hope played against dismay that she had finally failed him and was not there.

She backed away from the table and started toward the kitchen door.

I must see if Jane needs me, she was thinking. Jane is always left with all the responsibility while I flit around, thinking foolishness.

She paused again, hesitating between the two doors, when abruptly and silently, the door from the living room opened and there he was, wearing that cheap blue plaid jacket she'd wanted to discard for years, and that grin, that idiotic, no-better-than-Dwayne-Pickens expression that betrayed his childishness, his expectancy, his fright.

"Hazard," she said because the rest of the family was

gathering behind him, waiting to get to the table. But he just stood there, thinking that he was reading something new in her expression, something that sparkled on her face and made her look younger, even twenty-five years younger, like she had that first night he'd seen her when he'd felt with such shattering alacrity what he'd been all this time recovering from—here was the woman he'd always care about. This was the person he'd never want to lose.

"Old Mr. Tutoni had a heart attack and he's in the hospital and they've closed the restaurant till he gets better or else he dies. Either way, I don't see much future in it," he began.

He had never been so awkward in his life. Never had his hands seemed so big and useless. Never had his head ballooned and lightened as if he were full of air or smoke. He felt himself evaporating under her gaze. His mouth formed heavy, careful, unspoken words around his tongue. I've always been a salesman, he thought. A salesman, a con artist, a dancing man. His feet moved under him, starting a slow brush step.

Oh, no, good heavens, he's going to dance, Pansy thought with horror. And she raised her hand to stop him.

Hazard did stop, but it wasn't Pansy's hand midair that halted him but the true and crucial knowledge that she would that very minute protect him against himself, would put out those careful fingers, so reserved in touching, to catch him as if she truly believed she could.

"I want to marry you, Pansy," he said before he could stop himself. Then, knowing full well what he was risking, he abandoned himself to it: "I've wanted to marry you for twenty-five years and I figure it's time I give you a chance to refuse me, if that's what you're aiming to do."

If he had shot straight at her soul, he could not have pierced her more completely.

"Why, Hazard," she said as if he'd just invited her to the picture show, "Of course I'll marry you."

Jane was behind her, a platter of fried chicken held like an offering on her arms. "What's this?" she asked, setting the plate at Ben's end of the table. "You all come on to the table. Supper's ready. Casey, come help me, honey. I've just got to get the biscuits up."

They stumbled into their places like drunks, their faces blustery and wide with the spectacle they'd just witnessed while Jane slipped bowls between their shoulders to the table.

"Pour out the water, Pansy," she said.

In all those years Pansy had never failed to bring the pitcher from the sideboard to pour full each goblet. Now she rose and put her hands on the pitcher, felt the cool weight of it. It was such a precious thing, this wedding pitcher of Jane's. She had never noticed before how slender the handle was or what strength it assumed against the water. It pulled at her wrist and she put up her other hand to steady it.

"Hazard has asked me to marry him," she said to Jane, although she faced the sideboard and the pitcher, her back to the table where Hazard sat struck-dumb but with tears rimming his eyes. "He has asked me and I have accepted."

"Well, hallelujah!" Jane said, as if the decision had been made only seconds before her patience gave out. "Now let's eat."

5

Nobody slept well. Casey awoke with the early light to the damp, warm heat of her father's rumpled bed. She had dreamed about him.

He stood on the front stoop of their military duplex in his flight suit with a duffel bag over his shoulder. Her mother was in the doorway behind him, her hands on the screen, as if she were about to come out. Her father looked across the yard at a little girl who was running toward him. The girl didn't look like Casey—she was much too young and had blond curls—but Casey knew the girl was she and that her father was calling her to hurry up and hug him.

But just as he put out his arms to her, the military police appeared, one on either side of him, and her father dropped his arms abruptly and stood at attention, eyes blank, face set like a uniform-clad mannequin she'd seen in an "Uncle Sam Wants You" exhibit.

The little girl pulled at her father's pants leg and tried to squirm into his arms, but the M.P.s shoved her away. She attacked his duffel bag in a frenzy, but the bag was heavy and banged against her chest, knocking her off the stoop onto the ground. Still her father didn't acknowledge her but marched stiffly to the jeep between the M.P.s. The child sat on the ground screaming as he got into the jeep and it pulled away. Finally she got up and turned to the house, where her mother was still standing, her hands pushed through the screen. There were two ragged holes where her hands had gone through.

Casey lay on her back, trying to remember every fine detail of the dream, as if by recalling it perfectly she could gain some defense against it. She shut her eyes and then squeezed them tight in concentration. What had her mother been wearing? Her clothing had seemed to shimmer against the screen. One of those singing dresses, that's what it must have been. One of those silly sequined scraps of cloth she'd paid a small fortune for. Casey hated those dresses. She opened her eyes to make the image of them go away and then lay still, gnawing her lip. She knew the dream wasn't really about her mother anyway. It had been about her father. It had been about going to war as if he didn't really mind, like it was easy for him because he was doing his job and he didn't have to think about it. Like nothing mattered to him as much as flying did, even if it meant flying in a war. Why did he want to fly anyway?

It was a question she could never ask him, fearful perhaps that he wouldn't want to tell her, or, even worse, that he would admit he didn't know the answer. She didn't want his life to be a mystery to him, not like hers so often was to her. Grown-ups never seemed to have very good answers to the questions that bothered her, so she'd learned to look out for herself, imagining answers at least as satisfactory as the ones she futilely gleaned from other people.

So she lay there imagining her father alone above the world, looking down on trees that were thick splotches of green and rivers that were tiny stationary streams and cities like Christmas-tree villages. He couldn't see any people, she was sure of that. No children looking up to discover fanciful pictures in the clouds. No parents fearfully studied the sky. No worries of earthly things followed him there; she could imagine him exhilarated, complete, content. Those were good reasons for doing something, even if you couldn't say them out loud.

Down the hall in the bathroom, water was running. Casey got up, straightened her disheveled pajamas, and padded into Taylor's room. Empty, but alive with color. Pictures of cars, gleaming Fords, grinning Chevvies, Plymouths, Hudsons. A glossy of Taylor's stripped Mercury that he kept locked in the lumberyard between races was hung above his bed.

Taylor might spend his days in the lumberyard, but his mind was forever on racing. Cars were the only things he took seriously and the only subject about which he was reticent. Only from hearing him talk to her father did Casey know how he loved speed.

"Morning," Taylor said from behind her. He was wearing a towel and his hair was a mass of tangled rusty curls. Casey liked the way he let his hair grow instead of shearing it close on his neck and around his ears like her father did. She liked Taylor's not having so many rules to follow and his wearing sloppy clothes and scuffed saddle oxfords.

"Forgot there was a lady on the hall," he said, going past her to his closet. "Excuse me a minute." He ducked behind the door and came out wearing his pants.

Chapter Five

"I've got something to tell you, Taylor," Casey said. "Actually it's something to ask you. It's about Dwayne Pickens." She sat down on the bed while Taylor slipped into his shirt.

"No need to worry, sugar," Taylor said. "He's harmless. Dwayne and I go way back. He was your daddy's friend, you know, back before anybody knew he was retarded. It happened so fast, like somebody opened up his ears one night and all his brains spilled out. Just that quick, it seemed like. Of course, I was just a kid and I thought everybody was smarter than me. It came as a surprise, I can tell you."

"Grandma told me," Casey said. "This is something else. It's about me and Dwayne. You see, I met him yesterday and he thinks I'm a boy. Grandmother says he doesn't like girls very much."

Taylor stopped fiddling with his tie and looked at her through the mirror. The child he saw surprised him. He had never given Casey much thought. She was, after all, just a little kid who came twice a year with parents who hovered over her with good behavior and nutrition on their minds. She had always been outside his reach, always so delicate and quiet, even foreign to him, although he had to admit she had her daddy's looks. Still he couldn't remember ever holding her or even really talking to her. He had never felt like an uncle.

Yet here she was, his niece. How old? Twelve probably, and beginning to grow up. In two or three years she'd be going out with boys, then off to college, then married maybe. He didn't know. He didn't know her well enough to know if she wanted those things, if her dreams had frills and music in them. All he knew was that she understood something about Dwayne Pickens, she felt something for that bumbling crazy man in his dirty baseball cap. She was asking him to help her protect it.

"I won't tell him," Taylor said, turning to look at her straight-on.

"I didn't really lie to him," Casey said. She stood up and ran her finger across the photographed fender of a 1949 Ford.

"You don't have to explain, Casey." Taylor waved his hand at the pictures. "We've all got things we don't want to explain."

"Thanks, Taylor."

"Now let's get some breakfast. I've got three hours at the lumberyard and then a race at two o'clock."

"Can I come?" Casey wanted to know.

"Let's put it this way. If you're there, I'll give you a ride home. Just don't tell your grandmother. The best plan is to get money for the pictures. Thirty-five cents gets you in the gate and a bottle of pop." He dipped into his pocket. "Here's fifteen cents more for peanuts. What the hell, it's like being at a circus anyway."

HAZARD COULD hear them talking. He socked his pillow behind his head and looked at the ceiling. He couldn't help thinking that his restless, tumbling night was an omen of discomfort to come. Already he had a headache, and his stomach burned with indigestion—or was it hunger? He couldn't remember eating a thing last night. All he could remember was Pansy.

He hadn't talked to her, not the kind of talk he'd expected to have. People in their situation were supposed to make plans, to be heady with the future. But walking her home, the still warm night close against them, he couldn't tell her he didn't have a plan, had no intentions for the future except to marry her.

He had looked up, hoping for stars, but the clouds were as thick and low as fog. Pansy was worrying about the possibility of a polio epidemic, but he only half listened to her because he was thinking about himself and about her, too, but not about her life. Her job, her house, her daily existence, seemed too concrete, too indestructible. He wanted to think about stars or nothing at all.

"They've had seven cases of poliomyelitis in the next county already, and it's just the middle of June," Pansy was saying.

He put his hand on her arm, hoping his touch would stop her, but she went on. "Dr. Kemble says this might be the summer for us. You know how we've been spared. All these years and only a few scattered cases, most of them quite mild. But this might be our year for an epidemic." She had taken on her doctor's receptionist tone and her arm stiffened under his grasp. "I suppose I should have talked to Jane about it, but I didn't see how she could help but get Casey down here. There's polio in South Carolina, too, you know. Once hot weather comes, no place is safe. Still I wouldn't want the responsibility of a child this time of year."

"Well, here we are," Hazard said halfheartedly at Pansy's steps. "I reckon we should talk some, Pansy."

"Yes we should," she said with a sigh and moved to the porch swing while Hazard stayed on the step. Pansy seemed as unapproachable as the subject did.

The swing rocked gently, and Hazard watched the slight restless movement of her pale dress in the window light.

"I was born here, you know," Pansy said from the rocking swing. "My daddy was the only doctor in town for a long time and we could have afforded a finer house than this, but after Mama died, Daddy didn't want to move. He thought it would be like leaving her here if we moved someplace else. I was glad he didn't want to go. I like this house and there's always been Jane right down the street. We had good domestic help then, and I did for Daddy the best I could. Thank goodness, he thought women should have occupations. He taught me to keep his records and do the books besides being his receptionist. When he died and Dr. Kemble came, I knew as much about Daddy's practice as anybody. All the figures in the ledger were mine. Dr. Kemble can't manage without me anymore than Daddy could have."

"I'll need to look for a job," Hazard said. "I was thinking I might ask Ben if there's anything down at the lumberyard, just to get me started on something."

"We can talk about that tomorrow," Pansy said. She sighed again. "Come sit by me, Hazard."

Right then, at that moment when she was asking him to come to her, he wished he were younger. The wish overpowered him, even frightened him with its surge of regret. He wished her father would come out that very minute. They would shake hands like they used to fifteen years ago and then Hazard would stand, his arm firmly about Pansy's shoulder, and say, "Your daughter has agreed to be my wife and I hope we have your blessing."

Chapter Five

Is that what he would have said? Was that how it would have been so many years ago, if he had only understood that time didn't stand still, that he would someday be jobless, penniless. Fifty-two.

"What is it, Hazard?"

"I was thinking about your daddy. I was thinking about the past."

"There's no point in it," Pansy said lightly. "It's over and done with. Besides, I feel so happy tonight, so new. I don't want to think about regrets if we have any. I want to think about the future. Why, we have a wedding to see to. Even the most simple wedding requires careful planning. And then there's the wedding trip to think about."

Hazard could see her mind clicking through the details. There was nothing for him to do. He had played his part already, acted it out like a fool in front of the whole family. Now the rest seemed safely in Pansy's capable hands.

"Aren't you going to sit, Hazard?" she was asking him.

"Not tonight," he said. "I think I'll get on home. Like you said, we can talk about it tomorrow."

He waited for her to get out of the swing and come to him. The light through the glass front of her door edged her curls, put a shiny orb on her nose. He bent forward and pressed his mouth against her cheek, touching the light with his lips. Her face was warm. Her hands moved smoothly to his shoulders and he felt fingers through his damp jacket. Their faces moved spontaneously forward, but he knew she was hesitating, wanting to say something to him. He paused while his hands pressed into the curls along her neck.

"If you don't want to do this, Hazard," she said, "you must tell me now."

He couldn't answer her. For the life of him, no words came into his head that could say how scared he was, how happy, how completely undone. He pressed his mouth against hers and felt a little sigh as she accepted his answer, his confusion, his feeble entreaty that she was everything to him.

"Well, good night," she said.

"Good night," he muttered, kissing her lightly again. Suddenly he wanted very much to stay with her. He felt a swift, desperate panic that told him that by leaving her he would be losing something precious, some irretrievable moment in which to seal forever his intentions toward her, but nevertheless he stumbled off the porch and made his way down the walk to the Flanagans' without looking back.

If he had turned back, he would have seen Pansy turning the key in her front door (Why, he'd forgotten to unlock it for her!) and drop the key and her bag on the hall table. Then the house was suddenly dark, for Pansy clicked off the hall light and went through the shadows down the hall to her room.

There was no moon, just a hazy blackness outside her window, so she let up the shade and undressed by the distant window light from the house next door. Her bed was warm and her light summer gown clung to her skin, although she didn't feel the close heat of her house, only the sensation of being alive and healthy. She pulled the sheet up as if she anticipated a shiver, for she did. She expected every physical sensation she could imagine. She lay there waiting, remembering every word Hazard had said, every touch. She clasped her hands together across the sheet and remembered his kiss. She waited for every moment to relive itself, and while she waited, lying still in her bed with the thick buzzing air of summer around her, she went to sleep.

6

The noon whistle from the lumberyard had sounded and dinner had been served in the Flanagan kitchen before Casey saw Dwayne Pickens again. She was alone in the kitchen, having taken over the dishes from her weary grandmother, when she heard a clumping sound on the back porch and turned to find him peering in through the screen at her.

"Come on in, Dwayne," she said, although she hurried to wipe her hands and move away from the dishpan. What would he think of a boy doing the dishes?

Dwayne didn't budge.

"You can come in," Casey called again. She quickly spread a tea towel over the drying dishes and pulled the stopper out of the sink. The sudsy water gurgled away.

"I can't come in nobody's house," Dwayne said. He ducked his head and Casey saw only the oily stained crown of his baseball cap and the hands he twisted nervously in front of him.

"Why not?" she asked, pushing open the door. "I invited you."

"You did?"

"Sure I did. I said, 'Come on in, Dwayne.' "

He was grinning at her. "That's right, you did." He frowned and ducked his head again. "Mama says I don't go in people's houses."

"Then I'll come out."

They sat down on the steps.

"Hey boy, whatcha been doing all day?" he wanted to know.

"Nothing."

"I been cutting grass," Dwayne said, happy to have something to report. "Every Saturday I got to cut the grass at Alva's. Then come up here and cut the grass at Mama's. Mama's got a little yard, but Alva! You know my brother Alva? He's got that yard where we used to live, big as a ballpark near about. I fill up that gas tank and I pull that cord and there I go a-mowing and a-mowing. I hate that yard now Alva's got bushes in it and little flowers don't look like nothing but if'n I hit one, watch out! I get paid, though. Three dollars for Alva's. One dollar for Mama's. That's four dollars a week in the summertime to buy things with." He pulled his money out of his jeans and counted it on his knee. "One-two-three-four." He grinned. "See. Four dollars."

"What do you plan to buy with it?" Casey wanted to know.

"I don't know." He scratched under his cap. "Sometimes I buy some baseball cards or some comic books. One time I bought everybody in Hollis Drugstore a soda. It costed two seventy-five! Sometimes I just save it and get something big. I have to buy a lot of baseballs. Them and chewing 'bacca."

"I know where you could spend it today," Casey said. "We could go to the races at the fairgrounds. Do you ever do that?"

"Taylor goes there," Dwayne said. "I see him there in his car. He races—*va-ro-o-m* he goes around the track." He dropped the money and put his hands on an imaginary wheel. The wheel spun in his hands and he fought frantically for control. "He's spinning," Dwayne yelled in his announcer's voice. "He can't come out of the curve. That Ford's on top of him. They're gonna crash!" Dwayne made a skidding sound. "Pow! Bang! *Ba-a-m-a-lam!* And the cars are out of the race! What about the drivers? Here they come! They're all right! They're O.K.!"

Dwayne applauded madly. So did Casey.

"If we start now, we can walk out there by two o'clock, can't we?"

"You got to tell your grandma. You always got to tell somebody when you go off," Dwayne said, collecting his money from the ground.

"I will. I'll be back in a minute." Casey tiptoed through the dining room into the parlor where Jane lay with a cold cloth on her forehead.

"Grandma," she whispered from across the room. "I'm going out. I'll be back by supper."

No answer.

"Grandma?" Casey hesitated and then slipped back into the kitchen. "Well," she said to Dwayne, stuffing her own money into her pants pocket, "I told her."

IT WAS after two when they reached the fairgrounds on the other side of town, but walking along with Dwayne, Casey didn't really care what time they got there. She was too busy listening to him tell her about the stores they were passing and then the houses. It seemed that he knew everyone in town and had some opinion about each of them he didn't mind sharing.

They walked slowly, the afternoon sun boiling on their backs. Dwayne tossed a baseball in front of him, catching it effortlessly, as if it were as familiar an action as walking, and just as necessary.

"Folks named Post live there," he said, rolling his head in the direction of a big brick house with white columns and a carefully manicured lawn. "She don't like me. No-siree! One time my brother Alva, he wanted me to do yard work. He come up to our house and he says to Mama, he says—" Dwayne stopped and ducked his head to think. He wanted to get Alva's words exactly right. "He says, 'Mama, that boy's got to do something 'sides play ball. He's got to learn some responsibil-ity. He's got to cut grass.' " Dwayne laughed out loud, proud of successfully mocking Alva. "So Alva gives me this paper with all these people on it and he says, 'You take your mower down there and cut grass.' So I did. I came right here." He stopped again in front of the beautifully landscaped lawn.

"There was people all out there—in the back, too. Everywhere you'd want to look. They were walking around eating and talking and listening to music. But I went right on and cut that grass. I said, 'Excuse me,' but Lordy, it was hard going 'tween all them folks. They kept moving, you see, and they had those little tables with them little legs and lots of little chairs. Anyhow, that Mrs. Post, she come running out there and she says mean things to me. Ugly, ugly things, like you wouldn't hear me saying to nobody. And I says

Alva gave me this paper and it says I'm coming here to cut this grass. And she says you get outa my yard and don't you come back. Boy, was Alva mad at me. He was as mad as that woman was." Dwayne sighed and tossed the ball high. He ran forward a little to catch it in his bare palm. "I don't like cutting grass no way. I don't want a job. People yelling at you and all. You got a job?"

"Nope. I go to school in the winter and in the summer I just mess around. Who lives there?" Casey pointed at a yellow house with aqua trim.

"Oh, that's Monty's house. Ain't it the prettiest little thing! Monty's the man at the picture show. He takes the money and then he gives you half a ticket in case you want to keep it. He don't take money from me, though. I just go right on in. Monty says, 'Hey boy, where you going?' and I say, 'In here to see this picture show and it better be a goodun!' You be nice to folks and they be nice to you right back. That's one thing for sure."

"I think it's neat, your knowing everybody like you do," Casey said.

"Yeah." Dwayne puffed himself up a little and grinned at her. "I never lived no other place. Never been nowhere, neither, excepting that time they took me off to that school. Alva said it was a school, but I didn't see no school to it. First I went to the school right here, you see." Dwayne's smile had faded as he remembered. "I went a long time, but I got so tired of it. All them little kids. Every year, more little kids. Couldn't none of them play ball worth a hoot. So I quit going. Mama and Daddy and me was all right. It was Alva wanted me to go off to that place and learn something. So I went. Only there weren't no school to it. It was more like a hospital. They wouldn't let me listen to the radio there. That's what I didn't like the most. They says to me, 'Dwayne, them ballgames just get you all worked up,' and they took my radio away. Mama said they wanted me to rest up, but that weren't it. They didn't want no noise in that place. They didn't want nobody having a good time listening to the ballgames. That's all it was."

They walked on in silence. After a while, Dwayne tossed the ball again and ran forward to get it. "I ain't never going to that place again," he said. "Not ever."

THE RACETRACK was a ragged oval of dirt hewed into the middle of a pasture that lay inside the fairground fence.

"Long time back, they raced horses out here," Dwayne said. "When the fair comes, this is where you get to see fireworks, great big ones popping all over the sky." He pulled out his money and gave the man at the gate a bill.

"Hey boy," the man said. "What you doing out here at the races? You ain't planning to drive no cars, is you?"

"Don't have no car. I got me a bicycle, anyhow," Dwayne retorted, his hand stuck out for his change.

"We've come to see Taylor Flanagan," Casey said, dropping her money into the man's hand. "He's my uncle. Do you know where he is?"

"Over there in the infield, most likely. But don't you go over there. It's dangerous, ain't it, boy? Ain't it, Dwayne? You two just get a seat right there in the stands and you'll be seeing Taylor by and by. He'll come flying around here, big as anything in that Mercury of his. You seen that car run, boy?"

"Sure I seen it," Dwayne said impatiently, tired of having to prove himself. "I seen it lots of times."

Casey pulled him along, anxious to get a good seat before the race started. The stands consisted of three rows of weathered bleachers separated from the track by a chicken-wire fence.

"Let's go to the top," she said to Dwayne, wanting to get as high up and away from the other spectators as possible, where she could see everything.

The stands were filling up. They squirmed over pocketbooks and children to get to the far end of the third row. Once settled, Casey saw that most of the fans had driven their cars into the field surrounding the track and were perched on their hoods, awaiting the action. Some were leaning back against their windshields, their faces to the sun, mouths gaping while they napped. Others sat up straight, balancing on fenders while they drank beer and ate sandwiches out of waxed paper. A girl in shorts and halter lay on her stomach on top of a car with her bare feet hanging off the back, getting a tan. She flipped her head from side to side restlessly, as if she were suffering, and eventually she propped up on one elbow and called to the young man in a cowboy hat who was wandering around the other cars to bring her a soda.

"Anything cold!" she said. "You hear me, Frankie, something *cold!*" She sat up on the car, her legs crossed under her, her back arched, shoulders back, blond ponytail catching the sunlight.

Chapter Six

"That's Taylor's new girl friend," Dwayne said, bobbing his head in the girl's direction.

Casey was still watching her. So this was a racetrack girl. She was one of those girls Taylor brought through her grandmother's house like it was an inspection post. Well, she didn't see any reason why Grandma wouldn't approve of this one. She sure was pretty enough.

Frankie had returned with the bottle of soda, which the girl took from him. She lifted his cowboy hat off, twirled it mischieviously around on her hand, and plopped it down askew on his head.

"Don't Taylor need you?" she asked him. "Some mechanic you are!"

"Naw, car's running good, Gwen. He's all set."

"I sure do hope so. It's just too hot out here. I wish they'd get started." Gwen pushed her ponytail up on top of her head and let it fall again. "You tell Taylor I'll be right here after the race," she said. "I'll be steaming, too."

"I ain't tellin' him that." Frankie laughed. He patted the hood of the car. "You want him to keep his mind on what he's doing out there, don't you?"

"I guess so," Gwen said. She lifted the bottle to her lips, swung back her head, and took a big swallow. Casey thought she looked like a calendar model. Like she'd been studying poses and was proceeding to practice them one at a time.

"Well, I got to get going," Frankie said.

"Thanks for the cold drink," Gwen said sweetly. "Now you tell Taylor I'm waiting."

The girl flopped back down on the car, so Casey

turned her attention to the track itself. She could see Taylor in the infield beside his Mercury. The car had been stripped of its chrome and was painted a gaudy bright green. A big number three was stenciled on its door.

While she watched him, thinking how distant he was and yet surprised at how visible this secret life of his was proving to be, Taylor crawled through the window of the car and disappeared as if into a tunnel, gloved hands sinking last into the black interior of the gutted car. The automobile shuddered and sprang forward, followed by other cars that pulled out onto the track in some prearranged order. Their engines were like discordant music, each instrument trying to outsound the others as their drivers listened intently to their pitch and rhythm, the hidden strain of victory or defeat their cars predicted.

The crowd stood up in unison, as if the roar of the cars commanded them. Then the loudspeaker crackled over the idling engines and a parched rattling rendition of "The Star Spangled Banner" blared over them as Dwayne whipped off his baseball cap and Gwen, still atop the car, pretended to sleep so she wouldn't have to stand up.

The music warbled to a defeated halt, and Casey watched the flag fall in front of the cars. They lurched across the starting line, nose to tail, like rabbit dogs hunting a common scent.

"They're off!" the announcer shouted into the sputtering microphone.

Dwayne and Casey were still on their feet, giving the green Mercury their protective attention. Casey watched the cars moving into the first turn and felt her legs buckle. It was the same feeling she had when she saw an airplane taking off and knew her father could be in the cockpit, the instruments in front of him as familiar as his own face. As frightened as she was, she had to believe that he knew their sequence, that he understood their reactions and could reckon with their gauges. The plane became part of him, the panel was an extension of his mind communicating with the new and powerful body he had assumed, lifting its heavy wings against the wind, urging it through clouds, directing it to a black spot on his map. Suddenly she knew it was somehow the same with Taylor.

She dropped to the bench and shut her eyes. The frantic, excited noise of the crowd engulfed her. Spectators were shouting for different cars, names she didn't know, drivers who probably meant something to them—husbands, friends, sons, brothers. Only Dwayne's voice came out of the roar at her. "Looka there! Hey boy, look!"

She was being pulled to her feet and she opened her eyes to see the Mercury slide into the curve. It straightened itself miraculously and took a tenuous lead over a white Plymouth that was taking a rut closer to the inside.

"Taylor's ahead!" Dwayne yelled to the crowd. "That's Taylor's car!"

The track was short—only a quarter of a mile—but when Taylor was on the backstretch and lost to her in the dust, Casey sat down again and looked over at Gwen, who had come to life and was sitting up, her bare legs swishing on the windshield like a set of nervous wipers. She had put on sunglasses with red plastic frames and she held her ponytail off her neck with one hand while she slapped a frantic rhythm on the car with the other.

"He's winning!" Dwayne yelled. He bounced on the rickety bleacher and flung his arms in the air victoriously. "See that!" he yelled to the crowd. "He's winning!"

"Eight laps to go," Casey said.

Thick gray dust rose in front of them as wheels churned the dirt track. The cars were beginning to show abuse, their gleaming numbers dulled by dust, their paint jobs splotched and revealing dents and rust beneath their wax.

"He's gettin' 'em!" Dwayne shook his fist toward the track. "He's getttin' 'em good!"

Casey pulled at Dwayne to sit down, but he ignored her. Caught in the spirit of the event, he slapped himself and bounced on the bleachers, screeching instructions to Taylor and railing at the opponents.

"Look out!" he shouted. "He's coming on!" A car in the middle of the pack slung itself at the back of a Ford, trying to gain a position on the inside. The car under attack caught the blow on its rear, and like the recipient of a swift kick, lunged across the little ditch and into the infield where it banged into a parked pickup and settled down, its front squashed into the side of the empty truck.

"Oh, Jeez!" Gwen yelled, jumping off the car. "Look at that!" she called to Frankie, who was standing on the bed of the truck next to her. "That's my brother's truck! Look at that! Jeez!" She put her hands on her hips and studied the wreckage. "He was going to sell it," she wailed at Frankie. "He was going to sell that truck and the race car, too, and invest in a rig. He was gonna start hauling up into Virginia. We were gonna get rich, dammit. And now look!"

She stamped back to the car and hoisted herself onto the hood, where she stood up to see into the infield better. "Eason Warfield!" she yelled. "What you gonna do now, huh?"

The cars were coming around again.

"Fifth lap," Casey whispered.

The driver was crawling out of the smashed Ford. The audience gave him a little round of applause, although their attention had already returned to the possible winners. The Plymouth had overtaken Taylor on the last corner and it zoomed into the seventh lap half a length ahead of him. Now the same Chevy that had bumped off the Ford edged up on him, vying for second place.

"Watch out!" Dwayne yelled. "He's coming! He's a-comin' on!"

They went into the ninth lap with the three cars tailing each other like they were stuck, but in the turn the Plymouth lost a tire. The missile spun into the air, hit the top of Taylor's Mercury, and bounced off in front of the Chevy. The last car skidded into the loose rubber, maneuvered crazily around it, and straightened up within a breath of Taylor, who was trying to avoid the tireless wonder in front of him.

"They're gonna crash!" Dwayne roared.

Casey shut her eyes, closed her mind, stood suspended in the silence that overpowered the slamming of metal she refused to hear.

"*Wow-weeeeeee!*" Dwayne yelled.

Casey opened her eyes to see the Plymouth on its side against the fence and, in the backstretch, a screen of dust under which she could only hope Taylor and the Chevy were still battling. "What's happening, Dwayne?" she asked.

"He's winning. I knew he would! He's running good!"

Casey focused on the finish line, saw the flag waving, and then the green car screeching to a halt in front of them. The Mercury sat there in the dust as if stunned itself. It was quiet. The other cars passed around it and began pulling off the track.

The loudspeaker seemed to be belching on the dust. Every other word was lost in a giant swallow. "The ——ner ——lor Flan——gan. Driv—— a for-ty —— Merc—ry. Big hand —— Taylor Flan——gan!"

The crowd was cheering. Taylor might not be their husband, boy friend, cousin or brother, but he was the winner. He crawled out of the car, his body and clothes covered with a film of grime, disfigured by smudges of sweat and grease, looking inhuman.

He grinned up at the stands, acknowledging the crowd and shaking the trophy someone had slipped under his arm.

"I was supposed to give him that trophy!" Gwen shouted at them. "They told me I could be the one to do that!" She was jabbing her finger at the track manager, who grinned at her and shouted back, "You can give him something else, I reckon!"

The crowd laughed, but Gwen ignored them.

"It's hot out here, Taylor," she said, as if the rest of

the field wasn't listening. "You go on and get cleaned up so we can get outa here."

"She's wanting to go!" someone in the stands yelled down to Taylor.

"Yeah, she's *hot!*" another man laughed.

"I'm going," Taylor called. "Frankie, come help me get the car outa here." He dropped the trophy through the window into the seat and wiped his face with his sleeve.

"Hey boy!" Dwayne yelled. "Me and K.C.'s here!"

Taylor squinted into the stands.

"We come to see you win!" Dwayne called. "And we seen it!"

"Who's that, Taylor?" Gwen yelled, pointing at Casey and Dwayne.

"I'll meet you all at the gate," Taylor said. "All three of you!"

Gwen gave Casey a haughty look and slipped off the car. She stood there a minute, stretching her arms over her head with her stomach sucked in and her bottom pinched tight. Then she walked over to them. "I got to change clothes, too," she said. "I'm going to supper at the Flanagans' house tonight."

"So am I," Casey said. She was looking down into the halter top. "We'll see you at the car," she said, pulling Dwayne in the other direction.

"Wait a minute," Gwen called after them. "Who are you?"

"Casey Flanagan. Taylor's my uncle."

"Your uncle? You're kidding me. Taylor's not a uncle!" It struck Gwen hard that she had another Flanagan to cope with. She didn't like to think about

Taylor's having relatives at all. She didn't want anyone getting in the way of her having him just the way she wanted him, complete with a lumber business and a 1950 Chevrolet.

"Sure he is. I live with him, too." Casey was enjoying Gwen's obvious discomfort. "See you later."

"Wait a minute," Gwen said, edging closer to the bleachers. "Come here."

Casey leaned down so her face was close to Gwen's. She could see black bits of mascara sticking to her lashes and a little round blister of a pimple under the melting makeup on her cheek.

"Who's that with you?" Gwen whispered.

"He's all right. He's our neighbor, Dwayne Pickens." Casey tried to give Gwen a secretive look. "There's just one thing, though. He thinks I'm a boy."

"He what?" Gwen stretched her neck to get her ear closer to Casey's mouth. "He's crazy, isn't he? You tell me the truth now. I'm not going off with some crazy."

"He wouldn't hurt a fly," Casey said, "unless of course it was the person who told him I'm a girl. He doesn't like girls so that would probably get him riled up."

"Well-l-l." Gwen was backing off. "I reckon I'll see you at the gate in a few minutes." She slung her bag over her shoulder and gave them a little wave. "Good-bye, Mr. Pickens."

"You hear that?" Dwayne asked with an embarrassed grin. He slapped his cap on his leg and rolled his head. "She called me Mr. Pickens. Who ever heard of such?"

"Come on," Casey said. "Taylor's going to be waiting." She dropped to the ground behind the stands and headed for the gate.

"Can't we see another race?" Dwayne called. He jumped down and was stumbling after her. "Hey, K.C.! Can't we stay? Hey boy! Boy, can't we?"

Casey looked into the crowd expecting to hear someone correct him but nobody took notice of them. She turned around to watch him coming through the people who milled around the concession stand. He seemed so oblivious of the jostling cups of soda, the popcorn bags clutched in the crooks of arms, the obstacles in his path. Maybe he'd never seen any obstacles. Maybe there was no fear in him, no wariness.

Casey felt like a mother watching her child come to her. She could see in his face his one intention. He wanted only to reach her, a stranger already familiar to him. He was at her side, and she wanted to take his hand and make a pronouncement of her pride or at least say something about their being friends but she couldn't.

So they walked along, he bounding with excitement about the race, his arms flinging as he recounted the event that filled his mind, while she, subdued with the initial reality that he was truly a child, bent her head as the question just born in her mind spread like an anxious fever. How long could he exist this way? How long would the world, even a world as small as his, allow a full-grown man to be a boy?

7

Half past six found them waiting at Jane Flanagan's supper table while she forked cornbread out of bubbling oil and called to her husband to bring on the baked fish, a gigantic shad she'd smothered with onions, bacon, and potatoes, then doused with butter and milk.

Ben carried the dish into the dining room, the steam wafting into his face, and set it down at his end of the table. Then he sat down himself, his glasses misty with steam, and saw, through his two circles of fog, the faces around his table.

He knew Taylor had won his race that afternoon, although there had been no mention of it. He could tell by the way Taylor speared his boiled shrimp, popping them into his mouth greedily because victory had left him euphoric and believing for the moment that anything he wanted to do, even abandoning manners at his mother's table, was all right. Like inviting this girl to supper. He would have had second thoughts about bringing her if he hadn't won the race. He would have noticed she wasn't dressed properly, that the bare arms and shoulders her sundress exposed were hot and dry with sunburn, and that she had an uncouth twang to her speech that was made more noticeable by Pansy's proper enunciation and everyone else's silence. She was quite a talker, this Gwen, although being at the table seemed to have subdued her a little. She was quiet now, and watchful, maybe even a little apprehensive. Well, she had reason to be, although she and Jane had barely exchanged hellos as yet, so the girl didn't know what she was up against.

Ben speared a shrimp of his own and looked farther down the table at his granddaughter. She looked a little rosy herself. His guess was she'd been to the races, too. If he wasn't mistaken he'd seen her with Taylor when he hauled the Mercury into the lumberyard this evening. It looked like Casey and Dwayne Pickens in the back seat of Taylor's Chevy and this Gwen what's-her-name in the front.

Jane had told him about Casey and Dwayne, how the girl was letting him think she was a boy. He knew Jane was worrying about it, but he was trying not to. After all, what was the child supposed to do all summer? Well, she didn't seem to be wasting any time finding something. Two days with them and she'd already struck up an acquaintance with the village idiot and gone all the way across town to the racetrack with him. Ben smiled a little, chewing his shrimp. He was glad she was a spunky kid, more like Jane than Jane would be wanting to admit.

"Here's the bread—finally," Jane said, thrusting the plate onto the table. "I don't know what took it so long. Let's have the fish now while it's still hot," she urged. "Pass your plates down to Ben. There's the spoon, dear. Aren't you having any shrimp, Hazard? I thought you loved shrimp. Why, I fixed them especially with you in mind."

Hazard poked at his cocktail, got up a tiny shrimp and dropped it into his sauce, where he left it drowning.

"He doesn't seem to have much appetite," Pansy said, as if he weren't there or else were a child to be talked about.

"Off your feed, huh?" Taylor chuckled. He crammed the last of his shrimp into his mouth and sent his plate down the table to his daddy. "Well, I'm starving."

"How about you, Casey? Ready for fish? Pansy? Gwen? You look about ready to me." Ben dished buttery sauce over Taylor's fish and sent it back to him.

Gwen was picking at her shrimp. She didn't like seafood. Who would have thought it, her first and maybe only dinner at the Flanagans' and they had the one thing she couldn't swallow? Why, they could have had pig's feet and she'd have eaten. They could have had chitterlings or hashlet and she would have forced them down. But fish! What was she going to do? Her plate went down to Taylor's father and came back steaming with a rich, raw odor. The potatoes, she decided anxiously, her face and neck flush with indecision. I'll eat the potatoes. Avoid the onions where I can. And fork around the fish.

"I declare, I think I'm losing my mind," Jane said, heading back to the kitchen. "I forgot the shad roe and eggs."

Oh, God, Gwen thought helping herself to an adequate amount of cole slaw. Roe! What could that be?

The bowl Jane brought in passed under her nose. It looked like scrambled eggs speckled with brown globs. She'd seen something like that once before, but where? She put a tiny bit on her plate. The smell—Lord, it was rotten—whiffed into her face. It smelled like the caviar she'd tasted once at her rich second cousin's wedding reception. It was fish eggs. They expected her to eat fish eggs! Well, she wouldn't. She couldn't.

She felt like crying. No, she was afraid she was going to cry. What if she did? What if, when everything was going just the way she wanted it to—Taylor had won the race and finally invited her to meet his parents, even have supper with them, when she thought there was a chance she could be his special girl friend, maybe even marry him someday—what if now, with everything so nearly perfect, she went all to pieces over fish eggs?

Well, she wouldn't. She just wouldn't. She lifted her napkin to her lips, then pressed it under her eyes to make sure her mascara wasn't running. Her insides were crying even if she wasn't. Her eyes felt watery and her throat tight. She stifled a little moan, thinking how she needed to repair herself, heal the damage she felt she'd already done by not liking seafood. Why did she have to be born hating fish?

AT THE other end of the table, Jane was watching Pansy and Hazard, having determined earlier in the evening to avoid thinking about this girl Taylor had brought home. She'd have plenty of time for that. Besides, she wanted to give this girl a chance. No snap judgments this time. No subtle discouragement. At least she was pretty. That blond hair probably wasn't natural, but what did that matter? A lot of young women were peroxiding their hair nowadays. It didn't mean anything.

Hazard looked pained. He was toying with his fish, not eating any more than Gwen was. Like two people in love, Jane thought, and then paused in her thinking to look at Hazard seriously. Why, he *was* in love! Who said he couldn't lose his appetite and get weak-kneed just like anybody else? Well, here she was middle-aged and so set in her ways, she was almost past believing that people of her generation could fall in love. Romance seemed so frivolous to her now. Well, it shouldn't.

She knew she was still in love with Ben. *In love.* That was what she meant, although she'd have a hard time saying it, even to him. It was so much easier just to say she loved him. After all, she had spent years loving him, taking care of him. Her dedication to him and their sons had consumed her, energized her, probably even aged her, but still she was in love with him, could feel giddy when she looked out from the church choir to see him looking back at her, loving her over the distance of straight-backed women and drowsy, nodding men. There was a way he had of smiling at her that conjured up his look thirty-five years ago when they were courting and he'd come bounding onto her daddy's front porch as if he'd been coming all day long, every movement and thought at the lumberyard nothing more than another step toward nightfall and being with her. Good heavens, what a feeling that was, knowing someone thought about you all the time like that. Somebody cared about you that much.

She looked from Hazard to Pansy, these apparitions at her table. They surprised her a little, accustomed as she was to their ordinary behavior, their dependable combination of antics and solemnity. She'd been just as surprised when she'd walked down the street earlier today to ask Pansy to supper and had found her in her bathrobe, still at her morning coffee at ten o'clock.

Chapter Seven

"I feel so lazy," Pansy had said by way of an apology. "Come on and have some coffee with me." She hadn't even combed her hair, and there was a sleepy, drugged blush on her face. Jane thought she looked very innocent, very young, as if time had moved differently for them during the night, and daylight had found them years apart.

They had sat across from each other as they had many Saturdays before, although until today always at an earlier hour—eight thirty when Jane's men were off to work and Pansy was just up from her laziest morning of the week, the only day she didn't begin at six thirty.

Pansy had always gotten up with her father. Made his breakfast and tidied the kitchen before meeting him at his office at nine. By then he'd done rounds at the hospital and made house calls while she'd dusted the parlor or gardened a little and then spent a few precious minutes soaking in the tub, taking sweet advantage of the silence in her house. She liked being alone. She liked the aroma of bath oil and soap on her steamy bathroom walls. She liked being barefooted and robed in her kitchen, having the last of the coffee before putting on the stiff girdle that held her body in place by clamping wrinkles into stationary folds. And then selecting an outfit from among the shirtwaist dresses and soft skirts and blouses on which she wore her mother's jewelry—brooches, a delicate double strand of pearls, a cameo of peachy stone set in fine spun gold. She liked to wear the colors of roses, lilacs, peaches, plums. It pleased her skin to hover close to summer fruit and flowers. It made her happy to look through the closet, eyeing her one extravagance, searching for the perfect color to suit her mood.

In the doctor's office, amidst his antiseptic white, she was like a flower to admire, a hothouse fruit ripe for the picking, as she wrote numbers in her ledger books, accepted payments, wrote down appointments, listened kindly to complaints she'd trained herself to barely hear, much less remember.

She liked the figures in the ledger, even the perfectly lettered names she drew in the appointment book, but she didn't really like the people they represented. The people were sick. They coughed at her and left dirty tissues in her wastebasket. They handed her ancient bills from out of their soiled pockets. They had ringworm, strep throats, urinary tract infections. They sat stiffly on aching, arthritic bones and came too slowly when she beckoned them into the examining room.

It wasn't that she wasn't sympathetic, or even sometimes felt heart-wrenching pity. She did sometimes, against her better judgment. Sometimes, when all else failed, she consoled a sobbing child with a penny candy from her pocketbook or offered her arm to a frail body that shuffled weakly across her slick clean floor. But she didn't like to, didn't want to. She believed she did her job efficiently, even kindly, but she didn't want to care about those people. Once she started, where would the limit be? She was no nurse, it was not her inclination. That part of her life that needed a recipient of her care would simply have to go unfilled, unless, of course, Hazard Whitaker took it upon himself to fill it. And yesterday, he had done just that.

The two women studied each other over their cooling coffee.

"Taylor's bringing this Gwen person home for supper tonight," Jane said. "I thought you and Hazard could be with us, too, unless you've already planned something."

They sipped their coffee, each wondering how they could grab hold of the other. They had been friends for so long, as long as either of them could remember, but there had never before this been any apprehension between them, no fear that what they said to each other could do irreparable damage to their affection, no inhibitions that kept them from speaking the truth.

"Nothing has been planned," Pansy said tearfully. She got up suddenly, holding her mauve housecoat close to her breasts, and turned to the coffeepot on the stove although both of them still had full cups. "More?" she asked with her back to Jane.

"No." Jane studied Pansy's back. The housecoat made her seem taller and leaner than she really was. It camouflaged her softness, barricaded her openness with a wall of tightly woven defenses. Against what?

"What is it, Pansy?" Jane asked.

"I don't know." Pansy put her hands up to the coffeepot as if to warm herself, but she didn't touch it. "We didn't make any plans. That's all. First I didn't want to. I felt afraid to talk about it. I was afraid I'd just imagined his wanting to marry me. Last night was somehow magical, don't you think? I couldn't help thinking I'd created him, you see, and so I could make him say whatever I wanted him to." She paused and turned back to Jane. Her face was pale, stricken with her spoken fear. She smiled sadly. "Then after we came here and were sitting on the porch, I wanted to talk about it, but Hazard didn't. He said he had to go, and I didn't see any way to keep him, so he went. Not that I minded very much. I went straight to bed and slept. But now this morning, I feel so panicky, like I can't bear to ever face him again. What if he's changed his mind, Jane? Or what if, when I see him, I know I don't want to marry him. My life is so set, you know. I've been alone all these years. What if I don't really want Hazard living in my house? What—"

"What if," Jane interrupted, "when Hazard comes down here about lunchtime, as he will probably do, he finds you in your bathrobe, uncombed, unwashed, drinking cold coffee? What will he think then?" She laughed and thumped the table. "None of your questions are more serious than that one, Pansy," she continued, seeing the strain between them broken. There was no permanent barrier between them. Not yet. "Of course Hazard meant what he said. Everybody heard him and he was speaking from the bottom of his heart. I'm sure of that. As for plans, there's plenty of time. Start making some today—it'll give you something to talk about. And as for your not wanting anybody in this house, the truth is you've always had Hazard here, in your mind, at least. Why, these cups we're drinking out of, you bought because you thought he'd like them, not to mention the new parlor drapes and your daddy's chair you had reupholstered in that fine blue material. I never noticed blue being your favorite color."

She got up and put her arms around Pansy. It was an easy gesture, grateful acknowledgment that their friendship need not be hampered by Pansy's new situation. They embraced freely, with relief and pleasure, like comrades after an arduous journey. Then they stood arm in arm.

"You come to supper," Jane said.

"I will." Pansy felt herself tremble and then Jane squeezed her arm gently. "I suppose it's all said now, Jane."

"Maybe so, maybe not." Jane let her go. "It would be silly to remind you that anything worth doing is a little bit hard. We're neither of us children who need things like that explained to us. And yet, sometimes, I have to tell myself—like when I got Casey down here with all the responsibility that involves. When we commit ourselves to something important, like a child or a marriage, we have to realize all over again that it won't all be easy. And then we have to decide not to let that hinder us. Loving is truly the biggest risk a person can take, and the one that's the most worth it."

JANE CLOSED her eyes as if to clear her vision and opened them again to find herself in her own dining room and looking at Pansy, who was pressing her napkin to her lips to signify the completion of the meal.

"We'll have the pie later," Jane heard herself saying. "Out on the porch."

They were stirring. Taylor leaned back in his chair, rubbing his stomach and sighing. "Terrific, Ma."

Gwen had pushed her uneaten dinner away, as if she refused any responsibility for it. She smiled at Jane. "It was a good dinner," she said carefully. "I enjoyed it."

Not completely ill-bred, Jane thought, giving the girl a smile. Of course, the test would be if she offered to help with the dishes. Jane stood up and began collecting plates. "Now you all go on out on the porch where it's cooler. I'll be along in a minute."

"Let me help," Gwen said, grasping two crystal goblets by the stems as if she intended to squeeze them to pieces for fear of dropping them.

"Thank you, dear, but I can manage. You go on out with Taylor now and have a good time. Casey and I will do the dishes tonight."

Casey grimaced and took the goblets Gwen gratefully released to her. Gwen didn't think she could have stood the small talk women always got into over the kitchen sink. Dirty dishes and greasy water always seemed to release the kind of determined domestic chatter she abhorred. Family talk. Babies, deaths, illnesses. Depressing subjects, enough to give a person indigestion, if, of course, they'd eaten anything, which she hadn't.

She hoped Taylor would offer her a hamburger or something on the way home, or maybe the pie they were having later would tide her over. She didn't really want to stay through the pie. She wanted to be alone with Taylor even though her shoulders were burning like somebody'd set a match to her. She lifted her arms to pull free the tight hot skin cutting across her shoulder blades. Thank God, she'd worn this sundress with spaghetti straps. She'd have just died in anything else. She shuddered, imagining what a bra would be like on her back. She could feel Taylor's hand at her waist.

"Let's go then," he was saying. "Out of the way, girl."

They followed Mr. Flanagan and Hazard through the dining room and onto the porch, leaving the women and Casey with the kitchen.

"You go on out, too, Pansy," Jane said. "I'll call you to bring out some iced tea and the pie in a little while. You go on out there with Hazard now. Keep Gwen company. I declare, she looks like a little lobster with that sunburn. Maybe you can recommend something she could put on it."

Pansy did as she was told. It was easier than thinking for herself to follow Taylor and Gwen out onto the dark porch and sit down in a rocker between Hazard and Ben while the young couple took the swing. She could see Gwen settling close to Taylor and she considered mentioning the girl's sunburn, but she didn't. What did she care about Taylor's girl friend when Hazard was here rocking next to her? It was he she was supposed to take care of, not some racetrack girl who picked at her food and didn't insist on helping with the dishes. She reached over and took Hazard's hand, patted it gently, then rested it again on the arm of his chair.

What was that for? Hazard wondered. Maybe Jane had told her that Ben had given him a job at the lumberyard. Maybe it was a condolence that he'd had to ask his best friend for work. He sighed and rested his head on the back of his chair.

He could hear Taylor and Gwen whispering to each other. How could they have so much to say? They barely knew each other, he could tell that, and here they were chattering away. Hazard cleared his throat in anticipation of saying something to Pansy, but no ideas came to him.

Ben had lit his pipe and the cherry-flavored tobacco smoke hung in the summer night. "Do you remember the time we went fishing up Leggett Creek, Hazard?" he asked softly.

"Yeah." Hazard moved in his chair, setting himself to remember.

"I caught that shad long as a man's forearm. Remember that, Taylor?"

"Yes sir, I sure do, Daddy." The swing creaked.

"It was delicious," Pansy remembered. "As good as tonight's."

"I thought everything in the good old days was supposed to be better," Taylor chuckled.

"That's what some folks would lead you to believe," Ben said. "But we know better, don't we Hazard?"

Hazard sighed a noncommittal reply.

"Nothing is better than right now," Ben said, "give or take a few things like having David here with us and there being a cool breeze stirring. You won today, did you, Taylor?"

"Yes, sir."

Through the screen door Casey saw them like shadows that moved tentatively, mysteriously, catching light on her grandmother's porch. Their voices came to her in whispers as she leaned against the jamb, her head bent to the screen as if she believed she must hear a secret word of invitation if she were to open the door and disrupt their contemplations, cause shifting bodies and cleared throats to greet her. She didn't see a place for herself out there.

An aching kind of loneliness enveloped her. She looked up, wanting to recognize these shadowy forms that she knew held such a tenacious grip on her twelfth summer. Taylor and his girl friend on the swing, cuddling in the dark with their heads together and Taylor's finger tracing a soft line on Gwen's shivering arm. Pansy, sitting still and prim in her rocker, reasoning with herself that tonight when Hazard walked her home, everything would be different. Hazard slouching, his legs extended so that his feet rested on the porch rail, clicking his fingers on the arm rests, hoping someone would break the silence and fill the night with idle conversation to relieve him of that burden. And her grandfather, drowsy with a full stomach and his pipe, half listening for sounds from the kitchen, always wanting to know that Jane was about and taking care of things.

Casey ran her hand down the door frame until she reached the cool metal latch and pushed gently against it.

"That you, Jane?" Ben asked into the darkness.

"It's me, Grandpa."

"Casey."

She heard him sighing and knew the sigh was not one of disappointment but of contentment.

"We're glad you're here, Casey," her grandfather said.

And Casey gave the screen one determined shove and went out.

8

The house positively reeked of wedding plans. Ben Flanagan said it was a smell that held an uncanny resemblance to the odor of funeral flowers long after the body had been laid to rest.

"Too thick and sweet for healthy folks to breathe in," he added as he and Casey headed home from the lumberyard. It was dinnertime and Casey had been to fetch him, having nothing better to do since Dwayne had not appeared on the back porch that morning.

"Now that the date is finally set—the seventh of July, I believe they said—we'll just have to put our endurance to the test. Are you up to two weeks of frenzy, I ask you, because those women intend to squeeze every ounce of emotion into this occasion they can possibly muster? It's been a long time coming, and Jane, for one, has a whole lot of energy saved up for it. Only thing that could top it would be Taylor's getting married. What do you think about Gwen, anyhow?" Ben gave Casey a sly sideways glance that told her he knew she and Dwayne Pickens had spent the past two Saturdays at the racetrack.

"Oh, I don't know," Casey said. She slapped a crepe myrtle bush beside the sidewalk and came away with a handful of purple blossoms. "She's all right, I guess. She works at the candy counter in the five and dime, you know. Dwayne and I went in there one day last week and there she was, big as life in a little white jacket, scooping up chocolate-covered raisins. Dwayne wanted to buy something just to let her know we were there and saw her, and she smiled and called him 'Mr. Pickens.' Now he wants to go in there every single day and buy popcorn and M and M's. I guess her being Taylor's girl friend makes her O.K. with him." Casey let the crushed blossoms in her fist fall slowly, leaving a tiny trail behind her. She brushed her hand on her jeans.

"How long do you think you can fool him, Casey?" Ben asked.

"Until he doesn't care anymore," Casey replied.

"That time might never come, honey," Ben said. He wanted to touch her arm, but her body seemed suddenly stiff and defensive. She was tense just the way David's shoulders used to be when he felt himself about to be pressured into a parental point of view. "Casey, you don't know Dwayne very well. Nobody does. How can we when he doesn't know himself? But I believe he won't take to being duped anymore than you or I would. I know you think he wouldn't pal around with you if he knew you're a girl. I suspect you're right about that because he's always been kind of heated on the subject. People bait him about girl friends and such and that sort of thing embarrasses him. But it might just be that you're not giving him a chance to like you for who you are." He paused while Casey strode ahead, not wanting to listen. "Just think about it, Casey. It's something you've got to decide for yourself."

She hurried along in front of her grandfather, knowing she was being both rude and ungrateful. After all, the family had sworn to keep her secret and she knew they would. Even Gwen, who didn't seem very smart but who was at least half scared of Dwayne. And even Pansy, who was too involved with getting married to be giving any thought to the two of them.

Well, maybe she would tell him, Casey reasoned. After all, she had the wedding to contend with. She hadn't brought a single dress with her from home, but that didn't mean her grandmother was going to let her go to the wedding in pants. Maybe she could arrive in pants and put on some sort of skirt after she got there. Dwayne wouldn't be at the wedding, anyway. She'd checked the guest list to make sure, although she hadn't expected Pansy to include a crazy person in her wedding in the first place. She was hardly consenting to invite the people Jane thought were absolutely essential.

"You're not getting married but once," she'd heard her grandmother saying to Pansy, "and these people are your friends. They've known you all your life and they expect to be invited to your wedding, Pansy."

"I'm sure they do," Pansy had retorted. "They want to see it finally done so they can gloat." She was emphatically marking through names on Jane's list with a fountain pen. "Every one of these people has tried to fix me up with a man some time or the other. They've had me to dinner, to concerts, to picnics, to every social occasion you can imagine, with me so trusting and unaware every time that they had also invited what they called an eligible man who generally turned out to be a doddering idiot or else a widower with a mournful face who expected a continuation of his comforts at my expense.

They want to be there all right, but I shan't give them the satisfaction of a freak show. I shan't be the main attraction for them to *ooh* and *ah* over, while they're saying 'It's about time' under their breaths." She studied the list now disfigured with heavy black lines. "Well, that leaves about twenty people."

"But Pansy, this is just ridiculous, not to mention terribly embarrassing! These people consider themselves your friends, whether you do or not," Jane pleaded. "They expect to be invited. They want to help you and Hazard celebrate. And besides," she added solemnly, "if you're eliminating people who invited you to supper unawares, you best eliminate me. Don't you remember how you met Hazard in the first place?"

"Of course I remember," Pansy said. She patted Jane's hand to soothe the upset she was causing. "It was my regular Thursday night because Daddy was at his supper meeting. I remember that after we ate, you and I went on to choir practice just like always. Oh, how I wanted to stay on the porch that night! I remember I almost suggested that we skip choir practice since you had a guest and all, but I couldn't bring myself to say it. It was admitting too much. I was embarrassed to death just thinking it."

The two women sat beaming at each other.

"It seems like yesterday," Jane said softly.

"Yes." Pansy's smile faded. "But it wasn't. It was twenty-five years ago and over the years that followed, I've been harassed, Jane, truly harassed. By good intentions, I'm sure, but I can't condone them now. And I can't be putting on a show that makes them think they were right—that I really did want to get married all those years. Because it wasn't that way. I was never really sure I wanted to marry anybody, not even Hazard, until the moment he asked me. I've been happy alone, Jane. I've liked my life. I could have gone to my grave not married and known I'd had a good life."

Casey couldn't help thinking, when she remembered all those conversations she'd heard between her grandmother and Pansy, that there were more retarded-acting people in their neighborhood than just Dwayne Pickens. It was a secret kind of stupidity, but as childish and emotional in private as Dwayne's was in public.

People in love acted dumb, anyhow. Pansy and Hazard were proof of that, all the time smiling at each other like they had a secret between them when the truth was as plain as the grin on Hazard's face.

He looked just like Billy Pierce did that one week he was in love with Casey in the fourth grade, mooning around behind her and stumbling over his feet like she was eventually going to acknowledge his existence and even turn a smile his way. Which she never did. And so he gave up and faded into her classroom faces, although she knew both of them remembered. It was a good memory, too, without the embarrassment that had accompanied the event itself. That was how Pansy would remember her wedding, Casey thought, no matter who attended it. She would remember that she had been special to somebody, and there wasn't any better feeling than that.

She heard the metallic slap of the baseball slamming against the drum and ran farther ahead of her grandfather. "Dwayne! Hey!" she shouted toward the lot behind the trees. "Dw-ay-ne!"

She saw him pause on the mound and then watched while he scooped up something from the ground, jumped the fence, and trotted across the street with a package under his arm.

"Hey boy! Hey, I got you a present! Guess what I got you! Betcha can't guess!" He had arrived at her side and was pointing at the package wrapped in brown paper. "Betcha can't guess in a million, trillion years what I got in there."

He was grinning. Casey thought she'd never seen him so happy, not even at the racetrack or when he'd thrown Duke Snider out at third. Still she couldn't help feeling embarrassed.

"You shouldn't be getting me a present," she said. "It's not my birthday or anything."

"That don't matter," Dwayne said, undaunted by her lack of enthusiasm. "It's a real good present, the best present I ever bought anybody." He thrust the package into her hands. "Open it up, boy! Let's see it!"

Casey tore the paper away from the taped edges and let it fall as she stood staring at the gift in her hands. It was the most beautiful baseball glove she'd ever seen.

"It's a fielder's glove," Dwayne yelled, as if he were as surprised as she. "It's a fielder's glove, Mr. Ben," he called to Casey's grandfather, who was coming up behind them. "I went down to the hardware store this morning and I says to Mr. Wilson down there, I says, 'I wants to buy a fielder's glove,' and he says to me, 'They cost a lot of money, boy. How much money you got?' And I says, 'Ten dollars and fifty-two cents because Mama helped me count it out this morning,' And Mr. Wilson says, 'Well, that'll do her, all right.' And so I tried them all and I pounded them some and this was the best one!" He was dancing with excitement. "Hey boy, put it on! Put it on!"

Casey slipped her hand into the glove. The leather was solid and raw against her fingers as she worked them into place and then sunk her fist into the palm. Her hand was swallowed up and she worked her fingers slowly, flexing the leather. First she cradled the glove against her chest, then reached out her arm to see it better, turned her hand slowly to study the golden grain and to inspect the web stitching and the stamped signature of Ted Williams. She curved her index finger over the top of the glove and squeezed the pocket shut.

"We got to oil it," Dwayne said. "We got to loosen it up so it fits you right. Make it soft and easy on your hand so you can pick up them ground balls like they was dandelions. I tell you, that's a fine glove you got there. See, I told you I got you something good! I told you!" He pounded her on the back and then pulled the glove off her sweaty hand and put it on himself. "See it, Mr. Ben. Ain't it a fine one?" He shoved his baseball into the webbing of the glove again and again, methodically slapping the leather into shape. "We got to work it, though. Got to do some good work on it. Come on. Let's do it!"

"Casey's got to eat dinner, Dwayne," Ben said.

"I'm not really hungry, Grandpa," Casey had an urgency in her voice that made Ben want to give in to her.

"So you want me to offer your apologies to your grandmother, huh?"

"Would you?"

"It does seem like a special occasion to me," Ben said. What could one missed meal hurt? "You two go ahead then. But don't expect anything from the kitchen before supper, Casey. You know how your grandmother is about folks not eating at mealtime."

"I won't," Casey said, already starting across the street. "Thanks, Grandpa."

Ben bent down to pick up the paper they'd dropped and when he looked up again they were disappearing between the trees on their way to Dwayne's baseball diamond.

"Let's break it in some!" Dwayne called, running ahead of her. He sailed over the fence and trotted to the mound where he'd dropped his own glove. "I'll throw you some! A few light ones is all. Why, that thing swallows your hand up. You got a little hand for a boy, you know that?" He pulled his cap down closer to his eyes, bit off a plug of tobacco which he worked carefully in his jaw, then sent the ball flying in Casey's direction.

It sank into the pocket of the new glove. Casey flipped it out, curving her palm against the sting, and tossed the ball back to Dwayne, who fired another straight at her. She caught the hot missile in the webbing, then the next in the pocket, trying to alternate the stinging palm with the hot stretching fingers that still hunted a comfortable position between their stiff leather casings.

The noon sun was white around her. She wiped her arm against her forehead, blinking to see Dwayne, who seemed to shimmer beyond her like he was doing an exotic dance. She felt lightheaded, sun-struck with heat, and hungry—but she refused to quit. She couldn't let him know that her hand was on fire, that her fingers were swelling tight in the glove fingers, or that her shoulder motion seemed to rub bone against bone. The ball kept coming, and she returned it as vigorously as she could, although she knew Dwayne was not at all taxed. He was enjoying himself, congratulating himself on his purchase while Casey picked up the grounders he occasionally sent toward her and pushed herself into the hot sunny air, her head light and burning, to grasp the frequent high balls in the webbing of the new glove.

Finally she heard a voice coming through the trees. "Casey! Casey!" It was Taylor. He followed his voice across the street and into the lot. "What are you two doing?" He leaned against the fence.

"I got K.C. a good present," Dwayne said. "Go ahead and show it to him, boy. Go ahead."

He sent a black stream of tobacco juice between his teeth while Casey gratefully tugged the glove off her steaming hand. Her fingers were as red and swollen as she'd imagined and she rested them limply behind her, out of Dwayne's view.

"Mighty fine," Taylor said, examining the glove. "Mighty fine present you got there, Casey."

"Ten dollars," Dwayne said happily.

"Big spender," Taylor agreed. "Really big."

"Yeah." Dwayne grabbed the glove himself. "I got to oil it some. Loosen it up. That boy's got a little hand, you know that?"

"Yes, well," Taylor said, seeing the need to change the subject. "It's Wednesday afternoon, you know, and I was thinking what with the lumberyard closed and all, we just ought to go somewhere. I was thinking, how about the arcade? You been there yet, Casey?"

"No. What do you think, Dwayne?" she asked hopefully because she didn't want to abandon him when he'd just given her the glove.

"*Wowee!* Them machines you're talking about!" Dwayne turned his head to spit again. "Them cars to drive. *Var-oo-om!*" His face fell. "But I ain't carrying much money," he remembered. "Spent it all on that glove there."

"I've got two dollars," Taylor said. "You can play till it's gone and then we'll call it a day."

They piled into the front seat of Taylor's Chevy and went downtown to a little building that had housed a local market before the chain grocery set up business nearby. The building had been stripped of its produce bins and refrigerators and its raw ripped walls were lined with pinball machines bulging with shiny glass and blinking lights.

Casey's empty stomach rose into her chest as she stood peering at the mass of jangling, sliding slots, flashing lights, and metal pinging metal.

"What you want to try first?" Taylor asked her.

"That one!" Dwayne shouted. He was holding out his hand to Taylor. "Gimme some money."

"You got to get change from that man over there. See him at that counter making change for people," Taylor said, slipping a dollar to each of them. "Now don't race around here wasting this, you two. Watch the games people are playing the most and try them. And make sure you don't put your money in a machine that says *Out of Order*. See that sign right there, Dwayne. You'll be throwing your money away if you put it in that one."

Dwayne was nodding enthusiastically, hardly able to

contain himself until he was free to run loose in the room.

"Now I'm going down to the five and dime to see Gwen a minute," Taylor continued. "I won't be long, so you two stay right here until I get back. You got that, Casey? Right here."

Casey nodded. She didn't care where Taylor went as long as he stopped lecturing them. Nothing was more irritating than being given money and then having to hear how to spend it.

"O.K. then," he was saying. "You're all set." He could see they weren't listening to him anymore. "O.K. now. I'll see you in a little while."

Dwayne took off for the change counter, but Casey moved more slowly, wanting to take in the place, machine by machine. She still felt dizzy from having skipped lunch and having played baseball in the hot sun. The arcade was air-conditioned, and she stood in front of the blower for a minute feeling the cool breeze through her jeans on the back of her legs.

"Ain't you gonna play?" Dwayne asked. He was bobbing his head toward the machine nearest them and he jangled his fistful of coins at her. "I got the money."

He pushed a nickel into the slot and they watched the glass interior light up. The game sent a mechanical bear across the face of a woodland scene. Dwayne sighted through the rifle attached to the case and fired at the electric eye on the bear's side. The bear rose on its hind legs, glared at them, and then started down on all fours when Dwayne fired again. The bear rose again and slumped back onto the track, his light blinking. "I got 'im," Dwayne yelled. He fired again and again. The bear raised up and fell as if he were being pumped, his electric eye blinking furiously like a gaping wound until the lights went out.

"Let's do that one, boy!" Dwayne yelled over the noise of other machines. The place was getting crowded with boys off work for the afternoon. "This one!" Dwayne had arrived in front of a machine with two steering wheels. "Let's drive these cars!"

They inserted the money and watched the double-lane highway tremble. Then the landscape jerked into motion as trees spun by, rivers disappeared around the cylinder, and a little town blurred in the distance.

"Drive," Dwayne yelled. He gripped the wheel like a maniac, his jaw working, face set in dire concentration. "I'm gonna pass you!" he shouted. "Looka here, boy! I passed you. *Wooooo-eee!*"

Casey pushed hard on her accelerator and maneuvered into the lane ahead of him.

"That ain't fair," Dwayne said. "I'm gonna bump you offa this road, just like them drivers do out at the track!"

He gave her a spiteful grimace and then looked back into the machine to see his car wobbling on the road. "My car's broke!" He pressed on the accelerator with all his might but the car was coming to a gradual, defeated halt behind Casey's. Dwayne twisted his wheel angrily and let it spin back into place. "It quit," he said mournfully "Just when I was gonna beat you good!"

"Let's try another one," Casey suggested, wanting to get his mind off defeat. He seemed truly angry with her. "I've got to get some change. You go ahead and pick one. Pick a good one now."

With change in her pocket, Casey turned back to see Dwayne across the room, beckoning to her. He was playing one of the flipper games and she went to the machine next to him and inserted her coin. The play-field lit up and she snapped the lever, sending the steel ball up the shoot and into the field of thumper bumpers and bells. The ball eased through the maze, racking up points, and she worked the flipper buttons eagerly as if she were galvanized, part of the machine that sparkled and clanged with her winnings.

"I'm gonna do another one," Dwayne said and left her while she inserted another nickel to play the flipper game again.

"Over here, boy!" she heard Dwayne calling over the bells as the ball rounded the posts. "Come see this 'en!"

By the time she reached him, he had already pushed his coin into the slot and the interior of the machine had shown a faint light on a dark blue background. It was a night sky and Casey saw small lights flickering across it. They were the targets toward which Dwayne was aiming a machine gun.

"What is it, Dwayne?" she heard herself asking incredulously, although even then, at her distance, she knew what it must represent. A sky of planes. Tiny flickers of light appearing on the wingtips of animate aircraft. She knew, too, as she was rushing toward the machine and Dwayne was aiming down the sight, his finger clicking the trigger *ra-ra-ratt-t-t*, that she couldn't let him go on. She stood there, despising his inability to understand what she would mean if she told him to quit, to leave this easy victory and go back to killing bears. How could he understand? She stood behind him, unable to focus on the havoc inside the glass but looking instead at Dwayne's back, that crouched man's body leaning into his terrible task. He was so strong. His muscles moved under his khaki shirt, his arms flexed their bound-up strength. He could be a soldier, he could be any one of the thousands of men in uniform she'd seen in her life. He could have been someone who'd been to war and never spoke of it, someone who had flown beside her father, his eyes watchful for the plane that would spin out of the clouds to bring them down.

But he wasn't a soldier, no more than the plane he'd just hit contained the spattered, sinking remains of her father. It was a game, and a boy was playing it. Still, her ineptness to stop him astounded, even frightened her. She had no words to tell him her fear, the swift aching panic that had paralyzed her so that she could only stand staring at him with tears in her eyes. A boy crying in an arcade.

"Dwayne," she said softly, putting out her hand to touch his shoulder. "Dwayne."

He heard her over the din of his own gunfire and she saw that her voice, just the sound of it, must mean something to him because he released the trigger and turned to her. He knew something had hurt her and he must put all his strength into fixing it.

"My daddy flies in the war," she said, feeling her tears. She didn't want to cry. What would he think?

Dwayne was staring at her. His brain worked slowly through what he knew about this person. David's kid. The name stumbled into place. This was David's boy. David was in the war, and here was his kid in the arcade scared of something.

He wasn't sure of what. What in the arcade could scare a boy like that? He rubbed his head under his baseball cap. He could see tears in Casey's eyes. He could tell they were tears because his eyes were too shiny. Too round. Well, it was all right to cry. He'd cried when they took him to that place a few years back. Now Casey was in a new place, too, feeling maybe the same as him. If he just knew what to do about it.

"Let's don't play that game anymore," he said. "I don't like that one."

Casey wiped her face on her sleeve and came up with a dingy smear across her cheek.

"Boy, you got a dirty face," Dwayne said, handing her his handkerchief, which was permanently stained with baseball grime. He grinned, glad to be doing something for his friend.

"Thanks." Casey rubbed the handkerchief against the smear and then stuck the cloth in his hand. "You want to run those cars again?"

"I'm gonna beat you this time! I'm gonna beat you so bad! I'm gonna turn you every way but loose!"

"You don't know nothing about driving," Casey said, shivering back her tears. She headed for the steering wheels with Dwayne, but deep in her body the fear remained open and oozing. It would be as easy as Dwayne's aiming that fake machine gun, she knew. It would be that easy to have her daddy never come home, to have her life forever different.

They were still driving the cars when Taylor, Gwen in tow, found them. "Let's get outa here," he said. "Gwen's got the rest of the afternoon off and we're not spending it feeding these hungry monsters."

"We ain't spent all the money yet," Dwayne said, holding out the coins in his hand.

"We'll get a hamburger with it," Taylor said. "Anyhow, hadn't you rather do some real driving?"

"What are you intending to do?" Gwen wanted to know. She was wearing a little cotton dress with a Peter Pan collar and Capezio shoes with flowers on them. Casey thought she looked like a high school girl. Gwen twitched her ponytail and ran her hand up Taylor's bare arm. "I thought we were going somewhere, honey."

"We are," Taylor said. "And we're taking these two with us."

"Oh, Taylor," Gwen moaned. "I could be doing my hair."

"And miss teaching Casey how to drive?"

"I'm not old enough," Casey said, although the idea had an uncanny amount of appeal.

"Sure you are. You know right from left, don't you? You know stop from go, don't you? Why, I could teach Dwayne here to drive, couldn't I, Dwayne?"

"I reckon you could," Dwayne said with unexpected seriousness. "But first you teach K.C."

"Well, let's go!"

They headed across town to the lumberyard. Taylor unlocked the gate and drove in next to the little garage where he kept his stock car. He turned the Chevy around as it faced the open lot dotted with stacks of lumber.

"Ready, Casey?" Taylor said. "Come on up here."

Gwen, seeing for herself the necessity of sitting next to Dwayne Pickens, crawled angrily into the back seat where she leaned against the door, refusing to look at any of them. "If you all wreck this car, whatcha gonna do?" she asked finally, seeing that Taylor intended to ignore her for the business at hand.

He was explaining the dashboard to Casey. "Steering wheel, gears, radio, lighter."

"I know all the parts, Taylor," Casey said, wanting to get on with it now that she was in the driver's seat.

"All right. Clutch in. Turn on the ignition," Taylor commanded.

"He did it!" Dwayne yelled from the backseat. "Hey boy, you did it!"

The car settled into idle while Dwayne slapped the seat and roared and Gwen stared out the window, ignoring them all.

"Gears," Taylor said. "Reverse. Down for first. Up and over for second. Down for third. Clutch to shift. Wanna try it now?"

Casey nodded and pushed in the clutch while she eased the gear stick down to first.

"Great. O.K. Now. Start easing out the clutch and giving her a little gas. Not much now. We don't want to run into that pile of two by fours, do we?"

Casey did as instructed. All her concentration went into making the car move forward slowly and carefully. It went five yards and died.

"What happened?" Dwayne wanted to know. "Hey boy, you break this car?"

"Before long you're gonna be wheeling between the lumber like you were born on wheels," Taylor said. "This is where your daddy learned to drive. Then he taught me when I was about your age. Lord, I loved to drive. So did your daddy. But what he really wanted to do was sprout some wings. Wheels didn't go fast enough for him. Me, I like the dirt. I like the dust up my nose and the people yelling and cussin'. I like winning, too. But mostly I like trying those wheels on the track no matter what comes in front of me. Those potholes and flying tires aren't clouds you can sail through. They're obstacles. They'll put you out of business in a minute. In a second. But there's something about that, too, about it being dangerous, about putting what you can do to the test, not just against the track and the other cars, but against yourself. You know, Casey, if I could make a living at it and didn't have this lumberyard around my neck, I'd just drive."

He sighed and grinned at her, then looked back at Dwayne. Flushed with expectancy, he was awaiting his turn at the wheel. "Now let's get this baby going. Mama's gonna be wanting us for supper and it may take all night to teach Dwayne Pickens the rudiments of the motored vehicle."

9

C*asey wore a dress.* A few days before the wedding, she walked with Pansy two blocks east to Mrs. Lumby's to have it fitted. A hand-painted sign, thread letters with a wooden needle and spool attached, pointed them toward Mrs. Lumby's front door. In her bright, hot parlor, Casey stood on a large stool in her scratchy eyelet dress while Mrs. Lumby squatted at her feet, her mouth tight with pins that she briskly stuck into the fabric against the measure of her wooden yardstick. Casey had protested the dress weeks ago, in anticipation of wearing one, but even then she'd had a compromise in her head. She would wear it once and then only in the church. Her grandmother had agreed and had bought this miserable itchy material that made her look like a baby. At least none of her friends would see her in it.

"Your dress is two days away, Pansy," Mrs. Lumby said through her pins. She spoke as if she were bringing the dress from someplace far away rather than off her own sewing machine in the kitchen. "You can try it on, though. It never hurts to have another fitting."

Pansy disappeared into the kitchen and came back wearing the rose dress with its raw, uneven hem and gaping, zipperless back. The dress was the softest garment Casey had ever seen. She squirmed in her stiff blue eyelet while Pansy stood patiently, feeling the silkiness next to her powdered skin. The dress had a wide skirt and a bertha collar. Pansy's white chest rose against the collar that fell softly over her breasts and arms.

"All done," Mrs. Lumby said to Casey, dropping her extra pins into a tin box. "You can put on your clothes now. Let's look at you, Pansy."

Casey and the seamstress stood silent in the room while Pansy turned slowly, as if she were about to dance for them. She fingered the cloth of her skirt, lifting it and letting it fall back into place.

"I'm getting a hat," she said. "A big picture hat of the finest straw with fresh flowers on it. Roses, maybe, or camellias. Then some sprigs of baby's breath and fern. I'll carry a bouquet of roses and snapdragons and a white Testament I've been saving for an occasion such as this."

She was seeing the wedding. They were seeing it with her. The dress had transported them all. Mrs. Lumby stood with her hands folded across her apron as if the dress had been beautifully, miraculously finished, and Casey forgot her scratchy torment while they heard music, the organ from the Baptist Church down the street.

"I'll wear rose satin shoes and the sheerest stockings Broydan's sells, and perfume. Fragrance like rose petals."

They could see the wedding. Casey closed her eyes and was there. She saw herself slipping into the eyelet dress in the ladies room and squeezing her feet into the Mary Janes her grandmother had insisted she wear.

She could see Taylor and Gwen, Taylor in his blue Sunday suit and Gwen dressed to the teeth in a flowered dress with a lacy little jacket over it. She was wearing her Capezio shoes with a matching pocketbook and a tiny veil attached to her blond bun with silvery bobby pins.

When the wedding day arrived it was all just as Casey had imagined it. Jane and Ben were there on the front row as if they were the parents of the bride and groom, filling empty spaces in lives that had long been empty. Jane had a frantic look even though she was smiling, grateful the moment had finally arrived. She looked frazzled; she was functioning on borrowed energy and was destined to spend tomorrow in bed. Her old Sunday dress was wrinkled in the seat and her new hat leaned slightly to the side, blown there by the beginning of a summer storm.

Then Hazard in a white suit and white shoes. He came out of the Sunday school room with a grin on his face and a bounce in his walk as if he were prepared to perform the warmup while they waited for Pansy, the main attraction, to arrive. He clasped his hands in front of him trying to contain his nervous energy and winked at Casey. The organist was playing "O Promise Me." Miss Beulah Wendell, the choir soloist, began to sing. Her voice, old and thin, warbled out the notes of love while Hazard stared into space with a silly grin on his face and Casey twisted her shoulder blades against the pew, trying to get comfortable in the eyelet.

Pansy came down the aisle alone. Her roses quivered in her hand and she paused for a moment midway the church, looking at Hazard and the minister, who were both smiling encouragingly at her.

Chapter Nine

This is all for me, she thought. This is all because of me.

The idea made her suddenly so giddy that she wanted to lean against the closest pew and collect herself. As if she could, as if there were any collecting to be done. All her life she had been collected, in control, contained, even until three minutes ago when she'd been taking deep, rhythmic breaths in the vestibule, waiting for the wedding march. All her life she'd been waiting for this, not consciously because she had been truthful when she'd told Jane she'd been happy alone, yet she knew she hadn't wanted to miss this moment either, had been saving it like perfume until she'd thought its scent might have evaporated. Love unused became useless, became brittle and drawn, or vanished altogether. What if that had happened to her?

She resumed her walk, pushed forward by fear. If that were true, if she weren't capable of the love Hazard deserved, she would know soon enough. She would falter with it, drop it flat and useless between them, and they would have to deal with it. It was worth the risk. She hadn't come this far to deny the pain of risk taking.

They mumbled the vows, Hazard because he was scared, immobile with witless fear; he mouthed the words like a mute learning to speak. Pansy whispered, too, although it was not her inclination to show weakness or to falter in public. But she didn't want to embarrass Hazard by sounding more confident than he. It seemed to her that they should provide a solid if tremulous front even now, as they took their vows.

The minister was saying The Lord's Prayer. The words dropped on their bowed heads. Forgive us . . .

deliver us—words of contrition. The organ delivered them and Pansy felt Hazard's face against her cheek. Her mouth turned toward his and they pressed her bouquet between their damp trembling bodies.

During the reception in the church social hall, a summer storm blew up above them and dropped its windy lashing rain onto the windows. Miss Beulah had consented to play the piano during the reception. She sat straight and serious before the yellowing keyboard, fingering tunes from her head; across the room, at the refreshment table, Jane ladled pink punch into clear cups and urged cake and finger sandwiches she'd made on the guests.

Pansy was cutting the cake herself and wiping the knife carefully on a napkin between each slice. It was a duty she enjoyed because it took some skill and care. She turned her mind to it readily, accustomed as she was to fulfilling such tasks at wedding receptions. She hardly seemed the center of attention now that an atmosphere of celebration had taken over, but she liked that. She wanted to be efficient and unobtrusive—as a good hostess should be. She smiled to herself, seeing how relaxed and comfortable everyone seemed. Even Hazard, who was drinking cup after cup of punch, quenching a day-long thirst that had dried his mouth and shriveled his stomach. He was reviving before her eyes, turning rosy with satisfaction. How he loved a party. Pansy felt grateful for having provided him with one.

It would be as easy as this, she thought, shifting a slice of cake deftly onto a china plate. She could make him happy as easily as this. Hazard had certainly never demanded much of her in the past. His pleasures were simple ones. He was a simple man.

She was the complicated one. She was the one whose passions rose to discomfort her when he seemed so calm, so unperturbed by the impending events, the hours ahead of them. Looking at him now, it was hard to remember what had attracted her to him in the first place. Oh, she remembered the events well enough, but the emotions that went with them had faded over the years, and a carefulness had filtered into her early stirrings of romance. It was good they were married, Pansy thought, and not a minute too soon. She was not, after all, old wine; more likely, a spice that could lose its savor.

Hazard was directing Casey toward the piano. Casey looked pretty in her dress. She could possibly turn into a good-looking woman when and if she filled out and had her hair curled. Pansy thought she looked uncomfortable in her dress, but not foolish. Hazard was trying to get her to sing. Pansy could tell he was urging her because he had his arm around her and she was giving him a worried, plaintive look, the look of a girl who was expected to expose herself and her talents. If she had any.

It was Hazard who said the child could sing. He'd even wanted her to sing at the wedding, but Pansy had put her foot down. No twelve-year-old tomboy, not even one in a specially created blue eyelet, was going to ruin her wedding. No, she'd have Miss Beulah, who was at least dependable.

But Hazard would have his way. She could see him working his will on Casey now, nuzzling her like a sheepdog. He was conferring with Miss Beulah, too, who seemed delighted to contribute to the entertainment.

She began to play. Hazard backed away as if to give his floor show a stage. Rain washed against the windows and a chord of thunder rumbled around them as Miss Beulah took her introduction into a high register. The old piano thundered a little as she brought it down again into Casey's range.

Casey craned her thin neck out of the raw eyelet collar and closed her eyes. She was doing this for Hazard, a gift just for him, because since that first day when he'd come into her room and danced, the light touching him in such a fantastic, magical way, she'd loved him. Loved his puny jokes, his awkward manners, his nonsensical way of dealing with things, even his age, his ancient, timeless yearnings that told her that every year of her life could bring its special joys, its moments of dancing.

She heard her own voice. It came as from her mother's body, that tender delicate throat that could sing away pain and that Casey had long ago learned to mimic.

"You made me love you . . . I didn't wanna do it . . . I didn't wanna do it . . ."

Jane stopped the ladle midair. It was Casey she heard against the summer storm outside. It was Casey in a summer dress, her patent leather Mary Janes biting her toes, her hair brown and shining like David's. She was a girl. Jane could see that. Deep inside this child, the woman she would become lived and was slowly nourishing herself on songs like this one, on words from books, on nights when she must want to hug herself in the sheer magic of being alive and growing. A woman being born with as much pain and pleasure as being twelve could bring to anything.

"You made me want you . . . And all the time you knew it . . . I guess you always knew it . . ."

Gwen licked her lips smoothly and looked at Taylor, who was staring at his niece. What was he seeing? A transformation, that was for sure. Why, the poor thing looked half pretty in that dress even if her bony white knees did show above her socks and her hands, pressed to her stomach, were coarse and ragged-nailed. Half a tomboy was what Taylor was seeing, and he was looking at her as if he wanted to save that tomboy half, as if she was being lost to him right now while she sang those pearly notes, her thin chest pushing out her wind like perfectly tuned pipes resided there.

Well, Taylor could just turn his mind to other things. In a few minutes, they'd be out in his car going home, Gwen supposed, while Hazard and Pansy caught the train for their wedding trip, a honeymoon for old folks. Gwen wanted a honeymoon herself. She pressed her hand into the curve of Taylor's arm as if to tell him so.

"You made me happy sometimes . . . You made me glad . . . And there were times, dear . . . You made me feel so bad . . ."

Hazard looked across the room at Pansy. She seemed so far away from him, hours or miles away, like he'd felt sometimes in his room above Papa Tutoni's. But here she was, as accessible as steps were, as beautiful as he'd ever imagined anyone could be. Her hat shielded part of her face. He wished she'd get rid of it, show herself to him across the room with all those people between them. Give him some display of affection, some sign that she understood why Casey was singing, what had motivated him to put music to this event. Surely she knew it was his way of loving her. Surely she would understand . . .

"You made me sigh for . . . I didn't wanna tell you . . . I didn't wanna tell you . . ."

He wanted to dance. His feet, heavy and tight in his new white shoes, seemed to have found memory in the music. He did a slow grapevine onto the floor. He knew that if he ever danced in his life, this should be the time. Right now, with the people he loved most in the world in this room, he wanted to show them the delicate, complicated maneuvers of his art, the gifts of his childhood, his birthright. It seemed so precious a gift. He trembled against the fear that he couldn't do it justice, that his legs and feet, tired from years of dull, worthless waitering, from the waste of years, could not dance.

"I want some love that's true . . . Yes I do, 'deed I do, you know I do . . ."

He abandoned himself to it. It was the only way, the final release of all his fears that he and Pansy had foolishly let life go by and that this wedding was a sham of good intentions executed too late to save either of them. His feet were gliding, his body felt loose and agile in his skin.

Chapter Nine

"Gimme, gimme what I cry for . . . You know you got the brand of kisses that I'd die for . . . You know you made me love you. . . ."

Hazard danced.

10

They ordered a late supper on the *Southern Crescent* headed for Washington, although Pansy wasn't in the least bit hungry. What she needed was the comfort of the carefully set table, the beautiful manners of the waiter, the heavy napkin that covered her lap like a starched white blanket, the dull glowing silverware, the steaming dishes. Hazard sat across from her, looking out the window as the night flew by. The train seemed sure and swift; he watched lights fall away into shadows as the evening forest loomed beside the track.

"Would you care for dessert?" the waiter was asking him, although his plate had not been touched.

"Huh? Oh, no thanks." Hazard looked at Pansy, who was having her coffee, her eyes down as if to avoid his stammering, his lack of appetite, his malaise.

"No, thank you," she said, resting her coffee cup carefully. "We'll be going to the sleeping car soon." She looked at Hazard, expecting to see him smile at her willingness to admit the coming night between them.

But he was out of his seat and following the waiter down the aisle. She watched the two of them in conversation, Hazard slouching forward while the waiter stood straight, conscious of being watched, polite but regretful.

Hazard came back slowly while Pansy pressed her napkin to her mouth. She felt the stiff starchy coating on the napkin and wanted to crumble it in her hands as if such a feeble attempt at violence would relieve the torment on Hazard's face and keep her from having to hear whatever bumbling, stupid thing he was forced to say.

"We don't have a berth," was what he said, his head hung like a culpable child's. "I forgot to reserve a berth and they're all taken."

"You mean—" Pansy started and then stopped, not wanting to say out loud what a failure he was.

"It's just six hours to Washington," Hazard was saying. "It's midnight already, so we'll be there early in the morning. We can just sit here and talk. We can—"

His own words horrified him. What was he saying? That he and Pansy, after twenty-five years of waiting, would spend their wedding night in the dining car of the *Southern Crescent* bound for D.C.?

She stood up. She couldn't stand to look at him, but where could she go?

"The lounge car, ma'm," the porter said behind her. "I can give you pillows and a blanket."

"Thank you," Pansy said stiffly, not wanting to be appeased. Why should she be satisfied with a porter's duty when her own husband had failed her so miserably? Her husband.

She turned away from him and followed the porter down the aisle, past the white cloths and deserted places, through the narrow, blowing bit of dark into the lounge car. Empty, too, except for a few men already sleeping in their chairs. Pansy knew they were men accustomed to sleeping anywhere. They would awaken at the station and go blinking into the bright morning light, their hair in stiff points where they'd rested their heads, their stubble of beards smudging their sleepy faces. They would clean up in the station lavatory, maybe even pull a fresh shirt out of their bag of wares, and then be off to sell something, anything.

She sat down in the first chair she came to and closed her eyes. Hazard was like those men. He had spent years selling things, riding trains at night to get himself to another job in the morning. A chair in the lounge had been all right for him then. But now? And for her? How could he let it be enough for her?

She sighed and rolled her head on the back of the chair. Already she was aching, weary from the tension of her wedding day. She wished she were at home soaking in her tub. She wished she could shed her girdle and loosen the covered buttons on her blouse that were suddenly digging into her backbone like blunt little nails. She wished she were in bed with Hazard Whitaker, in a berth which, even in her most fanciful imaginings, had not been an ideal situation. She had worried about the cramped quarters, the proximity of the other passengers, the knowing looks she might face in the morning. She had felt dread, but not fear.

She heard the door open and close, felt the swift cool air against her legs. She knew it was Hazard. She could feel him looking down at her, thinking probably that she was already asleep. He wouldn't know what she was feeling, what humiliation she felt that he hadn't planned ahead, that he was letting their wedding night escape like this.

Chapter Ten

She felt a blanket touching her chest. He was pressing the folds around her legs, covering her regret, her vulnerable, needful body, with cheap railroad plaid. Well, she wouldn't sleep. But she sat still, waiting for him to move away. She didn't want to look at him. She felt with a chill that made her shudder under the blanket that she never wanted to see him again.

Hazard was awake, too. He sat by the window, looking out but also looking at Pansy, who sat too neatly to be sleeping but who nevertheless had her eyes shut. She was avoiding him, making it hard for him to apologize. It was just as well, even though he was truly sorry. He was more sorry than he could ever tell her, not because they weren't in bed together, but because he had hurt her already, so soon, like he'd always feared he would. Why, he had worried himself into this mistake just like a child who spills his plate because he's afraid he will.

He stared out the window. The night was passing him by. He leaned back and propped his feet on the window ledge. Over his shoes he could see a light here and there, dotting the black, sleeping landscape. He'd spent many nights just like this—on trains or busses, although he loved trains best. They were more than just transportation, they were a way of living. Why, a man who kept a room in the worst part of town and had one suit and paper in his shoes could be as rich as cream on a train.

With a few dollars and a sandwich in his pocket, he could hobnob with the best of them, read the paper, play a little rummy, and nobody would ask him where he was going or why. The trip itself was what counted, the camaraderie of the journey, the adventure of getting there. He could look successful even if he weren't, on a train.

At least he'd always thought so until tonight. Tonight, just hours after his wedding, he was living the result of the most monstrous mistake he'd ever made—not reserving a berth. The simplicity of his dilemma astounded him.

Here she was, his wife, not five yards from him, faking sleep to avoid him while he stared out the window, seeing nothing but knowing what was out there. He had visited all those little haunts between Greensboro and Washington. He'd sold shoes and pictures and a fine line of kitchenware in them. He knew those houses, kitchens stuffy with the close heat of a winter stove, the dank hallways, the parlors with their stiff, unused furniture. He had never wanted to own one of those houses. Never in all those years had he loved his destination as much as he did the journey itself.

Maybe he was destined to always be between places, riding the bus or the rails. Maybe he wasn't supposed to have married Pansy, who was as stationary as a pedestal and, at the moment, about as cold. He could see already that Pansy didn't like the traveling part, she scorned the adventure. She'd rather be at home without a honeymoon at all. Why, once they got back she'd probably never leave it again, and there he'd be, too, stuck in that fine, uncomfortable house of hers, working eight to five at the lumberyard, falling into her routine like a mouse on a treadmill, spinning himself dizzy but never dancing. Never kicking up his heels. Never forgiven for his minor mistakes, his bumbling attempts to make that woman happy. Well, by God, they'd just see about that.

He closed his eyes just as Pansy opened hers. The tiny lights along the rim of the ceiling cast flightly little shadows on them both. She was aching. Her elbows seemed stuck to the armrests, and her hands, so long folded together under the blanket, felt glued and useless. She tossed her head against the chair to force her brain into alertness. Hazard seemed to be sleeping. Well, good riddance. She didn't want to look at him, much less talk to him. How could he have made such a mess, he the world traveler who knew every station on the eastern seaboard? How could he have failed her so?

She was looking at him whether she wanted to or not. Something about his bent head, the thin forehead turned slightly toward her, the resting jaw, forced her to look at him. He was wearing his white wedding suit and looked incongruous in the dimly lit car, like a leftover party favor.

Oh, she loved him. And tomorrow in their hotel room in Washington, she would tell him so. She would forgive him, if by then she could remember why or how she had blamed him. It would be a funny story to them some day, the kind of story that was passed from generation to generation except that they would never have children to tell it to. Still, it would be part of their memory. They would laugh about it as one remembers the funny little tragedies that bind them to others, those most revealing, gentle knots of love.

She could see the beginning of day. In an hour or so they would be pulling into Washington, a city as foreign to her as San Francisco or Madrid would be, a place as rare and wonderful as any other in which to start a new life. She nestled into her blanket and sighed. She could be happy in Washington.

ONE OF their bags was missing. They were in a taxi more than halfway across town to their hotel when she missed her smallest case, the one transporting her toiletries, which she had foolishly let out of her hand in the station.

"We'll go on to the hotel," Hazard said to the driver, "and then I'll make arrangements to retrieve it."

The tone in his voice relieved Pansy. She heard a mixture of contrition and courage and knew Hazard had determined not to disappoint her again. At the hotel he had the desk clerk phone the station and learned that a messenger would arrive shortly with the missing bag.

"You needn't wait down here with me," Hazard said and sent her up to their room behind the bellhop, who opened the curtains and the bathroom door, snapped open her suitcase, and then left her.

She would take a bath, she thought, while she waited for Hazard. But she didn't have anything but a comb, a compact, a lipstick, and of course, the soap provided by the hotel. That would do, she reasoned, and she got out her new robe of peach silk with lacy butterfly sleeves.

But what if he arrived before she was out of the tub? What if he unthinkingly rushed headlong into the bathroom while she languished in the cool clear water?

Chapter Ten

She would lock the door, both the outside door and then the bathroom door. Hazard would have the key to their room, but would he be offended to discover the bathroom door locked? The only thing to do was to take a very quick bath, just long enough to take the restless night off her skin. She sat up straight in the tub, half turned from the door, and washed hurriedly while listening for the clicking lock that would signal Hazard's arrival.

Out of the tub, she rinsed it carefully and then applied what little makeup she had with her. She put on her underwear and the peach robe and sat down to wait. She was hungry. It was almost ten o'clock, but she decided to wait for Hazard to decide about breakfast. Or would they have lunch? Perhaps they would have brunch right here in the room. Over there by the window, she in her new robe and Hazard in his—she couldn't imagine what he would be wearing. A dressing gown, perhaps? Heaven help them both, his undershirt. Well, the white suit would be better—at least she was used to it.

She read the room-service menu carefully, selecting what she would have. Half a cantaloupe with assorted melon balls, a poached egg on toast, two slices of Canadian bacon, a brioche, coffee with cream. She stood the menu back in its fold on the dresser and opened the drawer. Stationery bearing the hotel insignia, a brochure describing some of the national monuments, a Gideon Bible. She closed the drawer. She was not yet prepared to read literature designed to compensate for loneliness or to make her feel at home.

The hands on her watch slipped toward noon. Then

toward one. The day was falling away soundlessly, like the turning pages of the Gideon Bible she held on her lap. She read the words slowly, forcing herself to think about the story of Daniel because it was a better story than the one she could envision closer at hand. This lone Israelite in the lion's den made more sense to her than she did in a hotel room in Washington, D.C., husbandless, a widow on her honeymoon, deserted either by intention or fate. She didn't know which.

She closed the Bible, knowing she had to find out. If he were dead, struck down by a car while retrieving her missing bag, she must know it. And if he had left her, she must know that, too.

She put on her apricot suit again, turned her diamond wedding ring straight inside her white glove, and closed the door behind her.

He was in the bar. She could see him through the open French doors leading from the lobby where she stood, peering into the dim recesses of the room from which she heard laughter and the clink of glass on metal trays. The white suit had a dingy cast to it now, as worn as the man inside it, for Hazard had a drunken glaze over his face, a will-less, stupid expression, although he was the one laughing the loudest, swallowing boldly, slapping his hand on the table while his two companions, men in similar states, laughed at him.

She stood, turned to stone, watching him even though she couldn't believe what she saw. It was not within her realm of imaginings. She simply did not believe that the man she was seeing was Hazard Whitaker, yesterday her groom. But then he turned to her. Like a thief who sensed apprehension, he looked her full in the face, his lips loose and foolish, his eyes barely focused but nevertheless seeing Pansy in her shiny summer honeymoon suit, that flower he had picked just yesterday.

He stood up to face her. It was his intention to draw her into his party. He would introduce her to these salesmen friends of long ago. He would order her a champagne cocktail, the first she would have ever tasted, and they would toast her, the goddess rising out of their celebration squalor, the queen of his kingdom, his own true love.

But she was gone. The ghost of her lingered for a moment before his sobering eyes, just long enough to tell him he had failed her again. Somewhere growling in his gut a fear sprang up. She had left him.

HE FOUND her in the train station, her hands folded in their white gloves, her hat perched defiantly on her head, while she waited for the train to take her home. He sat down near her, but not too near, just so she'd know he was there and she wasn't alone. He had collected their bags from the room, the suitcase of her things left open so he had to touch the soft silky fabric she had folded there. It seemed wrong of him to touch her things, as if he were defiling her; he closed the suitcase quickly, wanting to close his mind too, although that proved impossible. He could see where she had been sitting on the bed, the slightly rumpled coverlet, the pillow not quite in place. She had been there alone; in this room she had waited for the new beginnings of her life like a prisoner awaiting sentencing.

Now he watched her waiting for the train. It would be all night again on the train, again without a berth, he supposed.

"Pansy," he said softly, but she didn't acknowledge him. "Pansy, I'm so sorry."

She didn't turn her head, but he could see her chin trembling and a tear slip down her cheek into her collar.

"I'll make it up to you," Hazard said, still keeping his distance. He could feel the distance. "I know you don't think I ever can, but I'll find a way. I promise."

Still she didn't see him. She pressed her handkerchief to her face. He did not exist for her anymore.

11

That week the National League beat the American League 8–3 in the All Star Game. Stan Musial, Bob Elliott, Gil Hodges, and Ralph Kiner all hit homers for the National. In Tucson, Arizona, the mothers of two soldiers who had died in an undeclared war in Korea were denied the Gold Star because their sons had been killed in "peacetime." Jane Flanagan bought her granddaughter the sheet music to "Tennessee Waltz." Hazard Whitaker lay in his room next to Casey's when he wasn't working at the lumberyard. Wherever he was, he was subdued and silent under the weight of whatever had happened on his honeymoon.

Dwayne Pickens took Casey to see Susan Hayward in *I'd Climb the Highest Mountain,* during which Casey slid low in her seat and put her hands on her temples so he wouldn't see her cry. He also took her to see *King Solomon's Mines,* where he announced aloud what would be happening next because he had already seen the picture twice.

Pansy went to work as usual. Dr. Kemble did not question the length of her honeymoon or the tearful expression she hid periodically behind a monogrammed handkerchief. Five cases of polio had been identified among his patients by then, one of whom was already in a Raleigh hospital, being kept alive in an iron lung. The health department was considering a proposal to close the swimming pool, the racetrack, the arcade, all the places young people were likely to congregate. Dr. Kemble hoped the situation wouldn't come to that; meanwhile, he recommended that children stay close to home. He saw them around town anyway. They had not seen an iron lung or many crippled limbs. They had not been touched yet, and he could only be grateful for that.

On Saturday, Dwayne went to cut his brother Alva's grass as he did every week. It was the house in which his parents had lived, where Dwayne had been born and spent most of his interminable childhood. He knew every splinter of that house, he knew the smell and touch of it. Standing on the front lawn, looking up at the sparkling white two-story frame, he felt an urgency to return to it, to find himself there again. His mind curled, like a baby seeking fetal position, into the familiarity of the house, the warmth of his sudden acute memory of having lived there.

Alva's wife, Marge, was at home. He could see her big white Chrysler sticking out of the garage, so he knew he couldn't get into the house. Marge had changed everything, anyway. His room had a piano in it now, and there were heavy curtains on the windows that his mama had always left bare and open to the sun he'd loved to feel warming his wood floor, his bed, the models of trains and cars his daddy used to make for him.

Now those things were in his room on Chestnut Street. His mama had brought them in boxes on a big truck. He had unpacked them himself, but it wasn't the same in the new house. The sun didn't strike his window the same way, and his floor had a carpet on it, and there were no stairs to race up and down.

He turned back to his task. He knew Marge didn't want him looking up at the house like that. She'd be watching him. In a few minutes, after he'd started the mower and was at the far edge of the yard, she would come out on the front porch and call to him about watching out for the flowers she'd planted. He wouldn't be able to hear her over the machine, but he knew what she'd be saying. He could mimic her and Alva because they always said exactly the same things over and over again. It was like learning a song or a radio jingle. After a while, you couldn't help but have it rolling around in your head whether you wanted it there or not.

He started the mower and cut a path from walk to hedge where there were no flowers in his way. He liked to mow the straight lines and watch the cut grass spew into the freshly cut rows. He liked the smell of gasoline and grass and the sound of the engine when it was going forward at an even speed.

He heard Marge on the front porch and he looked up at her, pulling his baseball cap lower on his forehead so she couldn't see his face. He could see her mouthing the words of warning and he nodded once and began to mow again. He could feel the sun on his back and shoulders. It had to be late morning, what with the sun so high. He'd already mowed his mother's yard because he was planning to go to the racetrack that afternoon. He was going to ride his bike out there and then find Casey, who was coming with Taylor.

Casey had explained the whole thing to him, even how they'd put his bike up on the trailer with Taylor's car and pull it home. He liked that.

"What do you think you're doing, Dwayne Pickens?" Marge was saying right in his ear. He stopped pushing the mower and looked where she was pointing. He had grazed a little yucca plant and the spikey fronds were lying in a pile behind him. He was guilty, so what could he say to her?

"Mowing," he said. He revved up the engine and pushed away from her.

She came behind him, her flowery housecoat dancing around her bare feet. "Every week I ask you to be careful, Dwayne," she said, "and every week you mow something down. What are we going to do with you?"

Dwayne kept on mowing, his face set stubbornly away from her.

"You're going to hit that azalea!" Marge yelled into his ear, pointing at the pink bush that had appeared in his path.

Dwayne mowed right into it, hitting the tiny trunk and knocking blossoms all over the ground.

"Why, you stupid moron!" Marge yelled. "You did that on purpose!" She grabbed his arm and tried to wrench him free of the mower. "Stop that thing, dammit! You stop that thing this minute!"

Dwayne pushed the gear on the bar to "Off" and the mower sputtered to a halt. "I don't like you, Marge," he said straight into her face. "You are not a nice person."

Looking into her wide angry face, he knew she didn't like him either, and her dislike was more than the momentary feeling he had toward her. He knew she had never liked him and never would. He had to think what to do, how to escape her rampage.

"It's not that we don't love you, Dwayne," Marge was saying, still holding on to his arm but having relaxed her grip, turning anger into apology. "It's just that you don't pay attention, you don't remember."

He was listening to her. She had said it before, he remembered that. He knew he could remember things. He knew Marge was wrong, and Alva was wrong, and the people who loved him were right. He knew he could remember living in that house; he could remember when the lawn was clean and dark green, left open for him to play on. He could remember how his daddy played catch with him there, and how his mama came out on the porch to bring them something cold to drink. He remembered a Christmas tree in the front window and the ice storm one winter that left a solid sheet on the walk for him to slide on. He remembered the time the porch swing chain broke and sent him sailing head first into the wall. He remembered the sunlight in his room and the car his daddy used to have. He remembered how to drive.

He pulled away from Marge and headed for the garage. He knew how to drive. Marge was coming after him, her dressing gown flapping and her hand pressed to her panting chest.

"What are you going to do?" she screamed. "Dwayne, come back here!"

The keys were in the ignition. That was something else he remembered. That was how Marge always knew where they were. He turned the key and pressed the accelerator. The engine turned over and caught.

He remembered the sound. He remembered Taylor. He remembered the repetition of his instruction. Clutch, gears, accelerate. The pattern fell into his brain like learning to tie his shoes had, because it was something he needed to do. He backed the car out into the street with Marge running along beside him skirting the shrubbery. She was screaming at him, but he had the window up and didn't try to hear her. Her face was ugly when she screamed. He remembered he didn't like her and she didn't like him.

Out of the driveway, he had to decide quickly where to go. He knew every street in town, but his mind turned toward the open road where there weren't stop signs and people, where he could get away from Marge and her screaming. He went instinctively where he would have gone on his bike—toward the racetrack, toward Casey.

Two turns and he was on the road to the fairgrounds, less than a mile away. The road was almost empty of traffic because it was still too early for the drivers to be arriving. He drove slowly, his mind repeating Taylor's instructions. He didn't have to shift now, so he concentrated on the wheel. It was such a little thing to have such power. Why, with the turn of his wrist he could cross the white line where the cars coming toward him traveled. He knew enough not to do that. He felt the control in his hands. He could direct the car like he did a baseball, with his arms and hands. He wasn't afraid of what he was doing.

He turned at the big fairground sign and went through the gate that was open for the drivers. He idled the car for a moment, looking out at the track and the empty infield. In his mind he could hear the noise of the race. He could see the trailers and pickups in the infield. He could hear the sputtering microphone and the revving of engines. He could see Casey in the stands. He could see Gwen, too, and Taylor in his Mercury next to this fat white Chrysler that could most likely outrun everything in sight.

He pulled out on the track; he could see it differently now. The track had been washed down that morning. There was a sticky-looking surface on the packed, dry dirt. He could see the chugholes, the dilapidated fence, the curve that made the backstretch seem to disappear. He started slowly, feeling the dirt under the wheels. It was a new sensation, this churning dirt around him. Yet he remembered it, too—the dust choking him as his body churned into home plate.

He gave the Chrysler more gas and shifted into second. The car jumped with his uneven clutching and he remembered how his leg lifted and turned in one even, continuous motion when he threw a good pitch. On the next shift, the car responded perfectly. He could drive. He felt it in his hands and feet. His stomach heaved and he let go of the wheel for a second to shake his hands in the air. He could drive!

The track was getting familiar to him. He could take the first curve in second. With all that room out there and no other cars crowding him, he could take it in third. He could drive without shifting at all.

Casey saw the dust rising from the track before they got there. "Look!" she said to Taylor and Gwen in the front seat.

"I thought they were going to water that track down

this morning. It's gonna be like driving in a quarry," Taylor said, turning into the gate.

"It's a car," Casey said. "Taylor, somebody's driving out there."

"Oh, damn." Taylor pulled up near the track and got out. "Somebody's chewing the damn thing up!"

Casey was watching the car. She had seen it somewhere before but couldn't remember where. She just knew her association with it wasn't a good one. The car pulled out of the last corner and offered them a sideways view of itself in the dust. "Taylor, that's Dwayne!"

"You're kidding!" Taylor squinted at the backside of the Chrysler as it skidded through the first turn. "Good grief, I think that's Alva Pickens's car!"

"It is, and that's Dwayne driving it. I know it is!"

"Why, that man's crazy as a loon," Gwen said from between them.

"You've got to stop him, Taylor," Casey begged.

"How? Just tell me how? Walk out there and get smashed to smithereens?" Taylor gave his own car an angry, frustrated fist.

"He's gonna kill himself," Gwen said. "We're gonna stand right here and watch that ignoramus kill himself."

"Taylor, we've got to stop him!" Casey screamed. She put her fists over her eyes so she couldn't see him pass.

"I can't think," Taylor said, on the verge of tears himself. "Dammit, I can't think of any way to stop him, Casey."

"He sure is tearing the devil outa that track," Gwen said. "If this was a race he'd either win or die trying."

"That's it! That's it!" Casey was racing toward the

announcer's stand. "Taylor, how do you turn this thing on?"

Taylor raced up the steps behind her. "God help us, this had better work, because if it doesn't we'll have to wait until he gives outa gas or goes over the side." He flipped on switches and they heard the static of the speakers.

Casey picked up the mike and pressed it against her mouth. Her breath whistled out across the field. "Ladies and gentlemen! This has been a sight to see! Here on our famous track, the great driver Dwayne Pickens has just shown us a display of his skill and daring at the wheel of a white Chrysler, making better time than has ever been run here, even by that all-time favorite Taylor Flanagan!" She paused to get her breath while the car continued its careening laps below. "Ladies and gentlemen, Dwayne Pickens has won the race!" she shouted into the mike. "Dwayne Pickens is the winner! Dwayne Pickens, please bring your car in and accept the trophy!"

In the distance they could hear a police siren.

"Jeez," Gwen said. "What's the fuzz doing out here?"

"Dwayne does not own a car," Taylor said, his voice cold with frustration as he watched the track.

"Will the winner, Dwayne Pickens, please bring his car in!"

Dwayne could hear his name. At first, it was like the voice speaking those familiar sounds was coming out of the car itself, but then the rhythm changed and the sounds took on a frantic tone. He tried to peer through the dust to his right, but he couldn't see except straight in front of him. Still he heard his name. It was coming from the loudspeaker! He slowed down a little and rolled open his window. He had won! That was what they were saying. Dwayne Pickens had won the race! He should come get his trophy, the voice was saying. He pressed the brake and the car, caught at such speed, screeched, skidded and settled facing the spectators' stand. Dwayne crawled out of the window like Taylor always did and stood looking up through the dust at the announcer's stand.

He could see a police car coming, its siren whirring, and then Alva's second car behind it. Still he watched the announcer's stand, waiting for the appearance of his trophy. It was Casey who came down.

"Did you see me win?" he yelled to her. "I won! Did you see?" He bounced up and down beside the car. "I'm getting a trophy! Did you hear that!"

Taylor was getting something out of his car. It was a little silver-plated loving cup Gwen had given him to keep in the pocket of his Mercury. She had had *The Greatest* engraved on it.

"You can't give him that!" Gwen said, trying to pull Taylor back. "I gave you that. That was a present! Taylor Flanagan, if you give him that, you've seen the last of me!"

"Hush, Gwen," Taylor said. "And smile."

"The winner, setting a speed record unmatched on this track, is Dwayne Pickens!" Taylor shouted, setting the cup into Dwayne's waiting hand.

"Look at it, K.C.!" Dwayne said. "Look at it!" He thrust the cup at her.

"It's terriffic, Dwayne. It's the best trophy I've ever seen."

"What's going on here?" the policeman said to

Taylor, looking from one potential culprit to another.

"We had a little test run going here, George," Taylor said, moving away with him toward where Alva was examining his Chrysler.

"My brother stole this car," Alva sputtered. "He stole it and drove it out here without a license and practically tore it up racing around this track."

"Whose car is it? the officer wanted to know.

"Why, it's mine," Alva shouted. "You know it's mine."

"And you want to take action against your own brother?" the officer said. He was taking out his pad.

"No, he doesn't," Taylor said.

"You stay out of this, Taylor Flanagan. You're responsible for this anyway. Nobody else would teach a moron how to drive. It's you and these goddamn races. You ought to close this place down, Officer. Nothing but riffraff comes out here, anyway."

"I'm driving the second race this afternoon," the officer said to Taylor. "I guess you are, too."

"Yeah, if we can get the track back in shape."

"What about my car?" Alva asked, his indignation slightly dampened.

"Doesn't seem to be much damage to it," George said. "Any body shop can knock those little dents out in an hour. Get her washed up and maybe get her tires checked. This track is hell on tires."

"Officer," Alva said, trying to be calm. "My brother stole my car, this car, out of my garage with my wife standing right there, and he drove it without a license to this racetrack, where he proceeded to show himself for the moron that he is."

"George," Taylor said, turning his back to Alva. "It seems to me that whereas his wife saw him taking the car, he was more borrowing it than stealing. And whereas we didn't see him drive it out here, we can't say for sure that he did. And since the car isn't damaged, I don't see what the problem is."

"He's right about that, Mr. Pickens. Besides, everybody knows Dwayne."

"Then everybody should know he presented a danger to the public today," Alva said.

"To your car, maybe," George said. "But, so far, Dwayne has never, ever hurt a person, and he doesn't seem as likely to as the rest of us do. Now let's get your car outa here. I'll go by in a little bit and have a talk with your mama about this. We just got to make Dwayne understand he can't go around driving cars, that's all."

Taylor got into the Chrysler and drove it off the track. "There she is, Alva," he said. "We'll get somebody to drive it home for you in a little while."

"I'll do it right now," Gwen said. "I was leaving anyway, in case you'd forgotten, Mr. Flanagan." She slammed the door of the filthy car and drove it furiously through the gate and onto the highway.

"Gwen's kinda riled up," the officer said, slapping Taylor on the shoulder.

"Yeah, she's got a temper all right. Just one of the many charming things about her." Taylor grinned. "Listen, George, I'll keep Dwayne with me the rest of the afternoon. Casey here's a friend of his. They'll be all right. I'll see he gets home."

"That's right, Taylor," Alva said bitterly. "You take care of him. But you'd better decide if you are willing to do it every day, because if you're not, you better stay outa this. Somebody's got to be responsible for him.

He ought to have been in training school or somewhere years ago, before he was so set in his ways, but Mama and Daddy wouldn't have it. Now it's up to me, and I'm not going to have him all over town making a nuisance of himself."

"Just what does that mean, Alva? Sounds like out of sight, out of mind to me," Taylor said.

"We'll see," Alva said, "although it's none of your business what I do."

"Let's get outa here, Mr. Pickens," George cut in. "Don't want you mixing with this here riffraff."

They pulled away, passing a line of pickups and cars pulling trailers through the gate. Taylor turned to Casey and Dwayne who were sitting on the bottom row of the bleachers.

"You were great," he said. And each of them knew just who he was talking to.

12

Where could she put the pain? That was what Pansy Whitaker wanted to know after those first days when her grief stopped its spreading and she felt her body filled to the brim and leaking sorrow like tears. She knew she must contain it somehow, control the ache's relentless pursuit of her mind and spirit. She knew she couldn't suffer any longer, at least not so passionately, so willingly, for the pain had become too close to her, almost dear, like a companion she'd grown comfortable with.

At first, when feeling anything seemed such a blessing to her, she had welcomed the pain because she dreaded numbness, that undisputable sign of life's ebbing, most of all. In the beginning, she had reasoned that if Hazard Whitaker were not sharing her table and bed, then bereavement would.

But now she wanted to live, not mourn. Now she wanted the old, sustaining pattern of her days, the familiarity of her single life again. Yet the pain stayed and with it, its own little irritations. She didn't like the constant threat of tears or the wan, trembling face she saw in the mirror. She worried about meeting Hazard on the street, about meeting anybody for that matter. The only people she felt comfortable with were Dr. Kemble's patients. They were sick like her. They didn't know or care that her marriage had ended before it was begun. All they wanted was release from pain—and that was what she wanted, too.

Jane came to see her. Every evening between dusk and dark, she would leave Ben and Hazard on the porch and go down the sidewalk to sit with Pansy on her porch. The two men were always silent. So were the women, but it wasn't a natural kind of silence, not the comfortable silence between people who knew each other well enough not to need conversation. No, it was a looming silence; it was like a third person who kept them from speaking their minds sat between them.

Still, Jane came because she loved Pansy and because she refused to let Hazard come between them now, just as she'd refused to let Ben affect their friendship years ago. What she felt for Pansy was worth keeping, was worth this silence that pushed itself between them.

"I know I must go on living," Pansy said finally, and the silence she broke shattered around them like tiny shards of glass they must be careful not to tread on.

Jane waited, avoiding the glass.

"I know I must put the past behind me," Pansy continued. "But where do I put the pain? I don't know what to do with a hurt that can't be cured. There's no remedy, Jane. I've faced that."

Still Jane waited.

"Twenty-five, even ten years ago, Hazard and I could have been happy together, but now it's as I've always feared it would be. As the years slipped by, I knew it was going to be too late for us. I knew we'd missed our chance for happiness. Hazard knew it, too. We both knew, and yet we let ourselves be hopeful. Now I know we were foolish. So foolish."

"That's what Hazard is saying, too," Jane said. She rocked her chair gently and it creaked on the porch floorboards. "That's what both of you are saying—how it was doomed from the beginning. How you're too old, too set in your ways, too hurt. But, Pansy, I've been thinking about this situation for two weeks now, since that morning when Hazard showed up hangdog on the back porch with you down here in your house alone like you'd never intended to be again. I've been thinking ever since that morning that you and Hazard, both of you, are too lazy. That's what it is. Laziness. Sure I know you've got to feel pain for whatever happened in Washington. So does Hazard. But after that, you've got to stop making excuses for this mess and start doing something about it."

"I can't," Pansy wailed. "Don't you see? I can't speak to him. I can't even stand to think about him. You don't know what he did to me, Jane. You don't know!"

"No, I don't. But I know this. Whatever Hazard did, it wasn't immoral and it wasn't against the law. That means it's something you can forgive. After all, he's your husband."

Pansy hadn't thought of him as that, not since that morning when she'd waited for him in their hotel room. She had handed him her wedding ring when she boarded the train for home. Wordlessly, she had dropped it into his open hand and then quickly put on her glove, covering her naked finger. She wasn't used to the ring anyway, and by the next day she didn't miss it at all. She put her mother's dinner ring back on her right hand, where she'd worn it for thirty years, and it felt comfortable and right. She liked the ring, although it was a bit gaudy with too many large stones and a heavy gold band. Pansy thought it said something about her father rather than her mother because he had selected it more, she knew, for show than for beauty or sentiment.

Hazard was like her father in that—always one for the gesture, making a show of things, but weak on relationships and commitments. She had taken good care of her father, but she hadn't always liked him. He had been demanding at times and inconsiderate, and for someone who had received an expensive university education, not very cultured. Everybody always thought he was cultured, though. Doctors were expected to be. But Pansy knew all that training didn't mean he knew anything about art or beauty or that he read anything beyond the front page of the paper.

Of course, what did that have to do with Hazard, who probably hadn't graduated from high school? She'd never asked him that. In all those years, she hadn't asked him anything about his education, assuming of course, until now, that he had one. Hazard seemed like the kind of man who had many opportunities—he was, at least, more than a little clever—but had never bothered to take them. Pansy both despised and admired his unwillingness to care much what people thought of him. She wished she didn't care that the whole town knew they'd come home from their honeymoon separated. Well, if she was the one who cared, then she should be the one to do something about it.

"Why, Jane, I think you're right," Pansy said suddenly. "What's needed here is some plan of action. I should either take Hazard back or else I should get an annulment."

"An annulment? Why, Pansy, of course you're going to take Hazard back! Of course you are. And I shouldn't be down here pushing you. You need time. A lot of time. Now I think you should at least see Hazard, talk to him. Why, you could come for supper tomorrow night like always. Do that, Pansy. See him."

"I'd be delighted," Pansy said.

CASEY WAS worried. The house seemed full of mourners —Hazard stuck in his room, avoiding her and Jane as if he were ashamed of something. Taylor was silent too, because Gwen turned her back on him at the candy counter when he tried to talk to her and didn't show up for last Saturday's race. Taylor lost. A new driver, a boy in his teens from a neighboring county, had shown up in a 1946 Ford that looked unbeatable, and was. Taylor barely managed to hold second place, but Casey could tell his mind wasn't on the race, anyway. He was missing Gwen a lot more than he'd thought he would.

Jane was always down at Pansy's trying to find out what had happened that put Hazard back in his old room and had left Pansy teary-eyed and humiliated. That left Casey with Dwayne, who seemed oblivious of the trouble he'd caused by taking Alva's car even after the officer had come and talked to him and his mama. Alva had come, too, with a lecture that Dwayne knew by heart.

"Hey boy," he said to Casey, who was sitting on the porch swing in the heat of the day, biding her grandmother's warning that summer sickness struck the overheated more than other folks. She pushed the swing with her bare foot and sent it sailing. Dwayne sat down in a rocker and watched her.

"Hey Dwayne," Casey said. She leaned back and let the hot breeze wash over her neck and face.

"Whatcha doin', boy?" Dwayne asked. He pounded the arms of the chair restlessly.

"Nothing. It's too hot to do anything," Casey said.

"We could ride my bike," Dwayne suggested.

"Too hot."

"We could go to the picture show."

"No money. Besides, we saw it yesterday."

"Go swimming."

"Uh-uh." Casey had a swift vision of herself in her two-piece swimsuit and almost laughed out loud. "How come you don't like girls, Dwayne?" she asked.

"Oh, they ain't worth nothin'," Dwayne said, ducking his head. He stopped rocking. "They make me feel bad, that's all it is," he said after a while. "I starts to thinking how they look so pretty sometimes, but then I remember how they can't do nothin'. Can't play ball, can't run worth nothin'. All the time combing their hair and wearing them frilly clothes, afraid of a little dirty spot on 'em. They just ain't fun, that's all."

"But you like Gwen and my grandma and your mama."

"They're different," Dwayne said. "Why, Gwen, she's Taylor's girl friend, and your grandma, she's been good to me ever since I can remember. And Mama, shoot, she's my mama. Anyhow, ain't none of them girls."

"Let's play cards," Casey suggested. "I've got some

animal rummy cards in the house. We can play until it cools off a little and then we can ride your bike."

Dwayne drew and matched his cards carefully, like he'd seen men do playing poker in the movies. Casey watched him play, his bent-forward concentration as he studied the silly animals. He was so involved in the game, so absorbed. Casey knew that his concentration on whatever he was doing accounted for so much of his trouble—it meant somebody else had to be watching out for him, protecting him from the world he didn't seem to know existed. Like his not understanding about the war in Korea. But then, who did understand it? What if he forgot it was even going on and asked her, like he sometimes did, "Where's your daddy, boy?" When she told him, he seemed to understand better than other people, even if he had to be told again and again. He took what he understood personally.

The world he knew was so very close to him. The houses and streets and people he saw every day. The food his mama cooked and the popcorn and sweets he bought at the picture show. The tobacco he chewed. His own moving body, and the announcer's voice on the radio that brought Crosley Field and Yankee Stadium into his head so that he could see the plays as clear as day. The determination that let him take Alva's car and the pleasure Taylor's little trophy brought him. Dwayne understood it was better to win, even when the game was animal rummy.

So she let him. Sometimes he won outright, and a couple of games Casey won fair and square, but mostly she arranged his victories. She liked to watch his slow grin forming long before he knew it was there, when he saw he had a chance to beat her. She liked the way he slapped the final pairs onto the porch floor and rolled his head back with glee.

"Hey boy, I got you good. See, I got you."

He could keep playing all day as long as he was winning. But he wouldn't always win. Already Casey had heard that Alva was talking about sending him away again. She'd heard all the arguments—how he needed to be trained in a menial skill, how he needed to understand discipline, how he was too old to be playing baseball with an oil drum, how his mama wouldn't always be there to take care of him. The talk hadn't reached Dwayne yet—it was as far away as Korea—but Jane and Ben Flanagan had heard it, so Casey knew it was true. She couldn't really imagine what such a place was like, but she knew Dwayne didn't want to go there and that was all that mattered to her.

"Let's go downtown," she said suddenly, dropping her cards on the floor. She didn't care about any dumb polio. She just wanted to get away. She wanted to feel free, to leave the cares that plagued her house and run away from the summer's silent, endless lethargy. And she wanted to take Dwayne Pickens with her.

HAZARD WHITAKER brought his face dripping from the basin and up straight in front of the mirror into which he peered anxiously, as if he hoped to see another face there. He looked terrible. He knew that, even without Casey announcing it to him as she had that morning when she paused in the open bathroom door to watch him shave. Both of them had looked at his mournful drawn face, one side lathered like a clown and the other smooth and pink but sad.

His jaws hung down like a basset hound's. That's what Casey said, and she was serious about it, too. He had a good face, but it was a face that needed to smile, especially with the jowls of his middle years hanging on no matter how many chin-ups he did. His eyes were baggy, too, and he needed a haircut. Gray sprigs stuck out around his ears—ears that seemed to be getting bigger and were sliding down his head, soon to be located on his wrinkling neck. A basset hound—that was what he looked like. No wonder Pansy wouldn't have him.

He dried his face and neck and turned away from the mirror without looking again. He didn't want to face the truth, although it seemed to be bumping into him every time his mind starting turning over his problem with Pansy. He knew she hadn't minded the way he looked. She'd seen his aging, just as he'd seen hers. He could remember her perfectly from years ago when she was perfect, but that didn't mean he didn't like the way she looked now. He could think how she looked twenty-five years ago beside how she looked on their wedding day and he'd take the wedding-day look, fine-powdered wrinkles and all. So why hadn't he taken her?

Opportunity had knocked at his door, handed him the finest prize a man could ask for, and he'd wasted it in a hotel bar with a couple of cronies he'd had to introduce himself to because they'd forotten him. Damn! Ten years at least he'd ridden the train with those guys, and they didn't know him from Adam until he told them who he was and what he'd been selling. That's what identified him on the road—his product. Well, he didn't have a product anymore. No product, nothing to sell but himself, and he'd made one hell of a mess outa that.

He went back into his room and put on a clean shirt. He knew the rest of the family was waiting for him. Casey had gone down five minutes ago and he'd heard Taylor's car in the drive. Somebody was playing the record player. Jane and her Frankie Carle records. They were all she ever bought, but they sure beat that stuff kids were playing nowadays. "Mockin' Bird Hill" and Nat King Cole singing "Too Young." Hazard started humming involuntarily.

"They say that love's a word . . . A word we've only heard . . . And don't begin to know the meaning of . . ."

Damnation, once that thing got into your head, it was there for good. Hazard tied his tie, still singing softly to himself. "*We were not too young at all.*" No, we were too damn old, he thought, practically strangling himself with his knot.

He shut his door and started down the stairs. Before he reached the bottom, he heard her voice, softer than the others, but tuned to his ear like a whistle an animal hears. Stuck on the steps, he thought quickly of the modes of escape available to him. He could go back to his room and feign a stomachache. He could go out the window and across the roof to the kitchen, where he could shimmy down the porch post. He could race down the stairs and out the front door and not stop running till he reached Cincinnati. Or he could face the music.

He could continue down the stairs and into the dining room where he could sit next to Pansy like always with everyone pretending nothing was wrong. Surely that was what Pansy intended to do. She must want to do that. Why else would she be here when she knew he was here, too? Obviously, she didn't intend to let one mistake ruin their lives. Well, neither did he. Besides, he missed her. No matter how angry she was, no matter what kind of icy look she intended to give him, no matter how she planned to ignore him, he wanted to look at her. He knew when he looked at her, he would believe again that loving her wasn't wrong. He didn't want it to be wrong. Loving Pansy was the most right thing he'd ever done, even if he'd botched it up and lost her for a while.

He went into the living room. Through the open door into the dining room he could see her, much as she'd viewed him in that Washington bar. She was smiling, her hand covering Jane's on the table. She was at home and comfortable. Her face was serene, clear of the pain he'd seen in the train station. Everything was all right! Praise God, it's all right! he thought, and bounded into his place before he could stop himself.

The food moved carefully around the table. Casey, across from him, looked from Hazard to Pansy and back, searching for some clue to the mystery of their dilemma. Ben and Taylor concentrated on eating. Jane gave her attention to Pansy as if she felt she could deter a confrontation by talking about the weather.

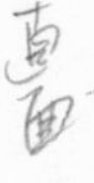

Hazard pushed his food around his plate. From the corner of his eye, he could see Pansy's hand on the table, her fingertips touching her water goblet. Her hand was perfectly shaped, so delicately curved, so bare. He wanted to put his hand over hers. He wanted to slip the wedding ring in his pocket back on to her finger and press his mouth to it.

She seemed to know what he wanted because her hand went swiftly to her lap, and she spoke, looking at Jane, but as if she were making a speech to all of them. "I saw a lawyer today."

It was what he'd feared most, and fearing it so, had made it the one possibility he could not consider. Hearing her words he knew there would be no reconciliation, no gradual renewal of their vows, no wooing. It would all be over unless he could stop her.

"But Pansy—" Jane started and then, seeing Hazard's face, fell silent. This is for him to do, she thought, and stared at her plate.

"I won't give you a divorce," Hazard said.

"You don't have to. I can get an annulment." Pansy still wasn't looking at him.

Her not looking at him stung worse than what she was saying. He wanted to see her eyes springing with tears. He wanted to see her quivering mouth.

"Look at me," he said. "Pansy Whitaker, you look at me."

To his surprise, she did. She turned sideways in her chair to face him. Clear-eyed, firm-jawed, without a hint of remorse, she stared him full in the face.

"You could have told me," Hazard began, more panicked than ever. "You didn't have to go racing off to a lawyer the first thing!"

"The first thing!" Pansy shouted. "The first thing! Two weeks, Hazard Whitaker. Two weeks since that fiasco in Washington! Two weeks and that's enough! No more feeling sorry for myself. No more moping around like I've lost my best friend, which, thank God, I have not! Jane said I needed to take action and I agree with her—"

"But I meant—" Jane started.

"I know, Jane, I know," Pansy said. "But you can't change him, I can't change him. I never could. I never even wanted to. I thought I could love him just the way he was." She turned back to Hazard. "But I can't."

He was the one who was going to cry. He looked at Casey, who was fiddling with her fork and pretending she was deaf. He wished she'd look at him. Maybe her face, her youth, would tide him over, but she couldn't lift her eyes any more than he could stop the tears that rolled down his cheeks.

"Don't," Pansy said in a normal voice. "Don't let this hurt you, Hazard."

"But it does." Hazard wiped his eyes with his napkin. "It was terrible what I did," he said to the table at large. "I know that. I mean, first I didn't reserve a berth and there we were, sitting up all night on the train. And then Pansy left her bag in the station and I was waiting for it in the lobby when I saw these two fellas from the old days and we had a couple of drinks and time just went away. Everything left me. Everything. Even you, Pansy. I admit that. I forgot about you up there in that hotel room waiting for me. I'm sorry for that. More sorry than I've ever been for anything I've ever done."

"You mean nothing happened?" Casey howled.

"Casey!" Jane slapped the table and the dishes rattled.

"Nothing happened," Pansy echoed. "And there's no changing that either. And because nothing happened,

I can get an annulment and have my old name back and my old house and my old life." She was sniffing.

"Then I'll just have to try to stop you," Hazard said, "because you're talking about my life, too, and I don't want my old life back. You want action, huh? Well, you'll see action!" He grabbed her hand out of her lap. "You see this?" He yelled. "I'm gonna put a wedding ring on that hand if it's the last thing I ever do!"

"And it will be!" Pansy said, wrenching her hand free. She pushed away from the table.

"Where are you going?" Hazard asked.

"Home." Pansy stood as straight and prim as she could.

"I'll walk you," Hazard said.

"No, thank you."

"Then I'll walk behind you." Hazard stood up, too.

"Hazard, please."

"Please what?"

"Please leave me alone."

"I can't. I love you and I've left you alone too damn long as it is."

"Jane—Ben." Pansy looked helplessly around the table.

Everybody ignored her.

"Casey—" Pansy was backing through the kitchen door with Hazard going toward her.

They heard the kitchen door slam and sat, their faces hot and their mouths struck with foolish smiles, while Casey raised her fists above her head and shook a Dwayne Pickens victory salute. "Nothing happened!" she crooned. "Nothing happened!"

13

The first weekend in August it rained. Late Friday, before the sun had time to fade into dusk, dark clouds swept in on a high wind and massed in dark patches on the surface of the sky. Jane Flanagan brought the geraniums in from the railing and leaned the porch chairs against the wall of the house. Dwayne Pickens scooped up his bag bases and slug them in his garage beside his bike, then yelled good night to Casey, who sat on the porch swing watching the moving clouds and waiting on the first hard crack of lightning that would send her scurrying into the house.

Taylor went to bed right after supper when the rain was just beginning to gust against the closed windows of his stuffy room. He lay there for a long time thinking about the race the next day, imagining how the track would be choked in mud, hiding new chugholes and spraying his windshield with a thick layer of mire.

He was thinking about Gwen, too. He couldn't seem to think about anything—not racing, not weekends, not even getting through his day—without thinking about her. He'd have his mind on the race and a spot of white light would catch his eye and he'd think it was Gwen, swinging that blond ponytail in the stands. But it wasn't. Hadn't been her for three Saturdays since he gave that stupid tin cup to Dwayne Pickens. Well, he'd get another cup, he'd get ten cups. But she wouldn't listen to him. She'd turned her back on him in the five and dime twice already, one time to wait on somebody, but the other time she was purely rejecting him. Showing she didn't care. Proving she didn't have a lick of feelings for Dwayne Pickins. He'd always suspected as much. But then, why should she?

Gwen hadn't been brought up with Dwayne. She hadn't seen him all those years struggling to fill up his days with something while everybody else grew up and had their days filled for them. She hadn't seen him when Alva took him away that time, like a convict or something, although Dwayne had been willing to go. And glad to come back. He'd told everybody in town, like they were as happy as he was. "I'm back!" he yelled to everybody in sight. "See, I'm back!" Like anybody cared.

The stuffy room had put a sweat on him. Taylor got up to open his door but then lay down again. He could hear Casey singing in her room, bored he reckoned, although she certainly never complained. This couldn't be the greatest summer the kid had ever had, not with her daddy on her mind and the only word from her mother a telephone call every Sunday morning. Casey always just said yes and no, or the shortest answer she could think of, into the phone. It was sad, her not talking to her mother any more than that. Taylor didn't blame it on Barbara, though. She was doing the best she could. They all were. After all, this was a war, a little one by some standards, but a war nonetheless. People were getting killed in it. People were getting worked up over it too, what with General MacArthur going around making speeches and worrying everybody about President Truman firing him just like people could get him his job back. Why the devil anybody would want that job was more than Taylor could understand. He didn't see why anybody would want to be president or a general or even a pilot. And if it didn't make sense to him, how could anybody expect Casey to understand it?

One letter she'd had from David. One lousy letter in two months. Well, what could he say? "Killed twenty Commies today. Wish you were here." or "Bailed out this morning. In hospital. Daddy is a gimp." At least the letter she got was a real letter. Two pages in David's tight, clear script. He didn't talk about the war at all, but about how he hoped she was O.K. and how he wanted her to be a good girl and how he remembered her and missed her. David could say things like that in a letter. His brain could pour out words his mouth would never say.

Taylor was like that himself. He couldn't imagine telling Gwen he loved her. If he did. Now there it was, the whole ball of wax. He couldn't even tell himself he loved her. He moaned into his pillow, kicked the sheet onto the floor, lay flat for a moment contemplating staying wide-awake for half the night, then got up and went across the hall to Casey's room.

She was reading, the book propped on her knees very close to her face. The lamplight shining on the page and the side of her face made her look spooky against the white sheet.

"Hi," Taylor said, thinking how much like David she was when she was quiet like this. He remembered

David reading with a flashlight, that eerie glow diffused on the bed and floor where he huddled with a book long after bedtime. Mama wouldn't have minded his reading, but there had been something fun about the secretiveness of those hours that made the adventures in the book more breathtaking. "Whatcha doing?"

"Nothing." Casey put the book down. She was glad Taylor had come. The night had begun so early because of the storm and she saw the hours stretching in front of her, a dismal, lonely time with the house so quiet and defenseless against the gusting rain outside.

"Still raining," Taylor said, peeping between her curtains.

"Yeah." She was thinking of her daddy and the lecture he liked to give her about the weather, explaining in long detail the formation of clouds, the wind currents, the peculiar combinations that resulted in hail and hurricanes and typhoons. He explained hopefully, as if he could make her never fear the elements, but always when lightning popped across the sky, she was frightened. The thunder always startled her by its closeness. Maybe that was why her daddy knew so much about weather—to keep himself from being afraid.

"Couldn't sleep," Taylor said, settling on the foot of the bed.

"Didn't try," Casey replied. "Grandma won't have the television on because of the lightning, so I thought I'd read."

"Good idea." Taylor picked up her book and read the jacket. He gathered it was some sort of romance, a book about teen-agers in love. "Any good?"

"It's O.K. Gwen gave it to me."

"She reads this stuff, huh?" Taylor flipped the pages as if he could discern the true contents in a second. He dropped the book back on the bed, defeated. "She won't talk to me, you know."

"She talks to Dwayne and me, though," Casey said encouragingly. "I think that's a good sign. I mean, she's not mad with all of us. In fact, I think she's getting to like us a little. She's always glad to see us."

"Even Dwayne?"

"Even Dwayne. Taylor, do you think Alva's still mad over the car?"

"Probably. What the hell, Casey, maybe I shouldn't have shown Dwayne how to drive, but there he was, as much a kid as any kid could be, and you could see how he was just aching to get behind the wheel." He picked up the book and dropped it again. "But maybe I shouldn't have done it."

"I heard Grandma say driving the car might be all Alva needs to try to send Dwayne to the hospital again," Casey said. "You don't think he will, do you?"

"Who's to know? Alva is a peculiar man, very big on his public image. He likes living in that big old homeplace, he likes being on committees and the town board. He's the sort of man who gets a kick out of his name on brass plates in public buildings. So here he is, saddled with Dwayne, and instead of enjoying him just the way he is, he thinks he's got to improve him or else hide him away."

"Is that what he was doing the last time?" Casey wanted to know. She felt a heavy, desperate clutch of fear that she knew wasn't associated with the storm. "Hiding him away?"

"Since there's no improving for Dwayne, I guess it was."

"And if he tries to put him away again?" Casey asked breathlessly.

"We'll try to stop him, I guess. We didn't the last time. That was before he moved across the street and we just weren't paying much attention to what was happening. Dwayne had sort of drifted out of our lives then."

"But now he's right here," Casey said hopefully.

"He sure is," Taylor said. "And I guess that makes him our responsibility. Somebody's got to look out for him, sort of like the way we're looking out for you this summer, not that you need much of that."

"Sometimes I do," Casey said softly.

"Homesick, huh?" Taylor put his hand on hers.

"A little. Sometimes Mama seems as far away as Daddy is."

"That's natural. Two miles and two hundred can be the same when you're lonesome." Taylor was thinking of Gwen.

"You're gonna get her back," Casey said, grinning at him, "just like it happens in this book." She flipped the volume at him.

"Then I better read it, hadn't I?" Taylor laughed. Then he was solemn again. "I'll make you a bargain. You don't worry about Dwayne and I won't worry about Gwen. Now let's get some sleep."

"Taylor," Casey said when he had reached the door. "I'm glad I came."

She went to sleep with dreams that had no storms in them.

Down the hall, Hazard Whitaker was devising a plan. The scene with Pansy in the Flanagans' dining room that past Thursday had convinced him. He didn't care what he had to do, he would get that woman back. So he'd followed her home that night just like he'd told her he would. Walked five steps behind her because she didn't want him up front of her. Followed her right up the steps, onto the porch, and would have been in the house, but she was too quick for him and slammed the door before he saw for sure that she wasn't going to give way and let him in politely.

Twice this week he'd gone to Dr. Kemble's office to see her, had stood right in front of her desk lined with violets, his back to the patients who waited to be called, and said, "I didn't come to see the doctor, although I'm sick, Pansy, sick at heart, sick to dying in love with you. Aching, giddy, sick with love."

She'd tried to hush him up. She'd whispered and stammered the first time, taken unaware as she was. But the second time, she'd been ready. He'd seen the fire in her eyes the minute he walked in, closing the opaque-paned door behind him so the bell jingled merrily above their heads. He had started his speech anyway. If nothing else, maybe he could wear her down. But she came from behind her desk briskly and took him by the arm as she introduced him to the waiting patients one by one while Hazard continued his entreaties, spouting poems he'd memorized from ladies' magazines. She ignored his raving. "He's deranged, you see," she would say. "But we must be tolerant, don't you think? He's not at all well, but I'm certain he's harmless." Until Hazard was exhausted and escaped her fierce grip like he was the one being harassed.

Now he turned his mind to something serious, some proof that he wasn't so harmless. He would camp out in her yard. Already he'd discovered Taylor's pup tent in the garage, along with a few old pieces of Boy Scout equipment. If it wasn't too wet, he'd move tomorrow. Maybe even if it was still raining. Maybe she'd get his meaning if the lightning was still dancing in the sky when he staked the ratty old tent down.

They all overslept, the smooth sound of rain washing down the roof lulling them past seven o'clock. Downstairs Jane was frying bacon and Ben stood at the bottom of the stairs and called up to Taylor that they were running late. Taylor could envision the bright wet stacks of lumber, and he turned over into his pillow to avoid his daddy's voice. Casey also lay in bed, listening to the rain and wondering what she'd do with a rainy, miserable Saturday. If it cleared off enough, she could go to the racetrack that afternoon like she and Dwayne had planned; if it didn't, it was a wasted day. She pulled the sheet over her head and went back to sleep.

Hazard was up, thinking he was late. He wanted to get out there with his tent first thing. Maybe he'd wake her up pounding the stakes in and she'd come out on the porch wearing that robe he'd seen in her suitcase, barefooted, her face heavy with sleep, and she'd say, "Come in, Hazard," and he'd know she was caught in a dream but he'd come anyway to make her dreaming real. Once in her house, they'd both see that was where he belonged.

After breakfast, he collected his duffel bag, a knapsack of supplies, and the little tent and went down the street to Pansy's. Her house was quiet, veiled in the soft morning rain. Above the rooftop there appeared a small slice of blue sky, as if the clouds were falling away from Pansy's house and their lives at the same time. He knew he was doing the right thing.

He lay the duffel bag on the front porch and went to work on the tent. The ties were stringy and brittle with age, but he pulled them as tightly as he could and swung the mallet against the metal stakes.

Pansy heard the sound, familiar yet close, in her sleep. Her eyes still closed, she thought she had dreamed the noise of Dwayne Pickens's baseball against the oil drum. But she was awake. She opened her eyes, still listening to the clang. It was too quick for baseball, too close, too definite. She got out of bed and slipped into her honeymoon robe, the peach silk she refused to discard even though the memories it held haunted her, and went to the window that looked out on the front yard. A dingy green tent was obstructing her view of the street.

Dwayne, she thought immediately. Although why would he be in her yard when he had a yard of his own? Of all his childish antics, she'd never known him to invade someone's property like this. Of course, Casey could be with him, which would make it all right, although she would like to object to stake holes in her front yard. As a matter of fact, she objected to a tent in her front yard, no matter who was putting it up. She rapped on the window and stood aghast at the figure who rose from the other side of the tent. It was Hazard, his shirt sticking to his chest, his hair slick with rain. He grinned at her over the top of the tent.

"Come on out here!" he called as she dropped the curtain, backing herself deeper into the dark parlor, out of his light. "Come on out here, Pansy!"

She stood in the parlor, her hand at her throat. She had thought he was harmless. She truly had. She had thought she could get an annulment and when Papa Tutoni got well, Hazard would go back to being a waiter and show up occasionally at the Flanagans', but not too often that she'd have any problem avoiding him. She had thought he would let go. But now she knew he wouldn't.

She pulled the robe tightly across her breasts, her arm against her chest like a shield, and marched resolutely to the front door. "What are you doing?" she was saying before she even got out on the porch. "What do you think you're doing?" She had to get the offensive. She had to attack, else she was lost.

But Hazard had already invaded, had already claimed the ground she'd thought was sacred. Standing beside the shabby little pup tent and looking at that wide-eyed, sleep-brushed face, he knew if he persevered, if he were willing to weather this storm, he could get her back.

"Camping out," he said calmly. He didn't smile. A smile would give away his victory. He was going to sleep that night in a soggy tent. Maybe the next and the next. Maybe the rest of the summer, until the leaves made a soft dry bed around him and the ground grew the white crystals of early frost. Maybe till then. But someday she would give in. He could see it on her face, that expectant look she would try to deny, that bewildered needful expression that told him she wanted to be led by the hand back into the life they had begun. But not yet. He wouldn't press his advantage yet. Camped outside her fortress wall, he would starve her out, make her hungry for his touch and his voice until she would see that his winning would be her victory, too.

14

The racetrack was in as bad a condition as Taylor had expected.

"Maybe we ought not run," he said to the track manager, who rolled his cigarette on his lip and looked thoughtfully out at the muddy oval. He was thinking about his money, how much he'd lose if these fools didn't get out there and sling their butts around in that mud puddle.

"Let's give it a try," he said finally, as if he'd been thinking the situation over carefully. "Run one race and then decide on the next. Got people on their way out here, you know. Feel like I got to offer them something."

"'Yeah, well, I'll run if everybody else does," Taylor said. He was watching the cars coming into the infield. There were two unfamiliar ones. "Who's that?"

"Fellas from up in the foothills. Called me up last week, wanting to come down here and run. Been running liquor up there for years and now they're thinking to make some money legit."

"What makes you think this is legit?" Taylor wanted to know. "You pocketing the cash and shelling out those little trophies not worth the writing on them."

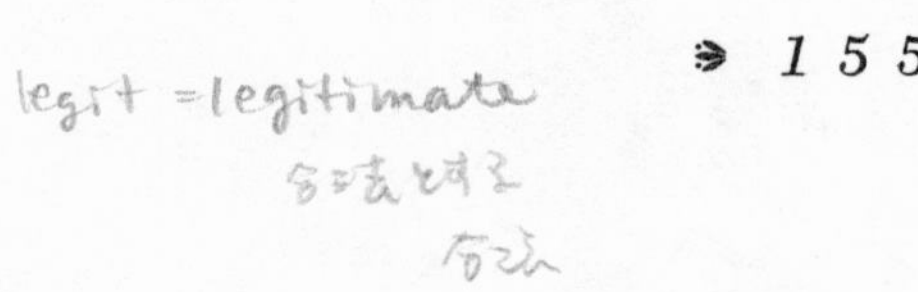

"You ain't gotta run, Taylor. Ain't nobody makin' you."

But Taylor had turned his back on the man and was looking for Casey and Dwayne. They were in the infield perched beside the Mercury on the trailer.

"Frankie, help us get the car off!" he yelled and clomped across the muddy track to his trailer.

The car was running good. Taylor had spent the last few nights in the lumberyard shack working on it. He loved the Mercury, but leaning over the fender, the light bouncing under the hood and his fingers slick with grease, he couldn't help but think about Gwen. He'd turned the radio on to that moody romantic music you could get late at night, and that little shack was the loneliest place in the world. But he knew Gwen wouldn't want to be there with him. He knew what interested her was the lumber business because she was always asking him about what they were selling and who bought it, about what the market was like. She didn't want to talk about cars. She wasn't interested in taking chances. Not Gwen. She was after a sure thing.

Now Taylor pressed the accelerator, listening for the clean smooth purr of his engine.

"It's O.K.," Casey said to him through the window. "Sounds good." She was wiping her hands on a grease rag like she knew what she was doing.

"You and Dwayne get on over to the stands," Taylor said, irritated with her. Why couldn't she act like a girl instead of turning into somebody he could rely on? Good grief, sometimes he got to thinking she was just trying to show Gwen up. Casey got involved in whatever was going on, she was willing to see the humor in things and make a good time out of nothing. Gwen just wanted to look good and strut around proud as a peacock. Well, he'd just about had it with her. If she wasn't here today, he was going to direct his attention elsewhere on a permanent basis, even if elsewhere turned out to be a carburetor.

He watched Casey and Dwayne sloshing through the mud to the stands. Out of the corner of his eye, he thought he saw a gleam of white there, but he refused to look. She hadn't come, wasn't coming, and that was that.

He slipped on his goggles and pulled his gloves tight against the tips of his fingers. The car grumbled under him as he eased out the clutch with a muddy boot. The other cars were pulling onto the track, too. Beside him was one of the new cars, its driver wearing a T-shirt and a cowboy hat. His gum rolled in his cheek before he spat it out the window and grinned at Taylor.

"How you do?" his mouth moved against the roar. Taylor nodded and looked back to the track.

They were playing the national anthem. Gwen was between Casey and Dwayne. She stood, her arms at her sides, face front but her eyes squinting toward the cars, hoping for a glimpse of Taylor.

She could see the car already rimmed with mud. He'll be filthy, she thought, and then stopped herself. She wasn't going to let that matter anymore. She wasn't going to care if he raced every Saturday for the rest of his life and gave every trophy he ever won to Dwayne Pickens. Not as long as he loved her.

The flag was down and wheels churned in the mud, trying to grip something solid. The spinning mire flew against the other cars, slapped windshields, and plopped into their sides. The good drivers moved on ahead, hoping their heat would begin to dry out the track. Nobody seemed to be really racing, just driving and trying to protect their cars. The laps moved slowly while the crowd twitched on the damp bleachers, bored with the lack of show.

Taylor was counting his laps and knew he was ahead. If he could win without damaging his car, that was O.K., too. Somebody had to get there first. But in the eighth lap, he felt someone moving in on him. It was one of the new cars, its sides thick with mud and its windshield wipers sliding over the splattered brown film on the glass. Taylor could feel the tension in the other engine, could hear the quickening power and the churn of intention the driver was putting into his anxious shifting. The new car couldn't be but one lap behind, not much under normal conditions but a lot when the track was bumper deep in mud.

Taylor could feel the car edging his backsides, and he started moving toward the fence to let the car pass. Give the kid a chance, he was thinking, although he knew he could get him in the backstretch where he knew the hidden holes like the back of his hand.

But the car wasn't trying to go around. Their bumpers touched and Taylor felt the heavy lunge of acceleration as the new car knocked into him. He's in a slide, Taylor thought, but he knew it wasn't so. The car had hit him intentionally.

He gave the Mercury gas and moved forward a little to give the car room to come around him. They were heading out of the first corner when the new car hit the gas and then slid into him broadside. It was no accident. Taylor looked across the car to his opponent.

He could see the glimmer of a smile under the dirty cowboy hat.

The new car moved on ahead of him, still a lap behind. Taylor slowed down a little, churning mud. He still didn't think the guy could win. But the new car was slowing down too, so they were abreast again, blocking the other cars when they took the last turn and came in front of the stands. Taylor saw the car moving in on him again, this time with unmistakable belligerence. He slammed into Taylor's side, the Mercury's mud-caked tires spun, lost traction altogether, and threw Taylor into the fence. He was out of the car in a minute, tearing off his goggles and gloves.

The new car was spinning its wheels, its slamming technique having momentarily crippled it. Taylor reached through the window and came out with a body struggling on his arm.

"It's a fight!" Dwayne was yelling from the stands. He dived over people, smashing hats and knocking cups to the ground as he headed for the track. The other cars were stopping behind the two front-runners and their drivers were crawling out.

The boy in the cowboy hat was dangling at arm's length from Taylor, grinning as if the prospect of a fight pleased him. He looked for his friend, who was coming around the cars behind Taylor, and then broke out of Taylor's grip to land a right under Taylor's jaw. Taylor slid against his car to get his balance in the mud and came out swinging.

"Where you goin'?" Dwayne said to the other new driver, who had broken through the circle of spectators. "Uh-uh! You stay right here." He shoved the wiry man against the car and turned to watch Taylor catching a blow in the stomach.

"Get 'em, Taylor!" Dwayne yelled. "Get 'em good!"

The man whom Dwayne had pressed against the car sprung to the side out of Dwayne's reach and headed for the action, but Dwayne went after him, catching him by the collar and spinning him around so that his fist could fit neatly under the fellow's chin. The man staggered backward and then slid down the side of the car, where his head settled heavily on his chest.

"Who's that?" Dwayne heard Gwen yelling from the sidelines. "Dwayne, see who that is!"

Two other strangers, obviously the mountain drivers' pit crew, were racing onto the track.

"Hey boy!" Dwayne yelled, catching one of them by the shoulder and decking him with a swing that would have meant a home run.

"Looka here, boy!" he said to the other one, pointing at the man he'd just decked. The startled opponent was still staring down at his companion when Dwayne landed him a right that sent him sprawling in the opposite direction.

"I'm gettin' 'em!" Dwayne yelled to his audience.

Taylor was still slugging it out with the cowboy, who came back grinning after every blow. The fight seemed to be what he'd been after all the time; Taylor, his head throbbing, one eye swelling fast, and his stomach still sucked in from the first hard blow, was tired of giving him what he wanted.

"Get in here, Dwayne," he yelled just as the mountain boy landed him a left that sent him down on his back in the mud. Looking up at the grinning face over him, he saw the sun behind his head darken for an instant and then heard the crack of bone as Dwayne let into the guy with his right. Blood sprang into the corner of the boy's mouth as he went down next to Taylor, dazed and oozing from the abrasions on his broken, bruised cheek.

"We got 'em!" Dwayne yelled. "Y'all see that? We got 'em!"

Taylor struggled to his feet and surveyed the damaged bodies in the mud. He was trying not to throw up. The smell of mud and heated engines was mixing with a burning stink in his throat.

"You all right, Taylor?" Casey was close to his face, a wet towel in her hand. She dabbed at his eye and cheek with the cloth and its rough texture grated on his raw skin.

"Yeah." He pushed the towel away to look through his one good eye as Gwen skipped across the muddy track, barefooted and holding her skirt out with one hand as if she were doing the minuet. "Taylor," she called. "Oh, Taylor."

"We got 'em," Dwayne said to her. "Cold-cocked 'em every one."

The mountain boys were coming around. George Greenwald flipped his badge out of his jeans in front of their teary eyes. "I could arrest you boys," he said, "but I ain't goin' to. Y'all too dirty to be messin' up the jail. But don't you come back here again. We all saw what you was doing."

"Picking a fight," Gwen said. She had Taylor by the hand and was leading him off the track. "Who you think you're messing with?" she asked the dazed faces. "This is Taylor Flanagan, that's who!"

"Y'all get on outa here," the track manager was

yelling to them from the sidelines. "I got a business here. I got to get them cars outa there for the next race."

"I'll drive yours off," Casey said to Taylor.

"No, we've had enough driving for one day. Let Frankie do it."

"Come on and sit down a minute," Gwen said. She was trying to direct Taylor without touching any of the places he hurt. "You poor thing."

The other drivers were backing off the track, spinning mud and laughing to each other. The fight had made them feel good.

"Who won?" Dwayne asked Casey as they went into the wet grass of the infield. Across the track, Casey could see Gwen and Taylor huddled together on the bottom row of the bleachers. He had his muddy arms around her.

"Nobody," she said, nodding in Taylor's direction, "unless maybe they did."

"I mean the race," Dwayne said trying to ignore the fact that Taylor and Gwen were kissing right in front of him. "Oh, shoot," he said, ducking his head. "*Yuk!*"

"Don't you think it's nice, Taylor and Gwen getting back together like that?" Casey asked, following him toward where Frankie was driving the Mercury up the ramp onto the trailer.

"*Pu-wee!*" Dwayne said, holding his nose and fanning the air with his baseball cap. "That love stuff makes me sick." He faked an upchuck into his hat.

Taylor and Gwen were coming up behind them, arm in arm.

"What's the matter with Dwayne?" Taylor mumbled, trying not to disturb his swollen face.

"Love makes him sick," Casey said.

"Well, you better get used to it, boy," Taylor said, gripping Gwen solidly around her shoulder, "because this here is a permanent arrangement."

Dwayne bent over to heave again, but this time it was for real. Peanuts floating in cola spewed over the trailer tire.

"He really is sick!" Casey said.

"Naw." Dwayne wiped his face with the towel Casey handed him. He gave them a half-sick, half-embarrassed smile. "I never hit nobody before, and it don't look like I take to it."

"Neither do I, Dwayne," Taylor said. He put his sore face against Gwen's. "Loving's got a lot more to it."

"Oh, shoot," Dwayne said, flailing the air with his cap again. But he was grinning at them. "Holy cow!"

"We can leave them here, making moon-eyes at each other," Casey said, "but that means we have to walk home."

"I want to ride," Dwayne said solemnly. "But, K.C., you got to get up there between them!"

"Not me," Casey said. "We'll just ride with our eyes shut. What we don't see won't hurt us."

"You two come on," Taylor said, pulling Gwen close to him. "I think we need to do some celebrating." He gave Gwen a long, breathtaking kiss.

"Holy cow!" Dwayne said. "There they go again!"

15

The next morning, before the sun was more than a red streak above the eastern woods, Taylor had stowed the rods and reels, his tackle box, ice chest, and a worn bedspread in the trunk of his car. Then he shoved a groggy Casey into the back seat next to Dwayne, whose jaw worked anxiously as he struggled to abate his excitement. He knew his whooping and hollering would wake up the whole neighborhood.

He had never been to the ocean that he could remember, although his mama said he went once when he was a little boy. She said he'd splashed right into the waves like they were ripples in the bathtub and had been sucked down and down until his daddy lifted him out, sputtering salty water and sobs.

He had nearly drowned, his mama said as she put his eggs in front of him this morning in her cluttered kitchen. It was still dark outside, like night, and Dwayne stirred catsup into the yellow scrambles and tried to remember what the ocean looked like and how it felt to be going down, down, where fishes tickled his fingers and crabs slipped sideways toward his toes.

He couldn't remember. In pictures, the waves were

caught, blue and solid, heavy lips rimmed with white foam. They were like walls to walk into. He could not imagine them liquid.

"You're not to go into the water," his mama said. She was frowning as he looked at her over his eggs, the harsh kitchen light above her head like a hot white halo, and he sensed her foreboding, her memory of almost losing him once many years ago.

"I won't, Mama," he promised, forking the eggs into his mouth. "I'll stay with Taylor and K.C. We're going fishing anyhow."

So here they were, Casey dozing and Taylor humming while the car lights spotted just above the asphalt as the skylight turned slightly yellow, dawning a golden Sunday morning. They headed out of town to pick up Gwen. She was waiting, her bare arm on the cold metal mailbox, her shoes damp from having rested in the dew. She slid her bag behind the seat at Casey's feet and huddled up close to Taylor.

"I'm shivering," she said, wrapping one goose-bumped arm around his neck.

"Not for long." Taylor pulled back onto the highway. "It's gonna be hot out there. Hey, Casey, you bring a hat?"

"Yeah." Casey sat up blinking and looked around as if she couldn't remember getting into the car, much less the purpose of the trip. "A hat and a long-sleeve shirt," she yawned.

"Me, too," Dwayne said. He was glad Casey was waking up. "You ever been to the beach before?"

"Yeah, sure." She looked at him in time to see his grin begin to fade. He wanted her to be as excited as he was. He wanted this to be the first time for her, too. "A long time ago," she said. "I hardly remember it at all."

Dwayne grinned. "Me either. Mama says I near 'bout drowned."

"Well, we aren't doing any swimming," Taylor said, giving Casey a wink through the rear-view mirror. When he'd first thought about taking them to the beach they'd dealt with the dilemma of Casey's swimsuit by deciding to make it a fishing trip, although Gwen was wearing a suit under her shorts because she intended to soak up some sun.

"We could wade a little," Casey said.

"Long as I don't get my hair wet," Gwen said. "I want to eat someplace nice. Can't we eat somewhere nice, Taylor?"

"That depends on how nice you consider hotdogs to be."

She plopped a loud kiss on his bruised cheek. "Someplace nice, Taylor. Someplace with prime ribs and sour cream on the potatoes."

"At the beach? At the beach, you're supposed to eat seafood."

Gwen sighed and moved a little away from him. "I have something to tell you, Taylor."

Everybody straightened up to pay attention as if they expected an announcement that would affect them permanently.

"I can't stand seafood," she said.

The ocean stretched lazily before them as if it were just stirring from a night's rest.

"Tide's out," Taylor said, surveying the dark rippled strip of packed sand near the water's edge.

Chapter Fifteen

Dwayne leaned against the car, the rods and reels clutched in his hand like spears. A wave rose a little way out and spilled over into the surf. It was green water, dull for lack of sun because a patch of clouds midway the sky was holding back the sparkling morning light.

"It'll be O.K.," Taylor said. "We'll be grateful for a few clouds once that sun gets a chance at us. You'll roast out there." He passed Gwen the blanket. "The wind will get you even if the sun doesn't."

"I think I'll fish a little," Gwen said, frowning at the clouds. "As long as I don't have to eat them."

"Or bait them. Or take them off the hook," Taylor laughed.

Casey led the way into the pier shack, which turned out to be one large room haphazardly divided into bait shop, sundries store, and restaurant. The trapped rotten smell of dead fish mingled with the hot odors of chili and sizzling hamburger on the grill. The ice machine dripped its overflow of shaved ice through the floorboards and into the tiny waves that lapped against the posts below. Behind the bait counter were pinned pictures from newspapers and greasy photographs of fishermen holding up their catch. Below them was a blackboard on which were listed the hours of the tide and the weights of the season's record fish.

"One chili dog!" the cook shouted, slapping the paper wrapped sandwich on the counter. "Who wanted this here chili dog?"

"I'll take it," Dwayne called back.

"You order it?" the man asked, eyeing his unfamiliar customer.

"No, but I'll take it."

"Ain't givin' it away," the cook said, taking the hotdog off the counter.

"You hungry already, Dwayne?" Taylor asked from the bait counter, where he was buying their pier permits. "Pin this to you." He handed them around.

Dwayne stuck the paper on his baseball cap and then put it proudly on his head. "Naw, ain't hungry. Just helpin' that fella out, seeing he cooked it and all."

"Where'll I put it?" Gwen wanted to know, looking down the front of her pink swimsuit. "I don't want pin holes ruining this elastic."

"Down there," Taylor said, eyeing her cleavage. "We can always get it when we want it."

"Aw, Taylor, you hush in front of these children." Gwen pushed the paper between her breasts. "I just hope it doesn't blow away."

"Not a chance." Taylor grinned and paid for a pound of shrimp the counterman brought dripping from cold storage. They followed him out the back door of the shack and onto the pier.

The weathered slats were like a track laid out in front of them and the pier seemed to drop down into the water at the end, following the curve of the horizon.

"Lordy, it's long!" Dwayne said, rubbing his head under his cap. He was still gripping the fishing equipment, as if he expected a sudden gust to blow both him and the rods away.

"Optical illusion," Taylor said. "We better go pretty far down, since it's low tide."

They followed him down the pier, Casey carrying the tackle box beside Dwayne, who kept looking down at the moving water between the boards.

"You'll be upchucking again," she warned. "Look out, not down."

Dwayne lifted his head to look at the expanse of ocean and sky surrounding them. "Who ever thought of so much water?" he said. "Who ever thought of so much everything? Look!" A gull was circling near them and they stopped to watch its sudden dip into the water.

"Having breakfast," Casey said.

"Don't you be getting my fish!" Dwayne yelled, shaking his fist at the gull, who was circling again. He laughed at his joke.

They were passing fishermen now, people who seemed asleep, their heads low against the ocean breeze, their permits fluttering on their clothes, necks and arms covered against the coming sun.

"Been out here all night?" Taylor said to one of them who seemed to be baiting his hook in his sleep.

"Since three. Nothing much," the man said, pinching off a bit of shrimp for his second hook. "Few spots. Expecting a run of croakers, though. Been expecting it two days now."

Near the end of the pier they found two empty benches side by side. Taylor divided the shrimp into a second container, put it between Dwayne and Casey, and then distributed the rods. "Three hooks to a leader, folks," he said. "I think the sinkers are about the right weight. When the tide starts in, we'll move up the pier a little."

Casey was already attaching her leader to the line. She slipped bits of shrimp onto the hooks. Fishing was something she felt comfortable with. Her father had taken her fishing, trusting her to maneuver the little outboard boat in the slow, brackish inlet water. They would spend the day moving slowly up the inlet, their lines dropping with no more than a single delicate splash, the only sound the deep chug of the outboard when they moved on and the steady click of their reels when they were still. They had caught pinfish, their chartreuse sides flicking between the dark water and the bucket in the bow of the boat. She could hear them flipping against the metal sides, shuddering life although their mouths bled and their gills fluttered. She had loved to fish as much because it was something they did together as for any other reason, although she liked the swell of moving water under the boat, the buoyancy that made her feel light herself, able to float, to swim, to dip deep below her world and lift out a treasure from another time, a primeval beauty welcomed with a spontaneous gasp of delight and a father's praise.

Dwayne had stuck himself with a hook and bent over his finger to conceal from Casey the thin trickle of blood he pressed from his thumb. He didn't want anyone to know he'd made a mistake. He wanted to do everything right.

"Got her ready?" Taylor asked him, having already sent Gwen's line out.

Dwayne wiped his hand on his pants. "Yeah."

"Then I'll show you how to cast. First thing," he said, taking the rod and reel from Dwayne, "is to make sure nobody's behind you. Caught a woman's hat one time. Took it right off her head and into the water. Then you do like this."

Taylor swung the rod over his shoulder with both hands, and the line spun off toward the water. "When the line's about down, start slowing it with your thumb." He let his finger lay gently against the spinning reel. "When it's down, you put the brake on until she's ready to reel in. Got it?"

"Yeah." Dwayne followed the steps carefully, an embarrassed smile edging his mouth. It was hard for him to learn things, he knew that. It took him a long time, and people didn't like to wait. Figuring on three hooks and this fancy business to let out and reel in made him nervous. He felt clammy with the damp wind blowing under his shirt. His thumb burned. He knew about fishing with a pole and some worms. Weren't nothing to it. Didn't catch much either, at least not in the creek outside of town, which was the only place his mama would let him go. Now this here was real fishing. This was serious business, and he intended to catch something at it.

The hooks and sinker sailed over his head and into the dark water below.

"Good cast, Dwayne!" Taylor said, grabbing his shoulder. "Atta boy!"

They settled down to fish while the sun moved slowly up, putting a sparkle on the water that now sent sloshing waves against the crusted pilings beneath them.

"I'm hungry," Gwen complained. She was holding the reel loosely in her hands, hardly paying any attention to the tension of the line. She seemed to be swaying with the pier, half asleep.

"I got something!" Dwayne yelled. His line was pulling away from him, straining in a slight curve toward the water.

"Easy now, boy," Taylor said. "Start reeling her in. Easy now. Don't jerk her."

The rod was dipping, too, pulling against the line that Dwayne slowly wound upward, out of the water. A croaker, its slick gray body glimmering with water and light, appeared above them as if by magic.

"A pound and a half if it's an ounce," Taylor said.

"I got one!" Dwayne yelled, holding out the fish still attached to the hook. "Looka here! I got one!"

"It's beautiful!" Casey said. "Here, I'll get him off. You go get ice to put him in."

"Naw, I'll take him off. You go get the ice." He put his hand out to catch the fish. The slippery body shivered in his hand. "You O.K., fish?" he said. He held up the croaker to a fisherman passing by. "See this one! It's a good one, ain't it?"

"Sure is, fella," the man said. "Best one I've seen all day."

"Hear that! It's the best one!"

Casey had arrived with the ice chest half full of shaved ice. "Get him off the hook and put him in here," she said.

"Naw. I wanta look at him."

"He'll rot," Casey said. "Just like that one." She pointed to a small shark left to shrivel on the boards. "He won't be good to eat."

"I'm not gonna eat him," Dwayne said. He got a tighter grip on the fish. "I'm gonna stuff him."

"Well, stuffed or not, he's got to go into the ice box," Taylor said. "Unless, of course, you want to throw him back."

"Uh-uh." Dwayne dislodged the hook from the fish's mouth and dropped him onto the ice. "That one's mine, though. You all know it's mine."

Chapter Fifteen

"I'm tired, Taylor," Gwen said. "I'm going on down and lie on the beach."

Casey felt a tug on her bait. "I think I've got something, Taylor," she said. "At least a nibble."

"Give it a few seconds. Too late and your bait's gone. Too early and you lose the fish, too."

Casey waited as long as she could and then started reeling in. They could see the silvery fish flipping and twirling on the hook halfway between the surface of water and the pier. Then the line was suddenly loose, the weight lost, and they saw the quick fall as the fish disappeared into the water.

"Lost him," Taylor said. "Too bad, Casey."

"He was a good one, though," Dwayne said. "Not as good as mine, but he was O.K."

"I'm going to eat a hotdog and drink a Pepsi and then go lie on the beach awhile," Gwen said. "You coming, Taylor?"

"Nope, I'll stay up here for now. You want to go with Gwen, Casey?"

"Yeah, I guess I will. Dwayne's having all the luck anyway."

They bought hotdogs and icy drinks in paper cups and took them down to the beach where they spread out Jane Flanagan's discarded blanket and sat down facing the water.

"So you're back together again," Casey said, having stuffed the hotdog into her mouth and washed it down with half the Pepsi.

"Thank God," Gwen said. She nibbled at the hotdog bun. "I was so lonesome, Casey. I didn't think I could get that lonesome. I mean, I always had a lot of friends.

I know a lot of people and all. I always had something to do, you know. But when Taylor and I weren't together, I just didn't want to do all that stuff. I just wanted him to come back. Of course, I knew he wouldn't. That day out at the racetrack I was so mad I just couldn't think how much I cared about him, but I wasn't halfway to town, driving that big old Chrysler, when I knew Taylor was right about doing something for Dwayne. I knew he was a better person than I am. I mean, he cares more than I do about people, but he's quiet about it.

"There I was in that big old car that rode so easy, like I was sitting on a pile of cushions and just floating along. But it was scary, too, like it could make me so comfortable I wouldn't notice how it was taking me away from what I wanted most in the world, until it was too late. I almost waited too late, didn't I, Casey?"

"I don't think so," Casey said, drawing a design in the sand with her finger. She put a stem on her flower, and tiny leaves. "Taylor was moping around there, him and Hazard, like they didn't have a thing to smile about. Couldn't get a laugh outa them for anything."

"He'd never tell me that," Gwen said. She held up her hand to shade her eyes. She could see Taylor and Dwayne on the pier. They were on the same bench, leaning against it more than sitting. She could see the points of their rods over the side and the bright yellow of Taylor's shirt. "He'll never say he missed me or that it was hard on him, too."

"Anyhow, he sure is smiling now," Casey said.

"Yeah, well," Gwen sighed and rolled over on her stomach. "He's got reason." She stretched her arm out off the blanket and let the sand fall between her fingers.

"One thing I've learned, Casey," she said, her voice muffled by the blanket and her drowsiness. "Don't ever make a person you care about have to choose between you and something else. Not if you can help it. Don't ever use yourself to bargain with. You ought to put a higher price on yourself than that."

Casey was still watching the pier. She could see Dwayne shaking his fist in the air, celebration for the fish that dangled at the end of his line. She knew not telling Dwayne she was a girl kept him from having to choose. She'd performed an act of kindness. That was what she'd thought. That was what she wanted it to be. But was it? Shouldn't she have taken the risk then, before they mattered so much to each other?

She lay back on the blanket beside Gwen. Through her shirt she could see the soft rise of her breasts. By next year this time she would be grown up, unable to hide beneath jeans and boys' shirts, unable to pretend. But not now, she thought, relaxing under the noon heat, her eyes shut against the brilliant sky. Right now I have this one last summer.

When she woke up, Dwayne was sitting on the blanket beside her. He had pushed his bare foot deep into the sand and was packing more sand around it to make a cave.

"That's a frog house," Casey said, sitting up beside him. "A house for toads or toes." She rubbed her hands through her damp, matted hair, freeing it to the breeze.

Dwayne pulled his foot out carefully and then watched the mound cave into the hole. "Hell."

"I'll get some water," Casey said, picking up her empty Pepsi cup. "If we wet the sand a little, it'll pack better."

"I don't want to," Dwayne said, smashing the mound flat with his foot. "Four fish," he said. "That's all. And then Taylor says to me, 'Me and Gwen are walking down the beach a little ways. You go down there and stay with K.C.' And you sleeping. You come to the ocean and you sleep. Hell."

"You ought to quit saying that, Dwayne." Casey dropped the cup and grabbed his hand. "We'll go walking down the beach, too, and look for shells. Maybe we can even find a perfect sand dollar or some angel wings."

He didn't budge so she let go his hand and sat down again.

"Whatcha doing?" he asked her.

"Rolling up my pants legs. I'm going in the water."

"Mama said I couldn't." Dwayne dug his foot into the sand again, refusing to look at her.

"She said you couldn't go swimming. She didn't say a word about wading. There." Casey stood up and wiped her hands on her pants. "I'm going wading and shell hunting whether you go or not. But I wish you'd come. What's the matter with you, anyway?"

"Four fish," Dwayne muttered. He picked up the paper cup and stared into it. "Half a day fishing and four fish."

"I bet yours are the biggest, though," Casey said. "I bet you caught the biggest fish on that pier today."

"Bigger than Taylor's." Dwayne grinned. He was feeling better. Casey could always make him feel better.

"And now I bet we find the best shells on the beach. Which way do you want to go?"

Dwayne nodded toward the least congested end of the beach. He took off his shirt and Casey could see the white skin around the edges of his T-shirt, skin too pale to withstand the salty, burning wind, too delicate to contain such careless strength and childish grief.

She could not look, so she ran down to the water's edge, letting the surf wash over her feet and ankles, feeling the water pull the sand beneath her weight.

Dwayne followed her and splashed into the surf, his fishing failure pushed aside by this new adventure she was offering him. He felt the pull as the water swept back, washing sharp bits of shell around his white ankles. The water sucked at his feet and he remembered his mama's warning. He remembered the thick sandy water washing over his head, the close swollen pain in his chest, the briny water in his throat and nose. But now he was safe. His friend was there in the water beside him. There was no need to be afraid.

Beyond them the waves were lifting, subject to some hidden force, and then falling, lapping over each other as they churned inward, leaving spindrift in the air. A dusky afternoon glow lay over the water, and her hand above her eyes to shield them from the sun, Casey watched Dwayne spinning in the surf, knee deep in the warm foam, his arms flailing the wind like a wind-up toy. He seemed to collide with the air, a lone combatant of the elements. Then suddenly, as if he'd just remembered she was there, he turned to her, his face open, memory clear of all regret, and above the rush of falling water, she heard him call, "I love you, K.C. I love you best of all."

16

Monday morning, Casey and Dwayne went down the street to inspect Hazard's new quarters. He was still there, squatting in front of a little Coleman burner over which an enamel cup of water was beginning to bubble.

"Making tea," he said, dipping a tea bag into the hot water. He looked bad. He hadn't washed in two days and his hair was sticking up in rebellious thatches all over his head.

"Grandma wants you to come down to the house and get cleaned up and eat a good breakfast," Casey said.

Dwayne was peering into the musty, sagging tent. "Holy cow," he said. "I wouldn't stay in there for nothin'."

"Neither would I. I'm staying in there for everything," Hazard said resolutely, swirling the tea bag in his cup.

"But you can eat, can't you? Grandma said what you did yesterday was your business, since it was Sunday. But this is Monday, a workday again, and there're certain things that have to be done."

"Like what?" Hazard blew on his tea.

"Liking eating, I guess, and shaving and—"

"Peeing," Dwayne added.

"Dwayne's right," Casey said. "The lilac bush may do in the dark of night, but this is daytime. Besides, you've got to go to work. Grandpa's expecting you this morning."

"She'll take the tent down," Hazard said. He looked gray, like a hobo sipping cheap wine over early morning ashes. "I know she will."

"She's gone to work, Hazard," Casey said. "Anyhow, I don't think she would do that."

"Yes, she would," Hazard said. "I'm an embarrassment to her. That's what she said to me yesterday. The only words she spoke in my direction all day was how I was an embarrassment and a disgrace."

"I had a tent once," Dwayne said. He had squatted next to Hazard and put his hands up to the fire although the morning was already warm and he had windburned streaks on his neck and arms. "Me and David and Taylor used to camp out in the front yard over on Plum Street. Sometimes at their house, too. It was a tent a lot like this." He turned suddenly to inspect the tent more carefully. "This is it!" he yelled, slapping the side happily. "This is it!"

"I hope you don't mind my borrowing it," Hazard said, looking even more dejected. No wife, no house, now no tent.

"You can have it," Dwayne said. "I wouldn't sleep in there for nothin'."

"Please go home, Hazard," Casey begged. "Just for a little while. Dwayne and I can watch the tent. You can even go on to work. Pansy won't come home until five o'clock like always."

"You'll watch it?" Hazard asked, looking from Casey to Dwayne and back again.

"We'll watch it, won't we, Dwayne?"

"Yeah, sure."

Hazard put out the stove and tossed the bitter tea into the flower bed. Then he trudged down the street toward a hot breakfast and bath, his every joint aching from the damp, cold ground and his mouth thick with remorse. Pansy had all the comfort. She had right on her side, too. She had everything.

He sat down on the back steps at the Flanagans', too weary to pull himself farther. She had won. Two days were all he could stand. Two days of potted meat and cheese. Two nights of wet, musty air too close to earth, too raw and solid for his old body. He put his hands over his face. He had lost her again, this time such a demoralizing defeat because he was simply too old, too full of pains, too tired.

"Hazard." It was Jane who lay her hand on his arm, reached around his trembling elbow, and pulled him up.

"There's breakfast on the table. Then I'll run you a bath and you can rest a while. Really sleep."

He heard sympathy in her voice. He heard her memory of their years together whisper in her gentle phrasing. He was the lost and found animal, the stray on her doorstep that she would love simply because he was there and needed her. Always before, he'd let her. Year in and year out, he'd willingly hung his head and nibbled at her generous hand. He'd rubbed himself against the Flanagans' warmth as if showing contentment would give him a permanent place there.

He lifted his eyes. "I'm going back," he said. "I have

to go back. My place is with Pansy now, no matter what I have to do."

"Today is not forever. It's just today," Jane said. "And if you don't win today, that doesn't mean you've lost. It just means you're holding your own. Some days that's all we can do."

"You think I'm foolish, don't you, Jane?" Hazard asked, letting himself be led to a chair at the kitchen table.

"No, Hazard, not foolish. I think you are brave, wonderfully brave. And if I were Pansy, I would love you very much."

DWAYNE WAS tired of watching the tent. After all, what was there to watch? At first, he inspected it carefully, crawling inside to look for David and Taylor's initials written with a crayon on the canvas. He found faint markings, but he couldn't read them. Then he crawled out and sat beside it, watching the flaps hanging loosely, and then the faded canvas that seemed to be smoking as the sun dried its moist surface.

"Let's go, K.C.," he said. "Let's go downtown."

"We told Hazard we'd watch the tent," Casey said. She was sitting on Pansy's step, out of the sun.

"But he ain't here so he won't know if we don't do it anymore," Dwayne argued.

"But what if Pansy comes home and takes it down?"

Dwayne's mind stumbled over that for a moment and then he brightened. "We could put it back up. Come on, K.C. Let's go."

"Well, for a little while," Casey said. She was bored, too, having long regretted promising Hazard their services. "When we get back, we can bring the gloves and ball over and catch some while we watch it."

They went downtown, having no mission but to confirm their freedom.

"There's the barbershop," Dwayne said, stopping to look through the window at the porcelain surfaces—black and white floor and counters gleaming like a photograph. "I get my hair cut in there." He waved at the barber, who waved back from beside a chair where he was bending over a man whose face was covered with a towel.

"Who's that?" Dwayne shouted through the glass. He pointed at the man in the chair.

The barber waved at them again.

"Who's that?" Dwayne shouted again, rapping his fingers on the glass.

The barber laughed and motioned them in.

"Hey boy," he said when Dwayne pushed through the door, pulling Casey reluctantly behind him. "Whatcha know, boy? Need a haircut?"

"Nope." Dwayne went right up beside the man still hidden under the steamy towel. "Who's that?" he wanted to know.

"Why, that's the mayor," the barber said, laughing. He was sharpening his razor on the strop. "Need a shave, Dwayne?"

Dwayne lifted the towel off the man's face so that a pinched, pink face emerged and blinked up at him.

"Don't look like a mayor to me," Dwayne said, dropping the towel back over the startled face. "Did he to you, K.C?" he wanted to know as Casey pulled him toward the door and out onto the sidewalk. She looked back to see the barber still sharpening his razor and grinning at them.

"Let's go see Gwen," Dwayne said.

They loitered along, looking in windows, catching their own reflections and grinning at their distorted sizes and foolish expressions.

"Look at that!" Casey said, stopping in front of a Schwinn bike in the hardware store window. "Just look at it, Dwayne!"

"You want that?" Dwayne asked, punching her lightly in the ribs. "You want that, boy? Well, hell, let's get it!"

"You don't have that kind of money, Dwayne," Casey said, pulling him away from the window. "Anyway, liking it doesn't mean I want it. Besides, I've got a bike at home."

They went into the five and dime, passed the magazines and school supplies, and right up to the counter where Gwen was scooping popcorn into long white paper bags and stacking them at one end of the warm popper.

"Hey," she said, smiling at them. "Want some popcorn?"

"No money," Casey said, pulling out her pockets.

"Me either." Dwayne grinned at her. He liked to see Gwen in her white jacket, looking so important and official.

"It's on me," Gwen said, handing a bag over the counter. "It's because yesterday was one of the nicest days I've ever had."

"Me, too," Casey said.

"Me, too," Dwayne echoed. "Except I didn't catch

enough fish. That much water, got to be a lot of fish down there." He shoved a handful of popcorn into his mouth.

"Next summer I bet we get a whole mess of fish," Gwen said.

"Hear that, boy?" Dwayne thrust the bag at Casey. "Next year we're going fishing again."

"Right now we got to get back to Hazard's tent," Casey said. "We got us a job watching it."

"What you all expecting it to do?" Gwen laughed.

"Nothin'." Dwayne frowned at her. "That's the whole trouble. It don't do nothin' and we don't do nothin'. Waste of a good day if you ask me. What we doin' it for, boy?"

"Because Hazard is afraid Pansy will come home and pull it down," Casey said.

"Shoot, it's about to fall down!" Dwayne hooted.

"Anyway, we got to go. Thanks for the popcorn," Casey said.

"You all have fun!" Gwen called after them.

"Ain't no fun watching a tent," Dwayne muttered as they went out to the street.

"Well, you don't have to," Casey said irritably. She had bargained with Hazard because he looked half sick to her, but she couldn't expect Dwayne to see that. All he saw was what he wanted to do. "Sometimes you act so spoiled," she said before she could stop herself, and then hurried off ahead of him.

"Hey boy!" Dwayne called, trotting along behind her, the popcorn bag clutched under his arm. "You mad with me, boy? You mad?"

Casey slowed down, thinking about what she could

say to him. "Just a little," she said finally. "Hazard wants to be married to Pansy just like you wanted to catch a lot of fish. Just like I want us always to be friends. It's important to him like that. And I want to help him because it's important to him. Do you understand, Dwayne?"

He stood grinning at her, then pushed the popcorn bag toward her. "Want some, boy?" he asked. "You're not mad at me anymore, are you?"

"No, Dwayne, I'm not mad." Casey brought out a fistful of popcorn, accepting the little gift he could offer her. But she couldn't believe he understood. She didn't know what love meant to him, how far beyond daily care and nourishment it went. Sure, he'd said he loved her yesterday, loved a boy, a friend. So easily he'd said those words she already found so difficult, sensing as she did, such commitment in them. Loving people was hard. It meant always trying to tell the truth. It meant figuring out when and how to give and take. Even love between friends meant that.

"Let's go watch a tent," she said.

Pansy was home when they got there, but she wasn't in the front yard ripping up the tent stakes or tossing Hazard's meager bedding in the trash can. Instead, she was standing on the porch talking to George Greenwald, the policeman Casey had met at the racetrack.

"Here they are," she said as Casey and Dwayne came across the lawn. "I just called the lumberyard," she said to Casey. "Your grandfather and Taylor will be here any minute. So will Jane."

"What is it?" Casey asked, her heart almost still with the dread that always struck first. "It's Daddy," she said.

"Oh no, dear. It's not about you. It's Dwayne," Pansy said, nervously fingering her brooch. "George here has a court order for him, signed by two doctors, one of which I'm ashamed to say is my own Dr. Kemble—what possessed him I'll never know—and, of course, the clerk of court." She shuddered out her breath, looking helplessly from Casey to Dwayne. "Alva Pickens is having him committed again."

Dwayne didn't seem to understand or else he wasn't listening. "The tent's still here," he said to Casey.

"You go watch it, Dwayne," Casey said. "In a minute Taylor and Grandpa will be here."

"They gonna watch it, too?" Dwayne scratched his head under his cap. He seemed to be refusing to acknowledge the policeman's presence or Pansy's frantic whispering.

Jane was puffing down the street. "I just went over to Dora's," she called, unable to hold back her news until she reached them. "She said Alva said it was the only thing to do since that fight he got into Saturday. She's distraught, poor woman, pulled between two sons like this. She doesn't want to let him go, but she wonders if it isn't the safest thing, the best thing for him. It's all for testing, you know. Of course, they've already tested him once and decided he was harmless, but that was before he took a swing at anybody." She had reached the porch and leaned against the rail, panting for breath. "My own opinion is that Alva's just been waiting for this. For something he could use to put that man away. Out of sight, out of mind. No blot on the royal family then. Sometimes I think Alva Pickens is the only person in this town who doesn't love Dwayne."

"I sure wish I wasn't having to do this," George said. He had his hat in his hand like he had come courting.

"We understand, George," Pansy said gently. "Better you than somebody who doesn't care about him."

"The worst of it is he'll have to stay in jail overnight. Somebody from the hospital is coming in the morning to get him."

"No," Casey muttered, surprised at her own self-control. She wanted to lash out, rip the papers from George's hand and tear them to shreds, but she just stood there staring at them and muttering, "No, no, no." They were adults. Why couldn't they be the ones saying no?

"Here's Taylor!" Dwayne called. "Hey Mr. Ben!"

"Hey Dwayne!" Taylor went right up on the porch and took the court order out of George's hand to study it.

"It's all legal, Taylor," George said. "Two doctors signed and the clerk of court. They examined him before he was taken up there the first time so they don't have to do it again. The clerk is a friend of Alva's, I reckon, because he sure as hell got this through fast. I got this thing about ten o'clock, but I just waited around, trying to think of something to do. Miss Pansy heard about it down at Dr. Kemble's and she came right home. Mrs. Pickens said Dwayne was over here, so this is where I ended up. Miss Pansy decided to call you." He stood breathlessly watching Taylor read the paper. "I don't think there's anything we can do."

"How long have we got?" Taylor asked.

"Somebody from the hospital is coming in the morning, but I have to take him into custody now. He'll have to spend the night in jail, but that gives us till morning to get this thing stopped. The law says this petition here can be withdrawn before the person is admitted to the institution, if the petitioner wants to."

"And the petitioner is Alva Pickens?" Taylor said. "I'll break every bone in his body."

"I think we better see a lawyer first," Ben said. "Right away. This afternoon."

"Well, I got to take Dwayne in, now that I've found him," George said. "His mama said he'd probably go with me all right as long as she wasn't around. She said she'd come down in the morning and see about him. That's who I feel sorry for," George said. "Mrs. Pickens don't want this to happen."

"Of course she doesn't," Jane said. "None of us do."

"I guess I'll tell him we're going for a ride in the police car," George said hesitantly. They were all looking out in the yard where Dwayne was tossing an imaginary ball and running, head back, to catch it.

"No," Casey said. "Don't lie to him."

"I'll go down with you," Taylor said. "I'll explain about going to see the lawyer. I'll tell him he won't have to go to the hospital." He rammed the porch post with his fist. "And that damn well better turn out to be the truth."

"I want to come," Casey said.

"No. Just tell him you'll see him tomorrow," Taylor said firmly.

"You might cry, honey," Jane said. "We all might, and that wouldn't help Dwayne a bit."

"Dwayne!" George called. "Listen here, boy!"

Dwayne stopped playing and stood between the porch and the patrol car.

"I got this paper here," George began reluctantly. "It's a paper about your going to the hospital for a little while—Oh, hell, Taylor, you tell him."

Taylor was already in the yard, his arm firmly around Dwayne's shoulder while Dwayne stood like a submissive child who expected punishment but couldn't remember his crime.

"It's because of the fight, Dwayne," Taylor said. "It's because you helped me out."

Dwayne grinned. "We got 'em all right," he said. Then he frowned. "But I didn't like fighting much."

"I know," Taylor said. "And that's what I'm going to tell our lawyer and the judge and the doctors and everybody in town, if I have to. But meanwhile you have to spend the rest of today and probably tonight down at the jail. That's what George's paper tells him to do."

"Take me away?" Dwayne asked. "It says to take me off somewhere, George?" he called, panic rising in his voice. He pulled away from Taylor. "It's like that other time, ain't it? I don't want to go there again, I told you that. I told everybody. I told you that, didn't I, K.C.? I can't have a radio there or a ball, even. I just sit there, waiting all day, and nothin' happens. I don't want to go there."

"You won't have to. I promise," Taylor said. "But right now, while I'm getting it fixed, you have to go downtown with George. I'll go with you."

But Dwayne was intent on talking them out of it. If

he could just keep talking, keep finding words to tell them why he couldn't go, it would be all right. They would understand and believe him. "K.C. and me were gonna play ball. We got to watch this tent, you see, so Miss Pansy don't tear it down, and we were gonna play ball while we watched it."

"I'll watch it, Dwayne," Casey called from the porch. She couldn't go any closer because she was crying. Tears spread their distorting film across her eyes and mucus trickled down one nostril. "I'll be right here when you get back."

He didn't understand why they were so far away, on the porch like that. Miss Jane and Mr. Ben, even Miss Pansy—why, they all knew him! They knew how he hated that place. "I don't want to go!" he yelled.

"Taylor'll fix it, Dwayne," Miss Jane called back. "You go ahead now, and don't be worried."

George went down to the car and opened the door so that Dwayne and Taylor could get in. The people on the porch were silent, watching the scene as if it were just that, a scene being acted with the clear knowledge of everybody concerned that it was only a play.

"Well, they're gone," Pansy said when the car had pulled away.

"Taylor will get it straightened out," Jane said. "I'm sure it can be worked out."

"We shouldn't have let him go," Casey said coldly. She refused to look at any of them. They were adults, they knew how to do things. They should have kept Dwayne safe. If they couldn't, then who could?

"Oh, Casey, you'll be learning there's little justice in this world," Pansy said wearily. "There's little that's fair." She sat down on the swing, her hands folded, and looked out at the tent in her yard.

"He'll be all right, honey." Jane tried to put her arms around the girl, but Casey pulled away.

"No, he won't. He'll be down there in the jail and he'll be scared all by himself and he'll be trying to figure out why we just stood here, letting him go," Casey said bitterly. She was holding back her tears, too angry to give way again. "We know him, Grandma! How could we let him go when we know him!"

"She's right," Pansy said. "Casey's right."

"Taylor's doing all that can be done. We just have to wait."

"Casey," Pansy said, "I want you to take that tent down."

"No!" She was staring at the road as if by closely watching she could turn today into tomorrow and have the car return with Dwayne still in it, never alone or frightened. "No, I won't."

"You are right, Casey, what you said about our knowing Dwayne," Pansy said softly, gently, as if she understood Casey's anger and could wait a long time for it to subside. "It's the same with Hazard and me. How could I let him go when I know him? How could I?"

So, later that afternoon, when Hazard came to Pansy's yard after work, the tent was gone. Only a rectangle of browning grass remained to commemorate his vigil. He stood in the yard, facing his defeat wearily, unable to think beyond this moment when his life seemed so wasted, so doomed to loneliness.

"Hazard," Pansy said from the doorway. She was standing behind the screen but he could see her, the outline of her fine figure imprinted against the waning afternoon light. "Come in."

He was afraid to move. What if his legs would no longer carry him? What if, this close, he stumbled?

"I don't ever want to hurt you again," he heard himself say. His voice lifted over the porch hedge, wafted against her house, her screen, her heart.

"I know you, Hazard Whitaker," she said, "and you are worth the risk."

17

The day dragged on. Casey fiddled with her lunch, but Jane didn't reprimand her. What was the use? Nobody felt like eating.

"I think I'll leave the dishes," Jane said. "I feel so drained this afternoon." She draped her apron over a chair and gave the cluttered counter around the sink a frown. She had expected Casey to offer to do the kitchen.

But Casey was silent. She stared at the melting ice in her glass of tea, refusing to look at her grandmother. They had all failed Dwayne, and she couldn't tell them it was all right. That was what doing the dishes would mean—that she was willing to let the day go on like any other day, doing chores upon which daily life subsisted, pretending nothing was amiss.

She wouldn't pretend she could trust them, either, she was thinking as the door swung shut behind her grandmother. And if you couldn't trust grown-ups who wrote and understood the laws, then who could you trust? And what about Taylor, mad as a hornet, but still not doing anything after he'd promised her he would? Talking to a lawyer. What good would that do when Mr. Greenwald said the papers were all in order? It was all legal for them to take Dwayne off to jail like he was a criminal. She expected more of Taylor than that. Of her grandparents. Even of Pansy and Hazard. They should never have let Dwayne go. They had all failed him. All of them, including herself.

She had thought, standing with them on Pansy's porch that morning and watching Dwayne and Taylor disappear into the patrol car, that what was going on was beyond her ability to prevent. She had muttered, subdued by an appalling willingness to let it happen, when she could have shouted.

All it would have taken was her yelling, "Run!" or, "Don't let them take you!" and chances were Dwayne would have done what she told him. That was what he'd wanted, someone to say, "This is wrong and we won't let it happen."

She'd heard sermons about such situations at chapel with half the congregation in uniform and the chaplain talking about duty, the distinctions between right and wrong, responsibility. But the chaplain wore a uniform himself under his vestments, and duty was always against a hypothetical enemy, some unidentified evil without a name or face. Moral conscience always meant country, democracy, the rights of men to govern themselves in these lectures that laced ideals with flowery language until the ideals themselves seemed vague and impractical, outside the reach of women and children. She had heard those sermons, listening with half an ear and absorbing only because of the constancy of the subject—sooner or later, you had to hear. But never before had she put real people to the principle, never had she cast the show with actors whose voices curled off the stage like empty, useless whiffs of smoke. "Just tell him you'll see him tomorrow." . . . "You have to go,

Dwayne." . . . "It's because of the fight." . . . "I'll watch the tent." Those faces on the porch—those people she had all summer been learning to depend on—they were the enemy, although she hadn't seen that until it was too late and Pansy was telling her to take the tent down. Pansy was taking Hazard back while they were abandoning Dwayne.

She got up and stuck her glass among the dirty dishes, then went out the back door. The afternoon was still with a breathless, vacant kind of heat, deathlike. People were napping, probably even Dwayne's mother, who had convinced herself there was nothing to do but continue with her day as if nothing were wrong.

Casey could see the empty lot through the trees. She felt a longing, as her body ached with muscles held too tight, to hear the thud of a baseball against Dwayne's drum. She went across the street and pushed against the door of his garage. In the hazy, warm dark she made out a rack of bats against the wall, and rummaging around it, she found the box of balls and collected some.

Out on the lot she took the mound. Dwayne never let her pitch, but she had watched him so often that the moves, although awkward, came to her. She watched the first ball glance off the metal near the base of the drum.

"Strike one!" she shouted.

The second pitch was more solid and nearer the center of the drum. "It's a base hit!" she screamed, dashing after the grounder.

She was beginning to sweat. Hatless, she squinted at the plate and let go another pitch that missed the drum altogether and rolled into the weeds along the fence. "Damn!" she shouted. "Damn, damn, damn!" Tears mixed with sweat on her cheeks, and she wiped her grimy hand across her face while she went after the ball.

Back on the mound, she went on pitching, calling the plays, retrieving the balls. Her arms began to pinch, stinging at the joints, but still she threw the ball because she had to be doing something, even if it were nothing. Even if it didn't help. She knew there was no redeeming her silence on the porch, but still she pitched, her body straining against its private inner ache because she had failed Dwayne Pickens.

Across the street, awakened from a restless doze by a familiar yet incongruous sound, Jane Flanagan stood at her kitchen door and watched, her own heart aching, as the girl burned out the rage they all shared but could not express.

"Oh, Casey," she said aloud.

The metallic thump of the baseball gave the neighborhood a new pulse, a heavy, lonely, throbbing sound. All through the long afternoon it toned, like a knelling bell, their lethargy, their indifference, their unspeakable failure, until Casey was exhausted and flung herself on the Flanagans' porch, her body heavy with sweat and dust.

She was too tired to resist her grandmother's folding arms around her, and so, her head heavy with heat, she leaned into the comfort she had all afternoon rejected, and whispered, "We have to get him back. We have to."

"We will, Casey. I promise." Jane stroked her damp, fragile head.

Chapter Seventeen

"We were wrong to let him go," Casey said.

"We were wrong, but I believe he will forgive us."

"But I won't, Grandma. I'll never forgive myself."

Jane held her, unable to say that age had taught her how people do forgive, even forget, the wrongs they've done. It was, she knew, one of the blessings of life, that lessening of pain by time until grief, once so vile a wound, was eventually a tiny scar, the result of slow, silent healing.

Still, at that moment, the wound was too deep for reason, and so she listened as Casey repeated the word over and over, a litany of remorse: "Never, never, never," knowing that there was no comfort beyond arms that held gently, restfully, accepting both the guilt and the love she now knew her grandchild capable of.

IT WAS after six when Taylor came home from the afternoon spent at the jail and in the lawyer's office. He dropped into a kitchen chair while the rest of the family clustered around him waiting to hear.

"George was right," he said finally. "The only way to stop them from taking Dwayne tomorrow is to stop Alva. I called his office ten times this afternoon but he's always out."

"Conveniently, I suppose," Ben said. "Well, we'll have to find him tonight."

"But that means Dwayne will have to spend the night in jail," Casey protested.

"I'm afraid so, honey, but I don't think that matters to him as much as staying out of the hospital does. He knows the hospital means a long time." Taylor took her hand. "We'll get him back," he said. "I mean that. I just don't know how yet."

"First we have to find Alva," Ben said, going to the telephone.

"Marge doesn't know where he is now," he said when he returned, "but she said he'd be at the town meeting at seven o'clock. I can't believe we elected that man to the town board."

"Then we'll go to the town meeting," Jane said. "That's a better place than most to confront him."

"Second only to the churchyard," Taylor said, beginning to smile.

"But how can the town meeting stop him?" Casey wanted to know.

"I don't know that it will," Jane said. "But it's worth a try, don't you think, Ben? There's no changing Alva's mind in private, we already know that much. He always was a stubborn, conceited boy. He'll have to be shamed into withdrawing that petition. Just what would embarrass him even more than having Dwayne loose?"

"Having the whole town know he was putting him away, that's what," Ben said. "He thought he could do it on the sly like the last time when he caught us napping."

"Well, I think we can wake them up tonight," Taylor said. He was feeling better. "Let's eat."

"So we'll go to the town meeting," Jane said. She busied herself with getting sandwiches on the table. "We'll all go." She smiled at Casey. "All the Flanagans."

The town meeting was already in progress when they got there. The Flanagans sat down behind the fifty or so citizens in the audience to get the gist of the proceedings. The mayor and six aldermen were sitting behind a table with stacks of papers in front of them. One of them was writing frantically. Smoke clouded the air above the table.

A black woman in the audience was addressing the men. She stood straight, her arms folded across her stomach, her flowered summer hat quivering as she moved her head emphatically. Only her head moved as she told them how the sewer system in her part of town was leaking again, the recent patching job having lasted only long enough for the construction company to collect their checks.

"We got sewage in the street," she was saying, her eyes flashing but her body still and her voice hushed because she knew the risk she was taking by being there at all. "We got a stench in our streets. We got children locked inside their houses in the hot summertime to keep them out of the mess bubbling up. But the smell comes in the house at us, anyways."

"Mr. Mayor!" One of the aldermen leaned down the table toward the mayor. "Harley, we got people coming at us every whipstitch wanting this and wanting that." He straightened up to look out at the woman. "Everybody needs something, woman."

"Hear her out," the mayor said. "Let's hear her out." He was smiling. "She pays town taxes just like you and me, even if she don't pay much. All according as they're able," he ended sanctimoniously.

Another alderman cleared his throat in preparation to saying something. Everybody waited. "We got that sewer system put in down there in colored town," he said in a slow, mournful drawl. "We got it in there where they didn't have nothin' but a slop jar and a outhouse. What I want to know is, ain't they ever satisfied?" He peered at the black woman.

"We're mothers here, speaking to you about our children," she said in a deep throaty voice. "We got hot weather and flies. We got sickness coming if it ain't cleaned up. We can't clean it up by ourselves. We're here about our children."

"That's right, Emmaline," one of the other women said. Emmaline sat down, her hat still shaking, while the women around her nodded, commending her performance as they watched with bitter, glancing looks at the men who mumbled among themselves at the table.

"Well," the mayor said, puffing himself up for a little speech. "I've contacted the company. They've been informed of the problem down there. They say they'll be in there doing something later this week."

"They promised that last week!" one of the women said, shaking her finger at the aldermen while the women next to her tried to ease her agitation by patting her shoulder and taking her hand.

"This is a firm commitment," the mayor said calmly. "We are doing the best we can, ladies." He smiled down at them, thinking he had appeased them by calling them ladies.

Seeing a break in the proceedings, Taylor stood up.

"State the nature of your business, Mr. Flanagan," the clerk called, glad to see a white man to contend with. Here was a friend, someone with more important business than a little leak in the sewer line.

"Personal, Howard," Taylor said firmly. "And then again, not so personal. I'm here about an issue that has to do with us as people. It's as serious as sewage and about as hard to get rid of."

The black women nodded and smiled, happy he was respecting their situation.

Alva Pickens leaned back in his chair and eyed Taylor over his glasses. He sensed the nature of Taylor's business, having noted the Flanagan contingency from the moment they arrived, but he thought it better to sit it out. Let Taylor make a fool of himself and then Alva could use the situation to his own advantage. He knew how to turn a situation to his advantage. It made him a good businessman and an even better politician.

"Today a court order was signed committing Dwayne Pickens to a mental institution," Taylor said forcefully. "It was signed by two doctors who examined him five years ago. It was also signed by the clerk of court and by the petitioner, Alva Pickens, Dwayne's brother." Taylor paused and looked around the room. He wanted to be sure everybody was paying attention. He needed everybody in the room rooting for Dwayne just like they would were he a great baseball player or the best racer on the track. Feet shuffled and people turned in their folding chairs to get a clearer view of the speaker.

"Now we all know Dwayne," Taylor went on.

"We do!" the black women sang out.

"We know him because he's been free to walk our streets, shop in our stores, attend our public functions for thirty years. He's even provided some public functions of his own with his baseball games. He's always been respectful. More than that, he's been good-natured in the face of taunting from certain quarters."

"That's right! I've seen it!" a white man across the aisle said. "He's good-hearted all right!"

"Now we know Dwayne's mind is not quite right. We know he's slow. But a lot of us are not as quick as we ought to be!"

The audience chuckled while Taylor got his breath. He could feel them with him. They were remembering Dwayne, each of them recalling those little encounters they hadn't even noticed at the time, his way of greeting them, his loose, careless gait, his unabashed enthusiasm that made them smile.

"The fact is Dwayne got into a little fight at the racetrack last Saturday. I guess you can see by my appearance, so did I." He touched his bruised cheek gingerly. "I was the cause of the fight, but nobody's locked me up. The fact is I called on Dwayne when things got a little thick out there."

Some of the men chuckled again, and Taylor flashed them a quick smile.

"God knows, Dwayne's got a swing. There's no denying that. But he didn't start that fight and when it was over, he threw up all over my trailer. It made him sick to hit a man. That's what he said.

"Now Alva Pickens here wants us to think Dwayne is dangerous. He wants us to treat him like he's a crazy person. Right this minute, Dwayne is over there locked up in jail for no good reason that I can think of. Dwayne doesn't understand why he's there and neither do I."

"Why is he, Alva?" a woman said from the audience. She popped her gum loudly and pressed her pocketbook to her bosom.

The audience and the alderman were staring at Alva,

who was refusing to look at anybody. He polished his glasses slowly to prove his control, put them back on his nose carefully, and then leaned over to speak to the men at the other end of the table. "This is a personal matter," he began. "I believe Mr. Flanagan is out of order."

"You're the one that's out of order," a new voice said from the audience. It was the barber Casey had seen that day. "Why, I've been cutting Dwayne Pickens's hair all these years. There's nothing dangerous about that boy. Nothing wrong with him except he acts like a kid." The man nodded at the Flanagans.

"That's right," the gum-chewing woman said. "I work the concessions at the picture show, and he's never caused no trouble there. Why, there's kids in there spilling all over everything, yellin' and carryin' on, them what ain't neckin' to beat the band. But not Dwayne. He's looking at the picture, I can promise you that." She sat back, satisfied.

"I know him, too," the mayor said, grinning down at the barber. "Met him just this morning."

"Mr. Mayor," Taylor thundered, seeing the point beginning to slip away. "I've come here tonight, understanding the terms and conditions of this petition Alva Pickens has signed against his brother. I've come knowing that the board of aldermen cannot stop this action any more than the Flanagans or God Almighty Himself can. But I've promised that boy he will not be sent away from his home, from his town, from the people who care about him. I'm not ashamed to say I love Dwayne Pickens. We grew up together. I know him, and I believe he has a right to reap the rewards of living in this fine community as much as you or I do."

"Amen!" the women chorused.

"It's for his own good," Alva said stonily, unable to tolerate dissent any longer. He pounded the table with his fist, betraying the frustration he'd felt mounting ever since Dwayne took his car. "I don't know what to do with him!"

"You don't have to do anything with him, Alva," Taylor said. "You never did. He's as much our brother as he is yours."

"Mama won't live forever," Alva said, wearily trying another tactic. He snorted into his handkerchief. "Mrs. Flanagan, you understand, don't you? You know how Mama takes care of him. What's going to become of him when she's gone? Who's going to be responsible then?"

"I don't know, Alva," Jane Flanagan said, rising to stand beside her son. "But why make him start living such a sad life before he has to? It'll come soon enough. He's a happy person, Alva. Let him have that much now, no matter what there is to come. No matter what you think is best for him."

"What can I do?" Alva moaned, slumping in his chair.

"First thing in the morning, you go back to the clerk of court and withdraw this petition," George Greenwald said, having just entered from the back. "You have to get the written consent of the doctors who signed this thing in the first place, and then the clerk of court will write up a motion dropping the whole business."

"How's Dwayne?" Casey called. "Is he all right, Mr. Greenwald?"

"Sleeping like a baby," George said. "I stayed right in there with him till he was asleep. He knows we're getting him out of there. I can tell he believes it."

"He's got more faith in human nature than I do," the mayor said. "A whole lot more."

Alva sat up straight again, as if he'd gotten a second wind. "I tell you, you people are mingling in something that's none of your business," he said, looking from the mayor to the Flanagans.

"What we've come here to tell you, Alva," Taylor said patiently, "is that Dwayne *is* our business."

"All you got to do is make a phone call, Alva," the mayor said. "That's all it'll take, isn't that right, George?"

"Yes sir. That's all. Just one little ol' telephone call to the clerk's office and he'll take care of the rest. I'm sure of that."

"Well, do *something*, Alva," one of the aldermen said, "or we'll be here all night!"

Alva looked around the table and then out at the audience as if he were tallying the opposition. He stood up, scraping his chair heavily. "I don't know what I'm going to do about Dwayne, but right now, I'm going home. And don't you come badgering me, Taylor Flanagan. I've seen enough fools for one night!" He slammed his hat on his head and marched out the side door.

"Hope he doesn't look in the mirror," Taylor said. The audience laughed with relief.

"Do you think he'll keep the boy home?" the mayor asked in the direction of the Flanagans.

"I think he will, Harley," Ben said. "I've known Alva

Pickens since the day he was born and he's not all bad."

"Just about half," the barber said.

"I think he's been shamed into keeping Dwayne home. I truly do," Jane said, hugging Casey to her. "We can pray for it now because we've done all we can do ourselves."

Casey was feeling better. She grabbed Taylor around the neck and kissed his uninjured cheek with a loud smack. "I just wish Gwen had been here to see you," she said. "You ought to be a preacher."

"That's what I told him when he was a little boy," Jane said. "Looks like it finally took on him! Now let's go on home and get to bed. Dwayne's going to be the only person around here getting a good night's sleep."

"But what about tomorrow?" Casey asked, following her grandmother outside.

"Tomorrow we'll just have to see if Alva has any redeeming qualities," Jane said.

"And if he doesn't, I intend to rearrange his face," Taylor added.

Casey went with Taylor to the jail the next morning. They didn't see Alva's Chrysler but they hurried inside anyway, Casey's empty stomach fluttering as she tightened her grip on Taylor's hand.

"Maybe he called," Taylor said, but Casey could see he was worried.

"He did it!" George said in the doorway. "I sure had my doubts, but he called just a little while ago. The clerk's over at the Courthouse getting the consents ready for the doctors. You can take him on because they'll both sign. I don't think they wanted any part of this business to begin with." He was grinning and he slapped Taylor on the back. "He's waiting for somebody to come get him. He's wanting to see you."

George hurried off as Casey let go of Taylor's hand and stood absolutely still, oblivious to the activity around her, waiting to see Dwayne come through the door. When he came, Casey was the first person he focused on, like the rest of them weren't even there.

"Hey boy," he called.

"Hey Dwayne," she answered. "You're coming home now. Your mama's waiting for you at your house, and Grandma's making a big cake and we're going to have a party tonight!"

"A party! *Wow-weeee!*" Dwayne slapped his thigh with his cap.

"Fried chicken, too, because I told Grandma that's your favorite."

" 'Bye!" Dwayne said to the officers in the station. "I'm going on home now. 'Bye!"

They climbed into Taylor's car and pulled away just as a state car pulled in behind them. "They're in for a surprise," Taylor said, looking through his rear-view mirror at the two men getting out. "Maybe they'll take Alva instead."

"We got to watch that tent today, K.C.?" Dwayne wanted to know.

"Nope, it's gone."

"Miss Pansy tore it down?" Dwayne looked distressed. "I told you all I had to watch it."

"It's not because we didn't watch it, Dwayne. It's because Hazard got Pansy back, just like he wanted to.

And we got you back, just like we wanted to." Casey had to resist her impulse to hug him.

"And I got you all back, too," Dwayne said, grinning. "Now let's us play some baseball!"

18

Casey felt the pain behind her eyes long before she opened them. She lay perfectly still, wishing the pain away while it crept across her temples, behind her ears, and into her neck.

I'll go back to sleep, she thought, and when I wake up it will be gone.

She dozed.

The air around her was warm and moist, too thick to breathe normally. She began to take shallow, light breaths that didn't hurt so much. She relaxed a little.

I'm tired, she thought, remembering that they had brought Dwayne home just yesterday and there had been a party last night.

She tried to remember the party, but her head hurt too much. Before her closed eyes moved quick, erratic pictures: Taylor and Gwen dancing the shag, Gwen's skirt floating out and then settling against her puffy white crinoline; her grandmother bustling between the kitchen and the dining room, Dora Pickens trailing after her wanting to be helpful; Hazard and Pansy looking at each other across the room, smiles hovering above their coffee cups; Dwayne, sprawled on the sofa watching everything and slapping his knees, calling to Gwen to dance with him, then his mama, then even her grandmother, who blushed and did a little Charleston step across the living-room floor. Dwayne happy. Dwayne rescued. Dwayne wrapped in love.

She was so hot. She wanted to get up and stir the air with her body. She wanted to move, but she didn't. She opened her eyes. The room was the same. The morning had broken over it as always, the same white spots across her daddy's desk, the same thin trickle of morning beneath her shade. The pain in her head made her vision blur. It hurt so bad. She wanted to pound her temples to make it stop, but still she didn't move.

In a minute I'll get up, she thought, pushing her mind to reason beyond the hot rushes of pain that swept through her on every swift, panting breath.

I'll be all right, she thought, closing her eyes. I'll stay here until it goes away. Minutes passed. She tried to turn over, but her head hurt too much. Her arms seemed heavy, elephantine.

She needed to go to the bathroom. It was a clear sensation, the only painless, natural feeling she could recognize. She felt such relief.

I'll go to the bathroom and then I'll be all right, she thought. She tried to smile, wanting to display her relief in some concrete fashion, but her cheeks were too dry and her skin too tight. The smile refused to come.

Suddenly she knew she couldn't move. Without even testing her legs and trunk, she knew. Her mouth opened, formed a silent, hollow O. She closed her eyes again, closed her mind against the sound she was so afraid to hear.

They heard her scream in the kitchen. It was not the

high-pitched, shrill screech of acute pain, but a throaty resigned cry of defeat. They went to her, Jane with her face ashen, aged by thirty seconds of despair between kitchen and bedroom: Ben, calm but with his breakfast napkin still tucked into his shirt; Taylor, racing ahead of them, believing he could and would conquer whatever awaited them.

Casey opened her eyes. They were there, leaning over her. Hands she couldn't feel touched her forehead, her arms, her hot bare legs.

"It hurts," she whispered through dry lips.

"Call Dr. Kemble," Jane said, her face set against her fear. "Get the thermometer, Taylor. And a pan of cool water." She had to be doing something. She knew there was nothing to do, but she would perform the rituals of care anyway.

Casey felt the cool water on her face. It dribbled down her neck and she opened her mouth and bit down on the towel, sucking moisture onto her tongue. The pain seemed better. Having them there gave her something else to concentrate on. She wanted them to stay with her, but she was afraid to try to say it. What if she couldn't? She wouldn't try. She fell asleep.

Dr. Kemble came and with him, Pansy and Hazard. They sat on the porch waiting while the doctor went upstairs. He was back again too soon, before they were prepared to hear.

"I don't know," the doctor said to them in the front hallway. "There are, of course, polio symptoms—high fever, pain, stiff joints, poor body movement. At the same time, I've seen some influenza cases like this. Polio is a virus, you know. It attacks the cells in the central nervous system. How strong the virus is determines how many cells it attacks. A few cells, a light case. A lot of cells, a severe case. That's about all we know. Other viruses can have the same primary symptoms. Unfortunately, only time will tell. If it's a simple virus, she could be well in three or four days. Even with a mild case of polio, she could be much better in the same length of time and with little or no permanent damage." He hesitated and then shook his head wearily. "God knows, I wish I could tell you something else. Someday there'll be a way to fight this thing, but I know that's little comfort now. I'll come back around noon. Try to get the fever down with alcohol rubs and sponge baths. Pay close attention to her breathing. If she starts gasping, call an ambulance. Otherwise we'll try to keep her out of the hospital."

"We'll take turns," Pansy said when the doctor had gone. "Two-hour shifts staying with her."

"I can't leave her now," Jane said. She hurried back up the stairs with Ben following her.

"You'd better stay, Pansy," Taylor said. "We're going to need both of you before this is over."

Pansy and Hazard cleared the kitchen. The familiar work calmed them a little, put a simple form of normalcy into their day. But they were silent. Hazard watched Pansy's narrow wrists dip into the suds in the dishpan. He saw the soft rise of her breasts as she drew quick breaths. He heard the sighs that floated between them like a dismal melody. Finally, he took her hand, drew it out of the soapy water so it appeared pink and dripping between them, and dried it carefully, touching her as lightly as he could.

"We're together," he said. "We can do whatever we have to do now. We can help them."

"But we can't save Casey," Pansy said. She was beginning to cry as she put her head against him.

"No, but we mustn't underestimate her, either."

"Oh, Hazard, don't you understand, there's nothing we can do, there's nothing she can do," Pansy moaned tearfully. "There's nothing anybody can do."

"I don't believe that," Hazard said, lifting her face to his. "Not any more. We are proof, Pansy, that people can do something."

"I wish it were that simple," Pansy said, trying to smile at him.

"There's nothing simple about it," Hazard said. "All I know is she's got to want to get well, we've got to make sure she wants it bad enough, no matter how she's hurting."

Ben came into the kitchen.

"How is she?" Pansy and Hazard asked together.

"The same. She sleeps and then wakes up for a minute. It's like she's unconscious most of the time. Jane is sponging her off, but she moans through it like the water hurts her. I don't think it's doing any good." He sat down in a chair and rested his head on the heels of his hands. "We shouldn't have let her go places like we did. Down at the racetrack every Saturday. She went to the beach just a couple of days ago. All over town with Dwayne Pickens. We should have kept her home."

Pansy was silent, thinking to herself that he was probably right.

"I know it doesn't do any good for me to say you

shouldn't blame yourself," Hazard said, "but I don't see how you could have prevented this, seeing how the doctors don't even know how people get it."

"Hazard's right, Daddy," Taylor said from the doorway. His face was splotched but he didn't seem to care that they could see he'd been crying. "We just have to make her as comfortable as we can. And pray it's not polio."

"I'll go help Jane," Pansy said. She wanted to leave the men alone together, comforting each other with the silence that was familiar between them.

Upstairs she paused in the open doorway of Casey's room to watch Jane bending over the still body, the white narrow bed. Jane was pressing a cloth to Casey's neck and shoulders, then dipping it back into the pan of water, squeezing it so a trickle of water fell back into the pan, then pressing the girl's skin once more. She moved silently about her task, her head bent, body intent on this saving, this salvaging of a life so close to her own. Nothing else mattered. Nothing counted but the woman and the child, the precious cooling of one body with the skill of another, the laying on of hands.

THE DAYS seemed endless, but for Jane Flanagan it was the nights, the sheer hot panic that came when no one was awake but her, which brought the most relentless terror. She would sit there beside the bed, listening to the breathing, hearing it closer than her own, and would think through the crucial days of her life, reacquainting herself with old griefs, remembering survivals and losses.

Chapter Eighteen

Illnesses spread themselves before her like languishing demons. Deaths draped their heavy shrouds around the dark room. Sometimes she cried. Just sitting there, her hand resting close to her grandchild's limp fingers —just in case—she would let the tears held back all that day come, spilling down her cold, determined cheeks. Nothing had prepared her for this.

She had not reached Barbara yet, but she knew she hadn't tried very hard, at least not since that first day. She didn't want to call her at work, so she'd tried at suppertime and then late at night when Barbara should be home from her second job, but wasn't. She'd let the phone ring for minutes, hearing it fill the hollow, vacant house so far away, until the operator cut in with her crisp, official, "Would you like to try again?" So Jane had waited another day, another little while, because she couldn't find words—she who was so quick with words—to tell a mother that her daughter might die.

For two days and nights she'd waited, doubting the possibility of a break in the fever, although Dr. Kemble came confidently morning and evening, telling her how the limbs were no worse, how the effectiveness of the alcohol rubs against the fever was a good sign, how Casey would not die. Jane didn't believe him. As much as she wanted Casey to live, as surely as she knew she would change places if she could, she felt somehow resigned.

It was as if knowing she herself could not make Casey live meant the child was doomed. Everything had rested in her hands for so long. Every comfort, every need of her family had been hers to offer, her sustaining gift to those she loved, until she couldn't believe they could succeed outside her will, outside her determined pursuit of their happiness.

Now everything was out of control. All those little things, like the small domestic tasks she'd always relished, had gone haywire; bigger things had, too, like Dwayne Pickens knowing Casey was a girl. She hadn't expected that to happen, not this late in the summer when Casey had put such effort into keeping her secret. Jane had even helped her by going to Dora Pickens that first day and explaining the circumstances of her granddaughter's lie, justifying a deed she had never expected to find justifiable.

But now he knew because he had been sitting on the front porch that first evening, waiting with the rest of them to hear how Casey was. He had been on the stoop, his back to them, when the doctor came out and stood in the patch of hall light on the porch like he intended to give a recitation.

"She's just the same," was all he'd said. "She's a sick little girl, but I think we have good reason to believe she'll pull through."

So Dwayne heard, and because the doctor's news was no news at all, Jane had looked at Dwayne instead, had seen him rise off the stoop like some threatened, angered monster, seen him flailing the air in the darkening front yard, his head back like a dog ready to howl at the moon, but silent, mute while his mind circled the truth. Casey was a girl. He loved a girl!

19

The fever took Casey in and out like a swinging door that slammed back in her face, having given her a glimpse of a cool place, a quiet, restful, shaded spot under the tree in her backyard at home.

She had the only full-grown tree on the block because the military bulldozer had plowed through the housing development site as if it had been commanded to obliterate every sign of life. Somehow, one straggly sweet gum had survived, refused to lie down and die under a pile of red clay, so Casey had a real tree while the neighbors struggled with dogwoods and flowering fruit trees still staked up after all these years.

In her fog of fever, she saw the tree like a mirage, shimmering and not quite there. Her head tossed on the pillow as she fought to keep the door open a little longer. She wanted to see the tree. She knew the full-leafed branches would cool her. She knew that if they would just take her home to the tree, she would be all right.

But the door slammed; the deep, leafy illusion was gone. Her mouth was dry and she couldn't swallow.

"I don't think she's breathing right," she heard someone saying. It was Pansy, her voice throbbing anxiously at Casey's temples.

"Sh-h-h."

The scent of alcohol stung her nostrils.

"It's all right, Casey. Just rest easy, honey."

She stopped trying to swallow. Saliva formed around her tongue. It seemed to be filling up her mouth. She would drown if she didn't swallow. She felt her throat opening and swallowed involuntarily, easily, without the gagging effort she'd expected.

"She's easier now," a voice said. But Casey knew it wasn't so.

SHE WAS cooler. Sunk like a stone deep within her empty gut, she sensed a coolness, felt it slowly begin to rise, floating inside her hollow stomach, pushing moisture to her skin's dry, shrunken surface. She felt slightly damp. The hot, dry bed seemed to draw at her flesh, collecting in tiny wet spots behind her knees and along her neck.

"Drink," she murmured, not opening her eyes. She knew someone was there.

A straw pushed itself between her lips and struck her teeth as she grasped it and sucked. The liquid spewed around her mouth, trickled down her throat. She gagged and coughed, her body heaving forward, her head spinning as it came off the pillow toward a hand raised in front of her. She opened her eyes. Taylor was holding her. He took her shoulders in his firm hands and lifted her against his chest, away from the wet bed and the dank, hot smell of her own body.

"I can move," she whispered into his chest.

"Of course you can," he said.

She could feel his chest, the heavy shuddering breaths he drew as he nursed her head, fingers at her dry, itching scalp, his arms enfolding her like her daddy's would.

"Mama. Daddy." Just the sound of the words made her heave again, but this time a sob came up, a plaintive whimpering sob that made Taylor want to cry himself.

"He's in Korea, Casey," he said. "Remember? You're here with us now."

Another sob came, and then another. Her body retched with sobs, her face and chest were sweaty with tears and the salty moisture that oozed up out of her skin.

"You're going to be all right, Casey," Taylor said, rocking her against his chest. "You can move. See?" He lifted her arm before her face. "You can feel." He rubbed her arm gently. "You can feel that, Casey. I know you can."

"What is it?" Jane was in the doorway, her face drawn and shadowed.

"She's cooler, Mama." Taylor lay her gently back on the bed. "She's sweating a lot and I think she can move all her limbs. Can you move your legs, Casey? Try to, Casey."

They were bending over her anxiously, their faces betraying the hours of torment she hadn't known existed. She was so tired, though. The damp bed seemed to pull at her, reminding her of sleep.

"Try, Casey, try."

She squeezed her eyes tightly shut, sending all her energy down her legs. Her foot moved. She felt the slight pressure of the sheet on her toes. Her ankle bent. There seemed to be pulse in her calves, a dull, throbbing ache that took all her strength to combat.

"She's all right!" Taylor said.

"Go back to sleep, honey," her grandmother said close to her face. "We'll be right here."

She felt fingers against her palm, trembling fingers spilling out their joy into her hand. She clutched the fingers to still them in hers, and went to sleep.

DWAYNE CAME. She was cool by then, the bed changed to crisp, dry sheets that didn't smell of fever; but still she didn't want to move, knowing she could. She was too tired. She saw him in the doorway, his baseball cap in his hand, the other hand behind his back, his head ducked in an embarrassed, hesitant tilt.

"Hey," she said softly.

"Hey boy," he said and came a little way into the room. He didn't look around but stared straight at her, as if her face were the proof he needed that she was all right.

"I knew you were gonna get well," he blurted out, "because I prayed for you, goddammit!" He grinned and slapped his cap against his thigh.

"Come sit down," she said, trying to put a familiar, healthy sound in her voice for him. She wanted to be just the way he remembered.

"Here," he said, thrusting a handful of daisies at her. Some of the stems stuck out from the squashed bundle. "I picked them all along the ditch bank. They grow wild, you know. Ain't no store-bought flowers."

"They're nice, Dwayne," she said, taking the flowers against her chest.

"Girls like flowers," Dwayne said. He put his baseball cap back on, but far back so that the bill stood straight up and she could see his face clearly. "I know you're a girl, Casey," he said.

"You didn't have to come see me," she said. Her eyes brimmed with tears that seemed too close lately, so eager. She wiped them away with her free hand. "I would understand if you didn't ever want to see me again."

Dwayne frowned, trying to figure out what she meant. "Sure I want to see you," he said. "We gonna play baseball all next week, but if you can't, we'll go to the show and to the racetrack and everything. Just like always, Casey. I want everything to be like always."

"But I'm a girl," Casey said. "And you don't like girls."

"Shoot!" Dwayne bobbed his head and then looked at her shyly. "You don't know nothin'! How you know that? How you know what Dwayne Pickens likes and don't like?"

Casey was silent, wishing she had an answer.

"Now you get well, you hear?" Dwayne was saying. He patted his foot restlessly and then stood up and pushed the chair back where he thought it might have been. "I got to go," he said. "See you tomorrow."

She heard him clumping down the stairs, his hand slapping the bannister, and she leaned back into the pillow, the wild daisies across her chest and the petals feathering on her skin. The back door slammed and the house became as quiet and peaceful as her own resting body. She was going to be all right.

Convalescence days were ice-cream days, cold supper nights, afternoons artificially cooled by the fan Casey's grandfather put in her bedroom window to suck out the hot, stuffy air close under the roof and replace it with a stirred warm bit of moving air.

Jane wanted to move her downstairs into their room, but Casey wouldn't leave. She had grown accustomed to her father's room; she liked its starkness, the dreary, empty look she could fill with visions of her own. Lying there, staring at the blank walls, she decorated them with pictures of airplanes, with college pennants, with the miscellaneous collection of memorabilia she had identified on Taylor's walls.

Being in his room made her feel close to her father. She knew she needed that, just as, since her illness, she'd needed to feel close to her mother. She cried when she heard her mother's voice on the phone that first time, her grandmother having already explained about her sickness, how she was on the mend and there was nothing to worry about. Still, bravery shattered when she heard that breathless, anxious voice that was so necessary to her survival. It was her knowledge of need that made her cry, sobs that mixed helplessness with gratitude. Her grandparents, Taylor, her mother—they all formed links in her circle of protection just as her daddy once had. Until this summer, her daddy had been the whole chain, but he couldn't be that again. Now there were other people.

"I'll be all right, Mama," she said, holding back tears.

"I'm just fine. We're all just fine." Although she felt so fragile, so tentative, almost unattached in a way that only good health could remedy.

"She ought to get back to bed," Jane said into the phone. "Dr. Kemble said she needs to rest in bed for a week and then another week of limited activity."

"You do that," her mother said, glad she had been offered a responsibility in the matter. "You mind your grandmother and the doctor." She sighed. "I wish I could come up there, Casey," she said. "Sometimes I wish I hadn't let you go at all."

"It's all right, Mama," Casey said. "I'm O.K. We just needed different things this summer."

"I guess you're right," her mother said. "But I miss you, Casey."

"I'll go back to bed now," Casey said to her grandmother when she'd hung up.

"I wish you'd stay down here," Jane said. "It's cooler and the bed is better."

"I like Daddy's room," Casey said. "It's just fine."

Jane took the phone from her, put her arms around her shoulders, and started walking her toward the stairs. "You know, Casey, I've always thought of that room as David's, but this summer it's really become yours. There are a lot of summers left for you to stay here if you want to."

"Where're you two off to?" Taylor asked through the screen.

"Casey's going back to bed," Jane said.

"Oh, no she's not." Taylor pushed open the door for them. "A ride in the car won't hurt her a bit. Might even do her good." He swung Casey into his arms befor Jane could protest.

In the front seat of the Chevy in her cotton robe, Casey started laughing. "You rescued me, Taylor! I knew somebody would! Where are we going?"

"It's a secret." Taylor was grinning.

They headed toward the lumberyard. "I've been thinking a lot about you lately, you know," Taylor said. "You gave us quite a scare when you were sick. It got me thinking about your daddy, too, more than I usually do. It's been a pretty long time since your daddy and I were close. He's got five years on me, for one thing, and then we took different directions when we grew up. At least, he took a direction. I've just been meandering along." He turned up a little path that ran into the woods bordering the lumberyard.

"Anyhow," he went on, swerving a little to avoid a bump, "I got to thinking about your daddy, about when we were kids, and I remembered something. So I came out here to see if it was still there and it is—at least it's sort of here. It's going to take some imagination on your part to make it right."

"What is it, Taylor?" Casey felt silly with excitement.

He stopped the car. "Wait and see. I'll have to carry you from here. We should have gotten your shoes on."

He lifted her into his arms and skirted the underbrush until they were in a small opening protected by a large maple. "There." He pointed.

She knew what it was. Splintered, ragged gray wood, sagging frame paint blistered to peeling patches, a propeller half gone, nose bent earthward. It was a plane, a boy's plane. A visionary, awkward, beautiful attempt at making a dream come true.

"He built it," Taylor said. "He had a picture from a magazine. A World War I plane, but I don't remember the name of it or what its history was. He got the lumber from the yard, scraps from the saw, the odd piece Daddy couldn't sell. He wanted silk for the wings, I remember that. It was the depression and he couldn't earn any money. Mama finally gave him the summer sheers off the living-room windows, but I don't think she ever came out here and saw it. Daddy, either. Just David and me. He let me help him sometimes, because one kid couldn't do it all. It was fun, but I didn't really understand what it was all about, not until I started fixing up my car. I didn't feel anything that strong when I was a kid, not like your daddy did."

"I want to get in the cockpit," Casey said against his shoulder.

"Lord, Casey, it's rotten. I'm surprised it's standing at all. It's been out here in the weather twenty years. I think it would fall apart completely if you laid a hand on it."

"I have to touch it, though," Casey said. "Don't you see that?"

He was silent, then took her closer to the plane and stood her on her bare feet in the mossy dirt. The wood was damp and soft under her fingers. She touched the fuselage gently, then the rib of the wing where once her grandmother's sheers had been.

"Sometimes I think that he'll never come back," she said. "I imagine what it would be like with just Mama and me, and then I'm so afraid, like thinking will make it happen. So I try not to think about it, but the thought is always there. What if he doesn't come back, I think, before I can stop myself."

"We can't make something bad happen just by thinking about it," Taylor said. "I know that for sure."

"What about good things? What about wishing Dwayne would like me until he did? And you and Grandma wanting me to get better so much that I did?"

"But you did something about Dwayne liking you. You tried to be the kind of person he liked. And we took care of you when you were sick. We tried to let you know we loved you, even when you were asleep. David wanted to fly, so he built a plane. Of course, it wouldn't fly anywhere but in his head, but that was enough. The important thing was he did something about what he wanted."

"I think he's coming home," Casey said, lifting her arms for Taylor to hold her again. She felt tired, but healthy, too.

"No doubt about it," Taylor said, hugging her. "And you're going to get well. And we're going to the races and I'm going to win until Gwen is up to her neck in trophies!"

"I don't know about that." Casey laughed. "But I feel good already."

20

Late August. The garden almost in, the last of the tomatoes weighting the spindly vine, wormy and not worth picking. Corn stalks had begun to shrivel, leaves edged with brown, and their yield was tough and had to be scraped off the cob. Only the weeds grew, standing high along the fence around Dwayne's diamond.

The final stretch of heat was smothering, and it didn't go away. Long into the night people walked the streets restlessly, speaking softly to one another across their hedges and from their porches. They watched the night sky hoping for a wind, any slight stir of breeze to dry their sweaty skin and cool the tin roofs of their smoldering houses.

Now and then it rained. Clouds formed magically and big, splashing drops soaked the grass and lawn furniture. But immediately the sun came back out and wilted the newly nourished grass and leaves. After the shower it seemed hotter than before.

Casey and Dwayne took turns deciding what they could do to entertain themselves. About every other turn, Dwayne would suggest they play catch or ride his bike, something he'd forgotten Casey was not yet allowed to do, and she would have to remind him of what the doctor had said about another week of rest, although she felt fine.

So they watched television, played cards, and read comic books. Casey found an old collection of wildlife stories that had belonged to her daddy and she read some of them to Dwayne while he lay on the porch floor, his head on a cushion Jane had provided Casey with in the swing, bare legs stretched out to get the breeze that the moving swing created around her. She read slowly, glancing occasionally at Dwayne's face to see if he was listening or if he was bored. Once he fell alseep, but when she nudged him awake with her foot, he denied his lack of attentiveness and told her what a good story it was.

Once when she was feeling restless and depressed, she told him he should find something better to do than hang around a sick person.

"You want me to go?" he'd asked, ducking his head.

"It's not that," Casey said. "I just don't want you to think you have to sit here with me."

"Next week we'll play ball," Dwayne promised. "We'll go to the races."

She couldn't bring herself to tell him that next week she'd be gone.

The family had talked about it even before she became sick, how she would have to be back home by the first of September when the school term began. Every week her mother reminded her, knowing exactly how many days were left. Her mother missed her during those hours between her two jobs and late at night when she was at home alone, no sleeping child in the house, no bowls left with drying bits of cereal or melted ice cream, no wet swimsuit on the bathroom rug, no one to speak to. She had only her own clutter, her own ironing draped over the chair, her own needs to take care of.

Casey knew there was something to be said for having someone depend on you. She'd learned that from Dwayne. Having responsibility made people responsible. Having someone to love gave you a chance to be loved yourself.

She looked down at Dwayne, his face screwed up in concentration over the words in a comic book. Perhaps once, years ago, her father had sat there with Dwayne beside him, and they had read and dreamed together—dreams of growing up, of adventure, of flight. They had traded secrets and bubblegum cards. They had acknowledged their disdain for girls and their dedication to whatever sport was seasonable.

But then they had grown up. Years that once seemed so endless had one by one fallen away, until now, on a muggy afternoon in August, they were miles apart, separated by some genetic mystery that was as unconquerable as Babe Ruth's home run record.

Casey had taken her father's place with Dwayne. She could see that now, how the pattern had repeated itself. And she could see how she would have to leave him, too.

She would grow up. By next summer she would be different. Already she felt the changes for which she had no words, no explanation that could make him understand how deep inside, where both her fever and her coolness had so recently been, there was a throbbing sense of life just waiting for a winter's nourishing. She would never be the same.

But Dwayne would. Next summer and the next. Then on and on until she was grown and maybe had children of her own. Dwayne would be the same. Oh, his hair would probably begin to gray, his eyes weaken as he squinted from the mound into the afternoon sun. He would stop playing baseball every day, and gradually his field would grow up, weeds choking home plate. He would lose the hard, quick agility of his body slowly and then loosen his belt a notch, surprised by the appearance of fat around his middle. He would sense the passage of time but never put his finger on it. He would grow old without ever having been a young man or a middle-aged man. Without the moments that are intended to get him ready for old age.

"Dwayne, let's go somewhere," she said suddenly.

He looked up frowning, the comic-book images still clouding his mind. Then her invitation registered and he was up like a shot, slapping his thighs and grinning at her. "You mean you got well? You mean we can do something!" And he bounded across the street to get his bike.

They would ride downtown, Casey thought. She would perch on the back fender, feet lifted away from the spokes, hands clutching the seat springs. Dwayne would pump, gathering speed against the burden of her added weight, and then they would coast, shirts blowing, eyes half-closed in the hot breeze.

The deserted streets would lay open like uncharted terrain, houses would be swallowed up by thick, steamy jungles. They would be sailing, soaring; there would be nothing to call them back. No warnings of the years to come. No reminders of the past. No hollow laughing voice to call a man a boy.

It was not, Jane Flanagan told Pansy, expected to be a happy occasion, but she had nevertheless told Taylor to bring Gwen and now she was inviting Pansy and Hazard to come for a farewell supper for Casey.

"I don't think I can stand to see her go," Jane said in Pansy's kitchen.

Pansy was dicing potatoes for a salad. She dug out the eyes carefully, swished the pared potato under the faucet, and chopped it with quick, efficient motions into the pan of water. The water turned milky.

"She's like my own child," Jane continued. "I always wanted a little girl, you know. I kept hoping for a third child, but—oh, well, we should be grateful for the blessings that do come our way. Two fine sons. A healthy, happy granddaughter," She sighed. "I just hate to think about her going back to Fort Jackson. She'll miss David more, I know that. Sometimes I feel so lucky that I'm still here where he grew up. I'm constantly reminded of him, you know. Every room has its own special memories of him as a boy. I miss him less this way."

"She has memories of him there," Pansy said, rinsing another potato.

"How much salad are you making?" Jane asked, watching it disappear into the pot.

"Enough for Hazard to have some in his lunch tomorrow. He loves cold potato salad in his lunch." Pansy smiled, glad she knew that about him. Every day there was something new to learn. It seemed strange to her and at the same time delightful that after all those years there still remained meaningful, daily habits to learn about him.

"So you'll come to supper?" Jane asked, returning to her original subject.

"Of course we will. It sounds like a lovely way to thank Casey for the summer. She's meant a lot to Hazard and me, you know. It's been good being around young people. They don't seem as confused about life as the rest of us, although I suppose they are. I'm just grateful that I don't feel so confused anymore." Pansy set the pot of potatoes on a burner and adjusted the flame.

"You're happy, aren't you?" Jane said.

"I don't think about happiness," Pansy said. "It seems like such an extraordinary sensation. I'm content, though. I feel loved. It's what I've always envied about you, Jane. You show love so clearly, I've always thought. It's so unadorned in you, so unencumbered by questions of degree or worth. It simply *is*. Now I think I feel that too."

"We've come a long way together, Pansy," Jane said, going to hug her.

"Tomorrow night, then," Jane said. "To say good-bye to Casey."

"Yes." Pansy smiled. "She'll be back, Jane. Surely the war will be over by next summer and David will be home. They'll all come. We have that to look forward to."

So the next evening they assembled in the Flanagan's dining room, everybody in their old places. They had all dressed up a little for the occasion. Pansy wore a new dress from her unused trousseau, and Hazard wore a pale blue shirt she had bought for him. Gwen was wearing a cool summer dress, but it had little capped sleeves and a touch of lace that made her look as innocent and wholesome as it did youthful.

Casey wore pants. Her only dress, the blue wedding eyelet, hung in the closet upstairs, never to be worn again. But her hair had grown over the summer and it framed her face softly, curling a little against her cheekbones. Maybe she would let it grow over the winter.

Supper was quiet. Between bites, someone would remind them of how quickly time went and they would agree. The summer had certainly gone quickly. They hoped the same of the winter.

Jane dreaded the winter, she said. She hoped it didn't ice up like it did last year. She recounted broken bones in the neighborhood. Ben recalled a snow from his childhood that stayed on the ground two months, turning yellowish, then brown, disfiguring the farmland almost until spring. They all hoped it would snow only once, a big fluffy snow that would last two or three days and could be easily cleared from the streets.

Gwen spoke up, shyly at first, as if this were her first time at their table, but then more boldly as her excitement grew. She was quitting her job at the five and dime and had enrolled in a secretarial course. She beamed at them, and Taylor took her hand openly and held it at the table. Casey thought they looked like two people with one future between them.

When the meal was over, Gwen followed Casey into the kitchen.

"We'll do them," they said to Jane and Pansy, who

were already putting aprons on to do the dishes. "We want to."

So Jane and Pansy left them to it and went into the living room where Hazard was fingering at the old upright piano Jane had owned since David and Taylor were in grade school.

"We should have a glass of wine," Jane said. "Wouldn't that be nice?"

"I have some homemade," Pansy said, remembering a bottle given her by a neighbor the previous autumn. "It's in the pantry, Hazard."

By the time the girls were finished in the kitchen, Hazard had returned with the bottle and Jane had dusted out the seldom-used wine goblets from the breakfront. Ben poured out the dark sweet wine and they sipped it eagerly and then smiled at each other.

"It's good," Taylor said.

"It's fine," they all agreed.

Jane put a record on the phonograph. They sat around the room, their glasses loose in relaxing fingers, and were silent, smiling at each other. They would miss Casey, but next summer she would be back. David would be back. Life went on.

Hazard stirred a little. The music had swept over him like a scent from his past that conjured up his best memories—places, times when he had abandoned himself to his mood and felt completely free.

"Casey, sing us a song," he said.

Casey felt the sudden flood of embarrassment she always felt, but then, looking around the room, she couldn't help but want to give them something, some gift that only she had to give. She remembered Hazard that first day when he'd come into her room, how he'd let her talk and how when she'd finished, she hadn't felt so out of place anymore. She remembered her grandmother's face when she'd stepped off the bus and her grandfather's tone when he'd tried to talk to her about Dwayne. She remembered Taylor teaching her to drive and Gwen's moment of truth on a sandy beach blanket. She remembered Pansy's quiet glow the night Hazard proposed. The hours spun into her head, as soft and warm as the wine on her stomach.

"I'll play," Jane said and went to the piano.

Casey flipped through the worn sheet music for a moment, then picked one out and put it on the stand.

"*It had to be you,*" she sang softly, looking at each of them in turn, her hand resting on her grandmother's shoulder. "*It had to be you . . . I wandered around and fin-al-ly found, some-body who —*" She smiled at Hazard. "*Could make me feel true . . . Could make me feel blue . . . And even be glad, just to be sad, thinking of you.*"

Hazard was patting his foot lightly. From his side, Pansy could feel the rhythm pulling at him, the urgency he felt to move his limbs in that graceful, yet somehow awkward, way of his.

"Hazard, dance," she said softly. "Dance."

He heard her over the trill of the piano, but at first he didn't believe it. It was too much for him to expect, too much to ask for. He felt her touching his arm, fingers easing him up so he found himself in front of her. He knew he was grinning foolishly but he couldn't help it.

"*Some others I've seen,*" Casey sang, "*Might never be mean . . . Might never be cross or try to be boss . . . But they wouldn't do . . .*"

"Dance." Hazard read the silent word form on Pansy's lips.

He moved his feet obediently, spinning on his toes, arms loose. The music from the old piano was like an orchestra. Casey's voice was Judy Garland's. And he, for the first and only time in his life, was Fred Astaire. And so he circled the room, hearing with every note and seeing on every face, the acknowledgment of Pansy's touching, final acceptance of him. She loved a dancing man.

THEY ALL went to the bus station. It was almost noon, so Taylor, Ben, and Hazard shut down the lumberyard before the whistle blew and came down to find Pansy, Gwen, and Jane already there with Casey and Dwayne in tow. Dwayne had lugged the suitcase, they said. He grinned at the men, proud of having been useful.

"It was heavy, too," he said to Taylor. "She's got bricks in there."

"No bricks," Casey said. "I've got my baseball glove, though."

"Don't you forget it next summer," Dwayne said. "We got to play baseball."

The bus roared into the station.

"Here it is," Hazard said. He had tears in his eyes. "We're going to miss you, Casey," he said, hugging her shoulder.

"We certainly are," Pansy added, patting her from the other side.

The three of them stood staring at the bus as the

door opened and the driver got off to load the new passenger's baggage.

"You've got those sandwiches, don't you?" Jane asked anxiously.

"And that candy to snack on," Gwen added. "It's my last day at the candy counter, so I thought you should get to try everything."

"You change buses once," Taylor said, studying Casey's ticket. "You'll know where, because this bus ends its run there. You'll have a few minutes. Time to get a drink and go to the bathroom."

"She got here just fine," Ben said, hugging her. "She can get home just fine, too, can't you, Casey?"

The baggage loaded, the driver slammed the compartment door shut.

"It's time," Casey said. She felt weak, like she was sick again.

They each hugged her once more, everyone except Dwayne, who stood a little to the side just watching, as if he were studying how to say good-bye.

"Well," they all sighed.

Casey stepped away from them toward the bus.

"Hey boy," a voice said behind her, just like she'd hoped it would.

"Hey Dwayne," she said softly, turning to the man who wore a stained cap low over his forehead and carried, bulging from his side pocket, a baseball. "Listen," she said, hearing tears in her voice. "You take care, you hear?"

"Next summer—" he started, then he stopped. He pulled out his handkerchief and wiped his eyes brusquely. "Oh, shoot."

"We'll all be here," Jane said.

"Yeah," Dwayne said, grateful she had rescued him from his bumbling. He smiled and opened his arms like he'd seen Taylor do.

"I love you, Casey," he said, hugging her hard.

She felt that body close for the first time, felt the power in his back and arms as he swung her off her feet against his chest. He would survive. She knew that now. All these people who loved him would help. She would help. But mostly he would survive because what he saw of life was so often good, and because he was willing to forgive what wasn't.

"I love you, too," she said.

THE LANDSCAPE changed. First the rows of houses fell away to scattered ones set in the middle of dried-up tobacco and corn fields. Then there were the woods, tall dark stands of narrow pines, their floors deep and brown with needles. Then the flat land, the endless miles spreading out before them, hot and silent.

Casey closed her eyes. The bus hummed its rolling rhythm. But what she heard was the metallic clang of a baseball against an empty oil drum. What she saw was a distant figure on a mound, his cap pulled low above his working jaw as he swung both hands high over his head, pushed off his left foot onto his right, swung his left leg into the air, dropped his right arm behind his back, brought it around to let the ball fly, wham into the drum.

"It's a hit!" a voice yelled in her head. "Hey boy, you see that? It's a hit!"

Sue Ellen Bridgers was born and raised in North Carolina, in the heart of the country she described so movingly in her first novel for Knopf, Home Before Dark. *Her stories have appeared in* Redbook, Ingenue, *and* The Carolina Quarterly.

Sue Ellen Bridgers lives with her husband and their three children in Sylva, North Carolina.